The Garden Lover's Guide to Canada

PRINCETON ARCHITECTURAL PRESS   NEW YORK

LARRY HODGSON

The Garden Lover's Guide to Canada

Published by Princeton Architectural Press
37 East 7th Street
New York, New York 10003

For a free catalog of books, call 1.800.722.6657.
Visit our web site at www.papress.com.

Unless otherwise noted, photographs are by Larry Hodgson, Horticom, Inc.

Series editor: Jan Cigliano
Design: Sara E. Stemen
Layout: Adam B. Bohannon
Copyeditor: Heather Ewing
Maps: Jane Garvie

Special thanks to: Nettie Aljian, Ann Alter, Amanda Atkins,
Nicola Bednarek, Mia Ihara, Clare Jacobson, Leslie Ann Kent,
Mark Lamster, Nancy Eklund Later, Anne Nitschke, Lottchen Shivers,
Jennifer Thompson, and Deb Wood of Princeton Architectural Press
—Kevin C. Lippert, publisher

ISBN 1-56898-279-8

Cataloging-in-Publication Data is available through the Library of Congress

PHOTOS
*Page i: Jardin Roger–Van den Hende Water Garden, Québec; Page ii:
Tangled Gardens, Nova Scotia; page iii: New Brunswick Botanical Garden's
flowery brook*

Contents

*Howard Gardens' perennial
border, Québec*

How to use this book

KEY TO SYMBOLS

Admission	💰
Refreshments in vicinity	🍴
Formal garden	❖
Landscape garden	🏞
House major feature	🏛
Historic garden	🏰
Kitchen garden	🌿
Botanic interest/rare plants	🌿
Topiary	🦆
Borders	🌾
Water features	⛲
Architectural features	♔

This guide was prepared for travelers who wish to visit the most interesting and beautiful gardens throughout Canada, from the gorgeous sunken gardens of Butchart Gardens on Vancouver Island in British Columbia to the extraordinary parks and gardens of Niagara Falls, Ontario, to the most complete botanical garden in North America, the Montréal Botanical Garden in Québec, to North America's easternmost garden, the Memorial University of Newfoundland Botanical Garden on the island of Newfoundland.

The book is divided into five chapters covering the major regions of Canada, from the Atlantic Provinces on the eastern coast to British Columbia on the west. Each chapter comprises an introductory section with a regional map and a list of the gardens, followed by entries on each garden. The numbers found on the regional maps can be used to locate the numbered entries within the chapters. These entries are accompanied by detailed at-a-glance information telling the reader about the garden's main characteristics and nearby sights of interest. The guide also includes five major gardens, beautifully illustrated by three-dimensional plans.

Entries begin with at-a-glance information on opening times, directions, nearby sights of interest, and how to receive further information.

Each regional map includes a numbered key to make finding garden entries easy.

Major gardens include watercolor plans that note special features.

Foreword

I don't know how other people travel, but for me, visiting gardens is my main pleasure. Sure, I'll throw in a museum now and then, and a few hours on the beach, plus some general sightseeing, but the first thought that comes up when I have a chance to travel is: "Do they have any gardens?"

Traveling in Canada is no exception. From my home in Québec City, I lecture quite widely, and as long as my trips take place during the right season—most Canadian gardens are only open from late spring to early autumn—I'll fit in a garden or two every time. The good news is that there are more and more Canadian gardens open to the public. The bad news is I couldn't possibly fit them all in this one book.

The gardens that *are* included are all remarkable ones, sometimes because of their beauty, sometimes because of their unusual characteristics, sometimes because of their incredible collections of rare plants. The competition was especially tough in Ontario, Québec, and British Columbia, as each province had more than enough gardens to fill a book of its own. In preparing this book, I included mostly public gardens or, at the very least, private gardens that are regularly open to the public. That means some very exciting gardens had to be left out, and I'm sorry about that. I suggest that, as you travel in Canada, you visit not only the gardens included here, but make a few phone calls (ask the local Chamber of Commerce to connect you to a garden club or horticultural society) to find out whether some private gardens might not be open during your stay in any area.

I hope you'll enjoy your visits to the gardens of Canada!

OPPOSITE: *Jardins du Grand-Portage, Québec*

BELOW: *Commissioners Park and Tulip Festival, Ontario, lily-flowered tulips.*

Introduction

For the most part, Canada is a cold country of plains, tundra, taiga, and forests, more suited to hunting, mining, and forestry than to gardening or even agriculture. Indeed, less than fifteen percent of Canada's soil is even considered arable! That said, gardening has nonetheless taken a firm hold there, practically wherever it is possible. That means that the vast and cold North, sparsely inhabited and where frost is possible and even expected twelve months a year, is essentially devoid of public gardens—and even home gardens are difficult if not impossible. Most of Canada's gardens are to be found in the southern third of the country, below the Arctic Circle, where summers are warmer and longer and soils generally deeper and richer, making gardening as we know it not only possible, but actually quite simple.

Another key to understanding Canada's gardens is to realize that it is a young country, officially founded only in 1867, although it was settled at least 10,000 years earlier by Amerindians and later the Inuit (Eskimos), and by Europeans since the 1600s. Native peoples *did* garden, notably in the southern parts of the country where agriculture is still predominant today. They traditionally used slash and burn techniques, producing, in fields hacked out of the forest, corn, beans, sunflowers, squash, and other New World vegetables to supplement the meat provided by hunting and the fruits gathered during the summer months. They had little time to grow flowers as ornamentals—just surviving was difficult enough.

The Europeans sailed to the New World with a stronger tradition of ornamental gardening. The first French settlers came to farm the land, not to hunt (although many *coureurs des bois* did take up fur trading, a way of life closer to the way native peoples lived). They brought with them not only farm animals and agricultural crops such as wheat, barley, and oats, but also medicinal herbs. Early plans of Québec City, founded in 1608, show it was dotted with formal French *parterres*, notably behind convents, providing healing plants to the sisters, whose role was to administer to the sick and needy. Early hospitals also had their 'jardin de simples' (herb garden). Since many of the herbs grown there were also ornamental (chamomile, chicory, hollyhock, lungwort, mauve, and tansy), these gardens were beautiful as well as practical. The *habitants* (the traditional name for French Canadian colonists) adopted the plants if not the patterns and used them in informal gardens planted near their homes. As a result, to this day, patches of escaped ornamentals dot the landscape throughout Ontario, Québec, and New Brunswick—traces of herb gardens long abandoned.

By the eighteenth and especially nineteenth and twentieth centuries, immigration, notably from Great Britain, but also

OPPOSITE: *Jardins du Grand Portage, Québec*

BELOW, TOP TO BOTTOM: *Nitobe Memorial Garden, Vancouver, BC; Jardin Daniel A. Séguin, Québec; Reford Gardens, Québec*

ABOVE: *Allan Gardens,
Ontario*

BELOW, TOP TO BOTTOM:
*Butchart Gardens, British
Columbia*

from across Europe and, more recently, Asia, South America, and Africa, was more massive and soon Canada was settled from coast to coast. Different peoples brought with them different gardening traditions . . . and different plants. Typically, pioneer families would bring with them seeds or even roots of flowers that reminded them of home. Often the family's peony was planted before the sod house or log cabin had even been built! Canada continues to be a country of immigrants, and Asiatic influences, notably, can be felt in most modern gardens.

Increased urbanization (appearances to the contrary, Canada is one of the most highly urbanized countries in the world, with the vast majority of its inhabitants living in cities and towns), especially since the end of the nineteenth century, has lead to a great deal of emphasis on often vast public parks as "lungs" for dense urban centers. Although some of these parks are mostly composed of lawns, trees, play areas, and sports fields, many include ornamental gardens, often quite elaborate ones: rose gardens, rock gardens, and Japanese gardens. Such urban parks are a prime source of Canada's public gardens. And urban renewal has spawned many parks and gardens in what were once the least appetizing areas; old warehouse areas in Toronto, Montréal, and Vancouver are quickly becoming "people places" with trendy restaurants and boutiques . . . and numerous gardens. Likewise, former landfill sites and quarries are festooned with flowers.

Other important gardens likewise came about towards the end of the nineteenth century, but from the private sector. Merchants who made it big inevitably built large homes on what where then the outskirts of Canada's towns and cities and surrounded them with even larger estates. Their country homes, used primarily as summer residences, were similarly grandiose and surrounded by gardens. They generally built houses recalling the majestic manors they had seen during their trips to Europe and for their gardens adopted European landscaping styles. Although many of these stately homes have been sold and their estates subdivided, a considerable number have been maintained and are now open to the public.

Ornamental gardens are no longer the privilege of the Canada's upper crust. Since World War II, the spread of suburbs, where most homes do have some green space to manage, has resulted in a veritable passion for gardening among average Canadians. Gardening is said to be the most popular hobby in Canada and some 80 percent of Canadian families garden. These days, given the wide availability of reasonably priced fruits and vegetables in commerce, most suburban gardens are ornamental ones. As with American gardens (not surprising seeing as the two countries experienced much the same influences at much the same times), vast, green lawns predominate, interspersed with plantings of trees and shrubs and, more and more frequently, flower beds filled with annuals and perennials. Many of the more interesting private gardens are open to the public, at least on occasion, and some are edging their way into the public garden sector.

Other public gardens have come about as part of restoration projects. Canada's history may be short, but the country is peppered with historic buildings that are well maintained and open to the public. In many places, entire villages have been recreated using period houses, stores, and farm buildings brought together on a common site. Generally these projects include both ornamental and vegetable gardens that represent styles and plants that would have been grown at the time.

A final source of public gardens of recent origin are those developed by garden centers and nurseries. Often designed originally as a showcase for their plants and products, some of these gardens have taken on a life of their own, becoming some of Canada's top showcase gardens.

Of course, you don't need to know the wheres and whyfors of Canada's gardens. They are numerous, attractive, and well worth a visit. Don't hesitate to include some of them in your next foray into the Canadian countryside.

Dr. Sun Yat-Sen Classical Chinese Garden, Vancouver, BC

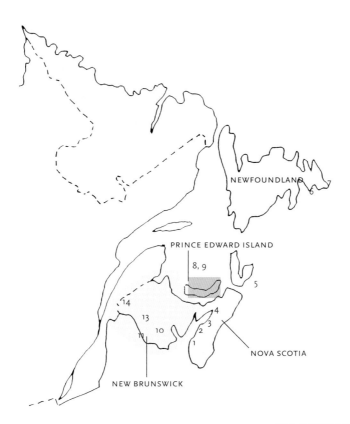

NEWFOUNDLAND

PRINCE EDWARD ISLAND

NOVA SCOTIA

NEW BRUNSWICK

ATLANTIC PROVINCES:

Nova Scotia, Newfoundland,

Prince Edward Island, New Brunswick

The Atlantic Coast of Canada is a rugged landscape of bays and inlets, lakes and rivers, rolling hills and alluvial plains, forest, bog, and farmland. Most towns and cities (and therefore most gardens) are located near the coast, where they profit from the moderating effects of the ocean, providing warmer winters and cooler summers than central Canada. Inland, winters are distinctly colder, but, due to higher elevations, summers are not much warmer. These geographical and climatic factors are major influences on the gardens of the Atlantic Provinces.

Atlantic Canada is divided into four provinces. New Brunswick, Prince Edward Island, and Nova Scotia are called the Maritime Provinces or, more simply, the Maritimes. When far distant Newfoundland is included, the term Atlantic Provinces is commonly used. The four are Canada's smallest provinces both in size and in population.

New Brunswick, which hugs the American border to the west and the Québec border to the north, is mainly a province of rolling hills descending to deep river valleys—whose waters eventually reach the Atlantic Ocean through a series of bays and straits. The center of the province is mostly forest, with most towns and cities being located on the coast or along one of the province's numerous river systems, the most important being the Saint John River, which runs almost the entire length of the province from north to south. As far as gardens are concerned, Saint

OPPOSITE: *New Brunswick Botanical Garden*

I

Andrews has to be the gardening capital of the province; long the summer haunt of rich Montréal, Toronto, and Boston merchants, it is filled with beautiful homes and attractive gardens, most still private but visible from the street. The reigning queen of the town, the elegant Algonquin Hotel, standing on a hill just outside of its center, has gardens of its own that you can visit at will, as does the neighboring inn, Pansy Patch. Kingsbrae (page 17) is the first of the formerly private estates to open to the public, but other gardens may well follow suit. Although comparatively new and located in the highlands and thus suffering from particularly cold winters and short summers, the New Brunswick Botanical Garden (page 20) is already one of the most exciting gardens in Canada. Only a stone's throw from the province of Québec and far from other major gardens in the Atlantic Provinces, it is more readily added to a tour of Quebéc's gardens.

Nova Scotia is the most populous of the Atlantic Provinces and also home to their largest city, Halifax, a booming metropolis of some 400,000 people—huge by Atlantic Canadian standards. The province is mostly one long peninsula, nearly surrounded by water except for a narrow stretch of land where it joins New Brunswick, plus a large island, Cape Breton, surrounding the salt-water Bras d'Or Lake, at its northeastern tip. The moderating effects of the Atlantic Ocean (the Gulf Stream flows not far off shore) mean the southern tip of the province and most of its shore are in Canadian hardiness zone six—quite balmy compared to most of Canada. Not surprisingly, most of the province's gardens are located in this warmer zone, including Halifax's popular Public Gardens (page 8) and one of Canada's most spectacular and beautifully arranged gardens, Annapolis Royal Historic Gardens (page 5).

Prince Edward Island is by far Canada's smallest province, only 139 miles (224 kilometers) long and four to forty miles (six to sixty-five kilometers) wide, and also boasts the smallest population. Entirely surrounded by the Gulf of the Saint Lawrence and Northumberland Strait, it was long relatively isolated from the rest of Canada, attainable only ferry and, more recently, air. It is now connected to the mainland (New Brunswick) by the Confederation Bridge, making it easier to visit. Largely rural, with proportionately more space given over to agriculture than any other Canadian province, Prince Edward Island is often called the "Garden of the Gulf" and is a popular spot for summer vacations. Private gardens are numerous and the islanders obviously love gardening, but the province was never very rich in public gardens. That is now changing, as tourist spots originally developed around other themes catch on to the fact that visitors love flowers. In some of them, like Woodleigh Replicas & Gardens in Kensington (page 15), beautiful gardens are now the major attraction.

Annapolis Royal Historic Gardens, Nova Scotia

Newfoundland was long an independent colony and only joined Canada in 1949. It is principally made up of what the locals call "The Rock"—huge Newfoundland Island—and Labrador, located on the mainland across the Strait of Belle Isle. Very rugged and deeply cut with glacial valleys and fjords, with more taiga and bog than true forest, Newfoundland Island is sparsely inhabited other than along the coast, as towns and cities, mostly based on the once-thriving fishing industry, have sprung up wherever there is a protected harbor. With the exception of a very few mining towns, fishing villages, and Amerindian and Inuit villages, Labrador is essentially uninhabited and has no gardens of note. Its very harsh climate would make gardening very difficult at best. The moderating effects of the Gulf Stream, however, make Newfoundland Island, and especially its southeastern tip, more amenable to ornamental gardens, although the very long, cold springs mean even many "cold hardy" plants fail to thrive. Most of the larger towns have attractive parks, but the capital, Saint John's, has the lion's share of the public gardens . . . and the population. The Memorial University of Newfoundland Botanical Garden (page 11) is a striking example of how to cope with a harsh climate and come out a winner! It on its own is well worth making the trip to Newfoundland, in spite of the long ferry ride or expensive plane fare needed to reach this isolated province.

Annapolis Royal: Annapolis Royal Historic Gardens

LOCATION: AT NO. 441 ST. GEORGE STREET IN THE HEART OF
ANNAPOLIS ROYAL

Although the Annapolis Royal Historic Gardens are relatively recent, dating back only to 1981, they have picked up, in that short time, the enviable reputation of being one of Canada's most beautiful gardens. They take a fascinating look at the history of gardening in the area, from the first gardens of the French-speaking Acadian people to Victorian period gardens. There are also some very modern garden ideas, notably in the *Innovative Garden*, which highlights the latest in plants and gardening techniques, such as dwarf, disease-resistant fruit trees and time-saving mulches.

The ten-acre main showcase features a rose collection of over 200 cultivars, recounting the history of roses from the species to the first hybrids to modern garden roses and includes a unique rose maze. The *Winter Garden* brings together plants of winter interest with unusual or attractive stems, bark, or evergreen foliage, even winter flowers. The *Acadian Cottage* is a simple homestead surrounded by a recreated *potager* or kitchen garden in the traditional French formal style, with four symmetrical raised beds containing vegetables that would have been grown at the time. Below is a unique

GARDEN OPEN: 8am to dusk, mid-May–mid-October

ADMISSION: $11 family, $5 adults, $4 students and seniors, free under 6 years.

FURTHER INFORMATION FROM:
Annapolis Royal Historic
Gardens Society
P.O. Box 278
Annapolis Royal, NS B0S 1A0
(902) 532-7018
fry@tartannet.ns.ca
www.historicgardens.com

NEARBY SIGHTS OF INTEREST:
Fort Anne National Historic
Site and Museum, Port Royal
National Historic Site

Perhaps the nicest knot garden in the maritimes is found in Annapolis Royal.

The Acadian Potager gives an idea of how people gardened in the early days of the colony.

example of a seven-acre salt marsh reclaimed from the sea by ancient Acadian dyking methods. Among the historical gardens are the *Knot Garden*, with trimmed plants trained in intricate patterns, the *Governor's Garden*, representing the early to mid-1700s, and the *Victorian Garden*, where brilliant color is provided by annuals with colored foliage or non-stop bloom. Other gardens of note are the Perennial Border, the Rock Garden, a spring garden, water gardens, a beautifully sculpted fountain, a bed of ornamental grasses, a collection of conifers, and a recreated pine forest that is developing very nicely.

It's hard to do justice to this fascinating and beautiful garden in just a few short paragraphs. Suffice to say it is attractive and informative enough that even non-gardeners will fully enjoy a 45-minute visit, while the more serious visitors will want to spend half a day! To make staying on longer easier, there is a restaurant/snack bar and a gift shop.

Vast perennial borders draw the eye.

2 Grand Pré: Tangled Garden

LOCATION: TAKE ROUTE 101 TO EXIT 10, AND TURN TOWARDS GRAND PRÉ, THE GARDEN IS THE FOURTH HOUSE ON THE RIGHT

GARDEN OPEN: 10am to 6pm daily, year-round.
ADMISSION: free.

FURTHER INFORMATION FROM:
Tangled Garden
Box 80
Grand Pré, Nova Scotia B0P 1M0
(902) 542-9811

NEARBY SIGHTS OF INTEREST:
Grand-Pré National Historic Site, Prescott House Museum

That a run-down old country home with equally dilapidated outbuildings could be changed into an exciting garden is quite amazing, but the most amazing thing of all is the beauty of the garden. The owners, Beverly McClare and George Walford, moved there in 1985 and basically "camped out" for the first few years. The house was scarcely livable, but their first priority was to create a vast garden for the dried flower and herb products business they wanted to start. The house now serves as their studio (both are also artists) and as sales area for their herb and flower jellies, vinegars, chutneys, sauces, and oils, and dried flowers, and as a gallery for their paintings and organic sculptures. The ceiling is festooned with dried flowers and an herbal scent permeates the whole boutique. But even herbal products customers aren't allowed to leave before visiting the gardens.

In some ways, Tangled Garden is just as jumbled as it sounds. Lush plantings of herbs and flowers mingle together and creep over fences and a vine-covered pergola, twist around sculptures, lean over the two ponds. But there is order in the seeming chaos and parts of the garden are undeniably formal in structure and planting, with just enough of a tousled look not to ruin the garden's reputation for free, unrestrained growth. Most of the plants in the one-acre garden are herbs or cut flowers, harvested for the business, and surplus plants (divisions, cuttings) are offered for sale to visitors. The paths meander through the back and side yards, then back to the boutique. Some plants are identified with hand-painted signs; others . . . well, stroke them and see if you recognize their scent. The informality of the garden extends to the visit. You can just show up and wander through, at no cost, although it's hard to believe anyone could resist the goodies in the boutique!

The weather-beaten, unpainted fences beckon to garden visitors.

Halifax: Halifax Public Garden

LOCATION: JUST OUTSIDE DOWNTOWN HALIFAX, KITTY-CORNER TO THE CITADEL, BETWEEN SOUTH PARK STREET, SACKVILLE STREET, SPRING GARDEN ROAD, AND SUMMER STREET

GARDEN OPEN: 8am to dusk daily, May 1–mid-October.

ADMISSION: free.

FURTHER INFORMATION FROM:
Halifax Public Gardens
Parks and Open Spaces
P.O. Box 1749
Halifax, Nova Scotia B3J 3A5
(902) 490-4895

NEARBY SIGHTS OF INTEREST:
Halifax Citadel National
Historic Site, Discovery
Centre, Province House

Back in the Victorian era, every major city in North America would have had a park like this: verdant lawns, artificial lakes and streams, ornate fountains, bright beds of annuals, a central bandstand, plantings of trees and shrubs, all arranged in the Romantic style with winding paths and natural-looking vistas. Most city parks commissions, however, followed modern trends and changed their central parks to meet the styles of the day. Often little remains of the original gardens other than a few sculptures or some photographs. Halifax had an advantage over other cities, though; the family of the original designer, Richard Power, remained in charge of maintaining the gardens for almost 100 years and strenuously objected to any changes in their ancestor's original plan. They were so successful that the latest major change to the gardens, the addition of the Boer War Memorial Fountain, dates back to 1901! Today the Halifax Public Garden is perhaps the best preserved Victorian park in all of North America.

The nearly square seventeen-acre park is surrounded by a wrought iron fence. Inside the park, gushing fountains, babbling brooks, rustling trees, and bird song cut off urban sounds, so it is easy to forget you're in a city center. Over 125 years (the park was first opened in 1874 when two adjoining gardens were combined), the trees have had time to reach maturity and have created shady walks. Many trees are of rare or unusual species, like weeping elms and oriental conifers (Victorians were very attracted to anything new or exotic), although not all are identified. A small spring-fed lake with resident ducks and geese draws children eager to feed them and there are likewise play areas for the younger set. Many of the

The abundant use of annuals in geometric patterns shows the Victorian origin of these gardens.

numerous flower beds are still planted with bedding plants common at the time of the park's opening—cannas, marigolds, salvias, dahlias—and there are several examples of carpet bedding in intricate designs, as likewise would have be current in the 1870s. The best examples of carpet bedding surround the jewel in the garden's crown, the Victorian bandstand dedicated to Queen Victoria at her Diamond Jubilee, where concerts are still given on Sunday afternoons at 2 pm, as they have been since the park was opened.

4 Truro: Nova Scotia Agricultural College Alumni Gardens

LOCATION: ON THE CAMPUS OF NOVA SCOTIA AGRICULTURAL COLLEGE

The Alumni Gardens are located immediately behind International House and DeWolfe House on the campus of the Nova Scotia Agricultural College. The rectangular garden is a popular meeting place for the community, with benches and green spaces and a bandstand for refuge in case of rain. Entirely wheelchair accessible, it includes many attractive features, among which the formal herb garden is perhaps the most notable. However, there are also attractive and interesting perennial demonstration gardens, a shade garden, and a dwarf conifer border.

The campus' gardens reach far beyond the Alumni Gardens, though; the entire site is a vast green park with remarkable and unusual trees and shrubs, shady corners, and benches, and is crisscrossed with footpaths. There is likewise a conifer collection, heather beds, an alpine garden, and a native plant demonstration garden. The TransCanada Trail runs through the campus.

GARDEN OPEN: dawn to dusk daily, mid-April–end of November.

FURTHER INFORMATION FROM: Nova Scotia Department of Agriculture and Marketing Production Technology Branch
P.O. Box 550
Truro, Nova Scotia B2N 5E3
(902) 893-6543
jmorton@cadmin.nsac.ns.ca
www.gov.ns.ca

NEARBY SIGHTS OF INTEREST: Nova Scotia Agricultural College campus and farm, Victoria Park

Clematis tangutica climbs into the feathery foliage of a cutleaf sumac in the Alumni Gardens. Carol Goodwin, Nova Scotia Agricultural College

9

5 Louisbourg: Fortress of Louisbourg National Historic Site

LOCATION: THIRTY-FIVE KILOMETERS FROM THE CITY OF SYDNEY ON CAPE BRETON ISLAND, VIA ROUTE 22

GARDEN OPEN: 9:30am to 5pm daily, May–June; 9:00am to 7pm, July–August; 9:30am to 5pm, September–October; buildings open during garden hours. November–April: advance arrangements required. **ADMISSION:** June–September $11 adults, $8.50 seniors, $5.50 youths. May–October $4.50 adults, $3.50 seniors, $2.25 youths.

FURTHER INFORMATION FROM:
Fortress of Louisbourg
National Historic Site
P.O. Box 160
Louisbourg, Nova Scotia B0A 1M0
(902) 733-2280
louisbourg_info@pch.gc.ca
www.fortress.uccb.ns.ca

NEARBY SIGHTS OF INTEREST:
Cabot Trail, Lighthouse Point, Sydney and Louisburg Railway Museum

The original fortress and town of Louisbourg thrived, mostly under French rule, from 1713 to 1760, then was destroyed by the British and later completely abandoned. However, the government of Canada began reconstructing it in 1961 as a historical site. Today the fortress itself and one quarter of the old walled town stand again and are made all that much more interesting by guides, soldiers, and residents in period costume. This is the largest historical reconstruction in North America and is well worth a full day's visit.

Naturally, the historical reconstruction of a town implies restoration of its gardens as well. There are several of them, all in the formal French style that would have been popular at the time of the colony. The gardens range from the simple rectangular boxes of the De Gannes and De la Perelle gardens, representing typical peasant gardens, to the more carefully planned starburst and rounded patterns of the gardens of the noblemen and bourgeois, represented among others by the De la Plagne, Bigot, and Engineer's Residence gardens. Though the formal styles make all the gardens attractive, it is worth noting that only useful plants—herbs and vegetables—were employed in these *potagers*, although many plants then considered kitchen or medicine cabinet staples, like calendula and primrose, do double duty are ornamentals. Even the hedges were made of medicinal plants like wormwood, and the clippings would have been carefully dried and stored for winter use. Note the wooden fencing around all the gardens, essential to keep marauding animals and strong winds out.

The De Gannes shows the rectangular, raised beds that peasants would have used. Fortress of Louisbourg National Historic Site

6 Saint John's: Memorial University of Newfoundland Botanical Garden

LOCATION: NO. 306 MOUNT SCIO ROAD, WITHIN A.C. PIPPY PARK, JUST NORTH OF SAINT JOHN'S

GARDEN OPEN: 10am to 5pm daily, May 1–November 30.
ADMISSION: $2 adults, $1 children 6–18 years and seniors.

FURTHER INFORMATION FROM:
The MUN Botanical Garden
306 Mount Scio Road
Saint John's, Newfoundland
A1C 5S7
(709) 737-8590
garden@morgan.ucs.mun.ca
www.mun.ca/botgarden

NEARBY SIGHTS OF INTEREST:
A. C. Pippy Park, Fluvarium, Art Gallery of Newfoundland and Labrador

Certainly one of Canada's most surprising botanical gardens and definitely a must-see if you like unusual plants, the Memorial University of Newfoundland Botanical Garden (called Oxen Pond Botanical Gardens or just Oxen Pond by locals) is located in what would at first seem a most unlikely spot: on the Canadian shield on the edge of a dense boreal forest, in poor, rocky soil, and surrounded by peat bogs and fens. It does have some protection from extremely cold winter weather due to its proximity to the Atlantic Ocean and, in fact, the garden is located at the limit between Agriculture Canada hardiness zones four and five, which is quite balmy for Canada. However the ocean likewise prevents the accumulation of any reliable snow cover, ensures blustery winds year round, and spells mostly cool summer temperatures—you'll probably want to visit wearing a jacket, even when it is quite warm in the city below. Many plants simply won't grow under these extreme conditions, but the surprise is that so many do. In fact, the MUN Botanical Garden has the finest plant collection of any garden in the Atlantic Provinces.

Flowers greet before you have even stepped out of your vehicle; a wide perennial border lines the parking lot, leading you to the *Field Centre,* which serves as administration offices, an information desk, classroom, and research station. From here, you have two choices: to go to the gardens first or to follow one of the nature trails, including one to beautiful Oxen Pond, actually a four-hectare (fourteen-acre) lake. Even those who normally prefer gardens to wild nature should at least take one of the nature trails. Rarely will you see so many wildflowers, including several native orchids and carnivorous plants, from the safety of a dry boardwalk! And bird lovers will find the trails well worth their while, with, among others, ospreys nesting in plain sight.

The gardens include many unique sections. The *Entrance Garden* houses a collection of acid-loving native plants, including the garden's emblem, twinflower (*Linnaea borealis*). One of the most charming gardens is the *Cottage Garden*, complete with picket fence. If you didn't look up to see the balsam fir forest in the background, you could easily imagine yourself in England! Nearby is the best known of Oxen Pond's gardens: the *Rock Garden*. Two sections, one in limestone, the other in more acidic rock, both with scree sections for those plants that need loose stones for healthy growth, are beautifully planted in alpine plants which seem to positively thrive under long, cool

Few places in North America have climates that better support alpine plants than here.

summer days of Newfoundland. An alpine greenhouse serves as a refuge for the less hardy species. Nearby winds the Ericaceous Border, planted with rhododendrons, heathers, and other plants in the rhododendron family. Other interesting gardens include the Woodland Bed, dedicated to forest flowers, the Dried Flower Garden, the Food Garden, the Bog Garden, the Medicinal Plant Garden, and the Wildlife Garden. Not to be missed either is the Heritage Garden, where garden plants collected from home gardens across Newfoundland (peonies, columbines, campanulas) are grown with, as a backdrop, a Quiggly fence, a traditional Newfoundland windbreak of vertically woven saplings. The botanically inclined should note that most plants are identified throughout the gardens.

GARDEN OPEN: 9am to 10pm daily, year-round.
ADMISSION: free.

FURTHER INFORMATION FROM:
The Bowring Park Foundation
P.O. Box 39085
Saint John's, Newfoundland
A1C 5Y7
(709) 576-6134
www.cs.mun.ca/k12media/bowring

NEARBY SIGHTS OF INTEREST:
Arts and Culture Centre, Newfoundland Museum

7 Saint John's: Bowring Park

LOCATION: WEST END OF SAINT JOHN'S, WITH TWO ENTRANCES OFF WATER-BRIDGE ROAD

Offered as a gift to the citizens of Saint John's by the Bowring family in 1914, the fifty-acre original park was designed in the Romantic style by noted landscape architect, Sir Frederick Todd, and that tradition has been well maintained over the years, with meandering walks following the South Brook and Waterford Rivers through rounded hills, rocky slopes, colorful flower beds, and majestic trees. A stroll along the Waterford River is especially interesting, with a natural waterfall at seemingly every turn, and some impressive statues, including the Caribou Monument—whose bronze caribou seem at first to be the real thing. The *Duck Pond*, where swans, ducks, and geese abound, is a favorite with children as they are allowed to feed the birds under the watchful eye of a delightful statue of Peter Pan. The *Conservatory*, recently reconstructed, is also in this section of the park and houses displays of cacti and tropical

plants as well as a changing seasonal display of flowers. It is open on a more limited schedule than the park and hours change according to the season. Most of the original flowerbeds still exist and are planted, for the most part, in annuals and shrubs, with a rose garden located near the conservatory. Many of the original trees, often rare specimens, still stand. Refreshments are available at several spots and there is a gift shop.

The Duck Pond is a favorite spot for children and adults.

A further 150 acres was added to the park in the 1950s; this new section is less intensively landscaped and used mostly for sports (it includes a lawn bowling green, a wading pool, and a swimming pool, among others). The *Fountain Pond*, a round reflecting basin surrounding a large fountain, is also located in the new section. This part also includes an extensive wilderness trail through open meadows and a wooded ravine.

Thanks to its natural setting, its trees, and its statues, not to mention the conservatory, Bowring Park is attractive even in winter—where it is a popular site for sledding. Even the Fountain Pond changes vocation, becoming an ice-skating rink.

A collection of hybrid tea and grandiflora roses is located near the conservatory.

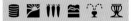

Vast perennial beds are a key feature of the garden. Betty Lou Frizzell Abbott

8   Hunter River: Perennial Pleasures

LOCATION: TWENTY MILES (THIRTY KILOMETERS) FROM THE CONFEDERATION BRIDGE ON ROUTE 227, JUST TWO MILES (THREE KILOMETERS) FROM HIGHWAY 2

Perennial Pleasures is a two-acre private garden in the very center of Prince Edward Island, the result of a labor of love by owner Betty Lou Frizzell Abbott and her husband Charles since 1975. Originally the house and barn, surrounded by rolling farmland located near the highest point on Prince Edward Island, boasted a remarkable view but little else. Mrs. Abbott began by planting trees and a hedge to supply a little privacy, then added more and more shrubs and flowers beds until, a quarter century later, the two-acre property is mostly covered in gardens.

There are over 100 different varieties of trees and shrubs, including a collection of rhododendrons, while the large perennial borders feature hundreds of flowering plants, including collections of daylilies and hostas, as well as numerous shrub roses. Among the whimsical features of this intensely personal garden are an outdoor living room called "The Cottage," a tree house, and strategically placed farm machinery.

9 Kensington: Woodleigh Replicas & Gardens

LOCATION: TAKE ROUTE 101 FROM KENSINGTON FOR THREE MILES (FOUR KILOMETERS) OR FOLLOW SIGNS FROM NEW LONDON OR CAVENDISH

Theme parks are often the very last place gardeners—who, on the whole, prefer quieter, calmer surroundings—would think of visiting when they travel, but it would be a mistake to miss Woodleigh Replicas & Gardens. True enough, visitors are usually drawn first and foremost by the thirty scale replicas of some of Britain's most famous buildings and castles, some reduced to only three feet high. They were built by a native Islander, Ernest Johnstone, who, after returning from World War I, wanted to reproduce the wonders of Great Britain on a manageable scale. To put his replicas in a suitable environment, he also landscaped the 45-acre site to resemble the beautifully manicured parks of Britain.

Today's park goes much farther still. A full ten acres are devoted exclusively to recreating a vast English cottage style garden. Elsewhere there are ponds, fountains, bridges, and verdant landscapes. Recently a new Shakespeare Garden, based on the works of the great poet and playwright and plants he would have known, has been installed around the models of Ann Hathaway's cottage, Shakespeare's birthplace, and Mary Arden's home. The result is a pleasing combination of history and gardens that can be enjoyed by all ages.

GARDEN OPEN: 9am to 5pm daily, June 1–30; 9am to 7pm, July 1–September 1; 9am to 5pm, September 2–October 15; gates close one hour prior to grounds closing.

ADMISSION: $8.50 adults, $8 seniors, $7 youths, $4.50 children (6–12 years).

FURTHER INFORMATION FROM:
Woodleigh Replicas & Gardens
R.R. 2, Route 234
Kensington, Prince Edward Island C0B 1M0
(902) 836-3401
woodleigh@pei.sympatico.ca
www.woodleighreplicas.com

NEARBY SIGHTS OF INTEREST:
Green Gables House, Prince Edward Island National Park, Cavendish Beach

The flower borders of Woodleigh Replicas & Gardens Woodleigh Replicas & Gardens

GARDEN OPEN: dawn to dusk
daily, year-round.
ADMISSION: free.

FURTHER INFORMATION FROM:
Horticultural Gardens
P.O. Box 784
Saint John
New Brunswick E2L 4B3
(506) 652-4050
www.tourismnbcanada.com/
web

NEARBY SIGHTS OF INTEREST:
Reversing Falls, New
Brunswick Museum, Aitken
Bicentennial Exhibition
Centre

OPPOSITE: *The Knot Garden
is just one of Kingsbrae's
features.* Kingsbrae
Horticultural Garden

BELOW: *Victorian-style
carpet bedding at the
Horticultural Gardens.*

10 Saint John: Horticultural Gardens/Rockwood Park

LOCATION: SEELY AND CROWN STREETS, AT THE SOUTHEAST CORNER OF
ROCKWOOD PARK

This urban park, established in 1893, is one of New
Brunswick's best preserved parks and still has a distinct
Victorian flavor. Surrounding a World War I war memorial, it is
a perfectly manicured, four-acre (1.5-hectare) green space featuring vast beds of colorful annuals and a rock garden rich in
perennials and shrubs.

The Horticultural Gardens also house the *municipal greenhouses.* These once were strictly working greenhouses, supplying the city's needs in bedding plants, but are now also used as
display greenhouses, featuring annuals, perennials, and tender
plants, the exact content varying according to season. They are
open Monday to Friday, 8am to 4pm.

The gardens adjoin vast *Rockwood Park,* one of Canada's
largest municipal parks. It is a huge 2,150-acre (870-hectare),
mostly forested recreational area that contains several sections
of interest to garden tourists, including flower beds and an
arboretum, plus a small zoo, thirteen lakes, picnicking sites,
nature and riding trails, camp sites, playgrounds, and a golf
course.

11   Saint Andrews: Kingsbrae Horticultural Garden

LOCATION: IN THE HEART OF SAINT ANDREWS JUST OFF PRINCE OF
WALES STREET

Both old and new: that's what strikes the visitor at Kingsbrae. This former private summer residence was only opened to the public in 1998. Although the original house was torn down in 1971, the gardens remain, and in fact they have been considerably augmented. The site covers 27 acres, including both gardens and a stand of old-growth forest, accessible through a winding nature trail. Parts of the garden are obviously very old, including some fully mature trees, but others are very modern, such as the obviously fresh plantings in the various thematic gardens. And the house, which serves as a cafe, art gallery, and boutique, plus the smaller admissions building, look old but are actually quite new; they were built in a rather ornate style, complete with turrets, that recalls the original home.

Kingsbrae Horticultural Garden is laid out as a series of garden rooms, including a white garden, a knot garden, a perennial garden, a cottage garden, and a therapy garden. There are likewise plant collections, including roses, herbs, heathers, rhododendrons, and ornamental shrubs. Water is

GARDEN OPEN: 9am to 6pm daily, May–October.
ADMISSION: $6 adults, $4 students and seniors, free children 6 years and younger.

FURTHER INFORMATION FROM:
Kingsbrae Horticultural Garden Inc.
220 King Street
Saint Andrews, New Brunswick E0G 2X0
(506) 529-4016
www.townsearch.com/kingsbraegarden

NEARBY SIGHTS OF INTEREST:
Minister's Island, Huntsman Marine Aquarium

also a prominent feature, with a winding brook and two ponds, the largest one complete with a functioning open replica (to one-third scale) of a Dutch windmill. Children will enjoy the windmill and also the cedar maze labyrinth, not to mention the Touch & Feel section in the children's garden. Serious garden visitors will especially appreciate the very tasteful landscaping and the care taken in identifying the plants, some of which are quite unusual.

Kingsbrae is maintained as a not-for-profit organization, thanks largely to a trust fund donated by former owners John and Lucinda Fleming. It is likewise an on-the-job training site for the Landscape Program offered at New Brunswick Community College—most people you'll see working in the garden are students of the college. It also prides itself in its respect for the environment; no topsoil is imported, mulch is made on the site, and an underground irrigation system recuperates and recycles water.

GARDEN OPEN: 8am to dusk, year-round; roads are not maintained in winter. Roosevelt Cottage open 10am to 6pm daily, late May–Canadian Thanksgiving.

FURTHER INFORMATION FROM:
Roosevelt Campobello
International Park
Commission
459 Route 774
Welshpool, NB E5E 1A4
(506) 752-2922
bailey@fdr.net
www.fdr.net

NEARBY SIGHTS OF INTEREST:
Roosevelt Campobello
International Park Natural
Area, Herring Cove Provincial
Park and Golf Course,
Mullholland Point Lighthouse

12 Campobello Island: Roosevelt Campobello International Park

LOCATION: SOUTHERN END OF CAMPOBELLO ISLAND VIA LUBEC, MAINE, AND THE FDR MEMORIAL BRIDGE; FERRY AVAILABLE IN SUMMER FROM DEER ISLAND

Odd, isn't it: a Canadian garden best visited by traveling through the United States! That's because Campobello Island, although in Canadian territory, is only linked to the continent by the FDR Bridge in Lubec, Maine. It's only a short drive from the Canadian border, though, and, in July and August, you can also take a ferry from St. Stephen, New Brunswick to Deer Island, and another from there to Campobello.

Campobello Island offers a refreshing change of pace for weary travelers. Long a private island, it became an exclusive summer resort with wealthy Boston and New York businessmen in the 1880s, including the Roosevelt family, whose son, Franklin would one day become president of the United States. Today, the southern part of the island is dominated by the *Roosevelt Campobello International Park*, established in 1964 as an international memorial to the close relationships between the peoples of Canada and the United States. It features the restored Roosevelt "Cottage," in actual fact an estate house of considerable size. The park likewise features beautiful drives through wooded areas, wonderful ocean views, and five kilometers of walking trails.

The Roosevelt Cottage, four other cottages in the park, and the visitor center grounds are beautifully landscaped. As would have been true when the island was still a popular resort, the

flower beds feature few permanent plants, other than hybrid tea and rugosa roses near the visitor's center, instead relying on mass plantings of colorful annuals, dahlias, and tuberous begonias to ensure non-stop bloom. Even the few perennials used are treated as annuals and removed at the end of the season. These temporary plantings mean the gardens change considerably from one year to the next. The plantings are designed to accentuate the appearance of the cottages, not to be historically accurate; the spirit of the old nineteenth-century carpet beds is there, but many modern plants, like the dwarf impatiens, have been integrated into the scheme of things.

The gardens are designed for maximum impact during July and August, when most visitors arrive, although there is already some color from late spring on, and by early fall dahlias reign supreme. Don't expect much color in the off-season.

A flowering border welcomes the visitor to the Prince Cottage, just next door to the Roosevelt Cottage.

13 Fredericton: Odell Park and Arboretum/Fredericton Botanic Garden

LOCATION: O'DELL PARK IS OFF SMYTHE STREET, JUST OUTSIDE OF DOWNTOWN FREDERICTON; THE BOTANIC GARDEN IS TO THE WEST, THROUGH THE PROSPECT STREET BALL PARK

GARDEN OPEN: 8am to 10pm daily, year-round.
ADMISSION: free.

FURTHER INFORMATION FROM:
Fredericton City Public Works Department
P.O. Box 130
Fredericton, New Brunswick
E3B 4Y7
(506) 460-2038
www.city.fredericton.nb.ca/community/parks.html

NEARBY SIGHTS OF INTEREST:
King's Landing Historical Settlement, Beaverbrook Art Gallery

Odell Park is a 388-acre (175-hectare), mostly forested park within walking distance of downtown Fredericton, New Brunswick's capital. It is the former estate of the Reverend Jonathan Odell and was originally known as Rockwood. The park contains meadows, a duck pond, a deer pen, but is mostly renowned for its virgin forest, easily accessible through 16 kilometers of hiking trails. The six-mile (2.8-kilometer) *Arboretum Trail* takes you deep into the park, where many of the trees,

Wildflowers, including these goldenrods, abound in the forests and meadow.

some over 400 years old, are identified by plaques. To the west of the deer pen is the *New Brunswick Species Collection*, containing examples of every native New Brunswick tree species in an environment of lawns, paths, and benches.

The western corner of Odell Park is occupied by the *Fredericton Botanical Garden*, a still very embryonic botanical garden that nonetheless grows in size and importance yearly. It features over 4.5 miles (two kilometers) of walking trails through a wooded hillside and several perennial beds, plus a collection of rhododendrons and azaleas. Plans are being made for twelve theme gardens.

GARDEN OPEN: 9am to 8pm daily, June–mid-October.
ADMISSION: $4.75 adults, $4.50 seniors and students, $2.25 children, free children 6 years and younger, $11.75 family.

FURTHER INFORMATION FROM:
New Brunswick Botanical Garden
P.O. Box 599
Saint-Jacques, New Brunswick E0L 1K0
(506) 737-5383
jardin@cuslm.ca
www.cuslm.ca/jardin

NEARBY SIGHTS OF INTEREST:
Les Jardins de la République Provincial Park, Automobile Museum, Madawaska

14 Saint Jacques: New Brunswick Botanical Garden

LOCATION: OFF THE TRANSCANADA HIGHWAY, EIGHT KILOMETERS FROM THE QUÉBEC-NEW BRUNSWICK BORDER AND SEVEN KILOMETERS FROM THE CITY OF EDMUNDSTON

That this beautiful botanical garden, one of Canada's most important horticultural developments of the late twentieth century, remains so little known is a mystery. Yet massive amounts of money were invested in producing a state-of-the-art botanical garden in a relatively inhospitable environment. Much of the planning of this garden was done by the Montréal Botanical Garden (page 35) and it shows; the garden is spacious, carefully planted, easily accessible to handicapped visitors, and all the lighting, irrigation, and other infrastructures were installed *before* planting, instead of as hard-to-hide afterthoughts as seems to be the case in so many other gardens. The piped-in classical music which makes visiting this garden so relaxing is a first in Canada.

The garden's location in one of the coldest corners of New Brunswick (Agriculture Canada hardiness zone three), meaning the flowering season starts late and ends early, but this also helps to concentrate bloom, with spring and early summer bloomers, or mid- and late season bloomers often in full flower at the same time. It also limits the choice of plants that can be grown, but that is hardly apparent, as there is wide variety of common and unusual trees, shrubs, perennials, and annuals that positively thrive in the cool summers. Most plants are clearly identified.

The show begins even before you officially enter the grounds, with striking displays of the latest developments in annuals just outside the Visitor's Center in semi-formal beds. The latter includes a small greenhouse housing a collection of succulents as well as admissions, administrative offices, and a cafeteria.

The most striking feature of the gardens is the magnificent *Alpine Garden*, which rises up from an artificial lake like a massive, craggy mountaintop and is strategically clothed in alpine and scree plants from around the world. A huge, very natural-looking waterfall drops into the lake from the rock garden and the rolling hills of the surrounding Madawaska Valley, densely covered in deep green conifers, make a perfect background—few alpine gardens anywhere in the world look quite as natural.

Other features include an *Economical Garden*, featuring vegetables, herbs, cereals, and textile plants, a *Natural Habitat Garden* displaying native plants in a humid setting by the river, a *Shade Garden* starring shade-tolerant perennials, a *pergola* hosting climbing and hanging plants, and, copied from one of the Montréal Botanical's finest achievements, the *Flowery Brook*, a winding artificial stream planted in a wide variety of perennials, including bulbs, lilies, daylilies, and ornamental grasses. The portrait is completed by two *arboreta* featuring hardy deciduous and evergreen trees.

The Economic Garden features such useful plants as vegetables, cereals, textile plants, and herbs.

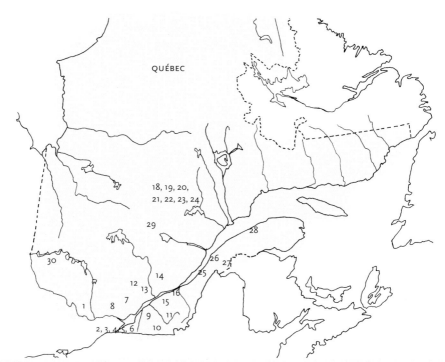

QUÉBEC

18, 19, 20,
21, 22, 23, 24

29

28

30

26 27

25

14

12
13
16

1
8
7

15

9
11

2, 3, 4, 5, 6
10

QUÉBEC

Two factors influence Québec gardens more than anything else: geography/climate and history/culture. Geographically, Québec is the largest of the Canadian provinces, covering 643,986 square miles (1,667,926 square kilometers)—about three times the size of Texas. The province of Ontario forms its western boundary while large bodies of water—Hudson Bay, James Bay, Hudson Strait, and Ungava Bay—delineate the province to the north. Labrador and the Gulf of the Saint Lawrence form the eastern borders while, starting from the east, New Brunswick and the northern New England states—Maine, New Hampshire, Vermont, and New York—are the southernmost limits.

Of this, nine-tenths is covered by a rocky, inhospitable shield left nearly bare of soil by the glaciers of the Ice Age, the Canadian Shield. Other than Inuit settlements to the north, along the coast from Hudson Bay to Labrador, and Amerindian settlements to the south and southwest, some scattered mining and forestry towns, fishing and hunting resorts, and hydroelectric projects, northern Québec is sparsely inhabited. In fact, the entire interior of this vast space is essentially devoid of human denizens: a land of mosses and lichens to the north and, in the center, the taiga—"land of the short trees"—where even Inuits and Amerindians rarely wander. The barrenness of northern Québec is such that road maps cling to the southern part of the province; there are no roads and therefore no practical reason to feature the north. Visitors traveling through the province, road map in hand, have therefore little reference to just how vast Québec really is.

From the point of view of European habitation, Québec essentially occupies a narrow strip of land to the

OPPOSITE: *Domaine des Fleurs, Saint-Pâcome*

south: mostly the valleys of the Saint Lawrence and the Ottawa rivers, plus a narrow extension up the Saguenay River to Lake Saint John. This is where Québec, Montréal, and Trois-Rivières/Cap-de-la-Madeleine, the province's largest cities, are found. The rivers are bordered by rich alluvial plains, wide in some sectors, very narrow in others, where many types of agriculture, from cereal production to market gardening and dairy farming, are possible. To the south, along the American and New Brunswick border and out to the point of the Gaspé peninsula, is the northern extension of the Appalachian mountains, a chain that reaches down into the United States as far as Alabama. The mountains themselves, well rounded and not particularly high, are undeveloped except for a few ski resorts and quarries, but the valleys below host a series of lakes and rivers surrounded by farmland. In the Southwest, the Appalachians are as heavily populated as the Saint Lawrence Valley, but populations decrease as the mountain chain angles towards the Gaspé peninsula, where colder temperatures brought by the cold Labrador Current make farming less productive. The vast majority of Québec's gardens are found in this southern sector of the province.

Québec's history gives a distinctly French flavor to its gardens. Of all Canada's provinces, only Québec is mostly French-speaking; of its some seven million population, about three quarters claim French as their mother tongue. European settlement began in Québec City (simply called Québec in French), founded by Samuel de Champlain in 1608. This was the first successful European settlement in what would one day become Canada, and the foundation of a French regime that would rule the entire interior of the North American con-

OPPOSITE: *À Fleur d'Eau Floral Park*. À Fleur d'Eau Floral Park

tinent, from New Orleans to Québec City, for almost two hundred years. The French installed a feudal system of land ownership—the seigniorial system— with seigniors or lords, often minor French aristocrats, obtaining rights to vast tracts of land which were then divided among the *habitants* or common folk. The seignior's duty was to provide basic services, such as a church, schools, and mills, to his subjects—who, in turn, were required to remit part of their crop to the seignior. Although the system was never as rigidly enforced as the feudal systems in Europe and the habitants had considerable freedom, it is worth mentioning in that several of Québec's gardens were originally seigniorial estates.

Québec City quickly became a booming metropolis, with 20,000 inhabitants by 1690, far outstripping the more modest British settlements of New England to the south. After a series of battles, the best remembered being that of the Plains of Abraham, in Québec City, in 1759, in which "New France" changed hands several times between the French and the British, it was finally ceded to Britain by the Treaty of Paris in 1763.

Interestingly, Britain did not attempt to erase French culture in Québec. They left most of its laws intact, even enshrining French, as well as English, as official languages, an unheard of concession at that time. As a result, French

culture and language continued to flourish in Québec in spite of British rule. The English-speaking population did increase over the years, though, especially after the American Revolution to the south created the now independent United States. Many English speakers, known as the Loyalists, unsatisfied with the new regime, left New England and moved north to the Maritimes, Ontario, and Québec. In Québec, they settled mainly in the hitherto undeveloped Eastern Townships, just North of New England, as well as along the Ottawa Valley and in the Gaspé Peninsula. Their descendants are still there, although an increasing French population overflowing into formerly English-speaking areas means that

Domaine Cataraqui

English speakers are a minority in most regions.

The history of English speakers in Québec City and Montréal is somewhat different. Many came over as administrators, military personnel, and merchants during the British regime. In fact, by the mid-1800s, both cities were mostly English. But as Canada's center of population shifted from Québec to Ontario after confederation in 1867, Québec's English population followed. Today, native English speakers are a tiny minority in Québec City, but still dominate in parts of Montréal, a bilingual city where both languages are spoken.

The grid on which many Québec gardens are today based is a complex one: a rigid, formal pattern dating from the seigniorial regime, but enlarged and softened by the influence of the English ruling class, then again modified as the French habitants ascended to urban life and the middle classes, and eventually to power. Perhaps the prime example of this is the Jardin

Domaine Maizerets. René Pronovost

Jeanne-d'Arc (Joan of Arc Garden) in Québec City (page 57), where the perfect cross made by the meeting of two straight axes, very much *à la française*, is overplanted with an English perennial border, to which has been added the brilliant color of annuals so beloved of the modern Québecers (or Québécois). Most gardens in Québec, if studied in detail, will reveal this mixed cultural background, as even during the period when the upper class British descendants dominated the garden scene they inevitably hired French-Canadian gardeners who managed to slip in their favorite plants.

Québec gardens are scattered throughout the inhabited parts of the province and are often located at great distances from one another. The province's best known and most beloved garden, Reford Gardens (Métis Gardens, page 67), for example, is a full day's drive from Montréal. Montréal boasts North America's largest and most diverse botanical garden, the Montréal Botanical Garden (page 35), a Mecca for gardeners throughout North America. And in numbers, the capital of the province, Québec City, boasts by far the largest number of public gardens. It would take three or four days to visit them all.

One note about garden names in Québec; some of the larger or older gardens have two names, one English, one French. In this chapter, the English name has been used in the title, while the French name is given in the text. Note though that road signs leading to the gardens will probably be only in French, so you should make sure you know the French name as well (hint: most start with the word "jardin"!). If you know a garden by its French name, you'll be able to locate it in the index at the back of this book. Other gardens have only French names and are listed under these names; no attempt has been made to translate them.

Also, most larger gardens have documentation (folders, maps, and so forth) available in both French and English. This is not as likely in the smaller gardens, so a smattering of knowledge of French can be helpful. In general, at least some of the gardens' staff are bilingual, so you can ask for explanations if you can't understand the printed information. And as always, everywhere in Québec, inserting a few words of French into your conversation, even if it is only a simply "Merci!," is always appreciated.

OPPOSITE: *The Mackenzie King Estate participates in Ottawa's Canadian Tulip Festival in May.* National Capital Commission

Hull: Mackenzie King Estate

I

LOCATION: NORTH OF HULL, TWENTY-FIVE-MINUTE DRIVE FROM OTTAWA, ONTARIO,
IN GATINEAU PARK. HIGHWAY 5 NORTH TO EXIT 12, THEN TURN LEFT ONTO OLD
CHELSEA ROAD. FOLLOW THE ROAD FOR TWO MILES (THREE KILOMETERS), THEN
TURN LEFT ON THE GATINEAU PARKWAY. FOLLOW SIGNS TO THE ESTATE

A stone's throw from Canada's capital, Ottawa, but on the
Québec side of the border, is the Mackenzie King Estate, also
called Moorside. It is located in the heart of the vast 87,968-
acre (25,600-hectare) Gatineau Park, mostly a beautiful natural
area of forests, nature trails, lakes, and streams, with abundant
wildlife. The estate is the former home of Canada's longest gov-
erning prime minister (1921–1948), William Lyon Mackenzie
King. He first bought a parcel of land here, called Kingswood,
on Kingsmere Lake, in 1903. He later bought the much vaster
Moorside Estate in 1924, and then other parcels of land, including "The Farm" (now the official residence of Canada's Speaker
of the House of Commons), and Shady Hill, a smaller residence. By the time of his death in 1950, the estate covered a
total area of 570 acres (231 hectares).

Mackenzie King was fascinated by gardening and sent for
seed from around the world to introduce into his garden. He
likewise personally oversaw the landscaping of the lands surrounding Moorside and Kingswood, adding flower beds, paths,
and ornamental features that have been maintained to this day.
The garden is perhaps best known as the outlet for Mackenzie

GARDEN OPEN: 11am to 5pm
Monday–Friday, mid-
May–mid-October; 10am to
6pm weekends and holidays,
mid-May–mid-October.
House open during garden
hours. **ADMISSION:** $7 per car.

FURTHER INFORMATION FROM:
Mackenzie King Estate
National Capital Commission
20240 Elgin Street
Ottawa, Ontario K1P 1C7
(800) 465-1867 or
(613) 239-5000
dmessier@ncc-cnn.ca
www.capcan.ca

NEARBY SIGHTS OF INTEREST:
Gatineau Park, Hull-Chelsea-
Wakefield Steam Train, Hull
Casino, Canadian Museum of
Civilization

King's curious attraction to artificial ruins, which he dotted throughout the Moorside section of the estate. They include the "Window on the Forest," the "Arc de Triomphe," and the "Abbey Ruins," all built from materials and architectural relics he purchased in Canada and Great Britain. They include stones from the original Canadian Parliament buildings (burned in 1916), the British Parliament Buildings in London, Westminster Abbey, the British North American Bank, and several other sites.

Besides the gardens, ruins, and nature trails, you can visit two of the residences, including *Moorside*, the ground floor of which is now the Moorside Tea Room, while the upper floor is the Moorside Museum, housing artifacts relating to Mackenzie-King's life. There are theaters in both Moorside and Kingswood showing films about the prime minister and his gardens.

The Mackenzie King Estate is used throughout the summer for a host of activities—lectures, concerts, workshops—and participates in the Canadian Tulip Festival, in May, with a display of over 8,500 tulips. Most activities are offered in English and in French.

GARDEN OPEN: 7am to 9pm daily, year-round.
ADMISSION: free.

FURTHER INFORMATION FROM:
Société du Parc Jean-Drapeau
Île Notre-Dame
Montréal, Québec H3C 1A9
(514) 872-0797
www.parcjeandrapeau.com

NEARBY SIGHTS OF INTEREST:
Parc-Plage, Île Sainte-Hélène,
La Ronde, Biosphère,
Montréal Casino

2 Montréal: Jardins des Floralies

LOCATION: FROM MONTRÉAL, EITHER TAKE THE SUBWAY TO STATION ÎLE-SAINTE-HÉLÈNE AND FOLLOW THE SIGNS TO ÎLE NOTRE-DAME OR, BY CAR, TAKE THE JACQUES-CARTIER BRIDGE TO THE ÎLE SAINTE-HÉLÈNE EXIT TO ANY OF THE PARKING LOTS, THEN REACH THE GARDEN BY FOOT. ALTERNATIVELY, FOLLOW SIGNS TO THE MONTRÉAL CASINO AND USE ITS PARKING LOT AS A BASE FOR YOUR VISIT

Three major international events put Montréal on the world map in the twentith century: the Olympics (1976), Expo 67 (Montréal World Fair), and the Floralies (1980), a summer-long international flower show. The latter two took place on two islands in the Saint Lawrence River, directly in front of Montréal: Île Sainte-Hélène and Île Notre-Dame. Today the entire archipelago is a public park called the Parc Jean-Drapeau—a recent name change: you may still find the park listed as Parc des Îles de Montréal—after the mayor who helped bring all three events to the city. Both islands are characterized by vast landscaped green spaces, forest, and waterways, with plenty of pedestrian and bicycle paths, not to mention the Montréal Casino and Québec's largest amusement park, La Ronde.

Garden lovers will enjoy strolling the walkways on both islands, but Île Notre-Dame will hold the greatest interest, as it is home to a more concentrated complex of flower gardens called the Jardins des Floralies, a mixture of some of the remaining pavilions of Expo 67 and the gardens of several of the different countries and states that participated in the Floralies: England, France, Israel, Italy, Some gardens are green and park-like, others full of flowers: perennials, annuals, and roses. Some, like those of Spain and especially Mexico, are largely made up of exotic plants (olive trees and palms in the first case, agaves, cactus, yuccas, and succulents in the second) that are overwintered in city greenhouses and planted out for the summer. The walled garden representing England is particularly charming, while that of Israel, with its ruins and potted citrus, is also very original. There is even a working peat bog, a recreation of the type of vegetation found further north in Québec. The entrance to the Montréal Casino, although not officially part of the Jardins des Floralies, is always beautifully planted in mostly annual flowers and well worth a stop. The building was originally the French pavilion during Expo 67.

Although admission to the Jardins des Floralies is free, you'll need to pay for parking. There are several restaurants on the island. Recreational activities include paddle boats and a public beach, plus bicycle paths.

Ruins featured in Israel's garden.

Montréal: Montréal Biodôme

LOCATION: IN OLYMPIC PARK JUST OUTSIDE OF DOWNTOWN. TAKE SHER-
BROOKE STREET TO ANY OF THE OLYMPIC PARK PARKING LOTS OR THE PIE IX
SUBWAY STATION

GARDEN OPEN: 9am to 7pm
daily, June 24–Labor Day;
9am to 5pm after Labor
Day–June 23. **ADMISSION:**
$9.50 adults, $7 seniors and
students, $4.75 children 5–12
years, free children 5 years
and younger.
**GARDEN AND NATIONAL
BIODÔME ADMISSION:** $15.25
adults, $11.25 seniors and stu-
dents, $7.75 youths, free chil-
dren 5 years and younger.

FURTHER INFORMATION FROM:
Montréal Biodôme
4777 Pierre-De Coubertin
Avenue
Montréal, Québec H1V 1B3
(514) 868-3000
www.ville.Montreal.qc.ca/
biodome

NEARBY SIGHTS OF INTEREST:
Montréal Botanical Garden,
Olympic Park

Following the Montréal Summer Olympics of 1976, most of its
sports installations, such as the bowl-shaped Olympic Stadium
with its tall mast, were put to good use, serving for sports
events and numerous other activities. The Velodrome, however,
built as an indoor bicycle racetrack, was not living up to its
potential and was empty much of the time. A decision was
made to recycle it to better use, and in 1992 it reopened as the
Montréal Biodôme.

It is hard to decide how to classify this vast indoor space. Is
it a garden? Or a zoo? Or an aquarium? It's all three in many
ways, but lovers of rare plants will certainly want to call it a garden. The concept of the Montréal Biodôme is not to build
"enclosures" or "beds," but rather to recreate entire ecosystems
indoors. There are four of them, three of interest to gardeners.
The largest and perhaps the most exciting is the *Tropical Forest*.
Plants and animals imported from Central and South America
evolve together here with relatively little human intervention;
they include, from the animal world, capybaras, caimans, parrots, monkeys, sloths, and piranhas and, from the vegetable
world, lianas, strangler figs, orchids, and bromeliads. Even the
columns that hold the roof up have been disguised as the massive trunks of forest giants. The temperature is hot year round
and humidity is often over 80 percent; you'll almost be able to
imagine yourself in Costa Rica or Venezuela.

The *Laurentian Forest* is an indoor version of the type of mixed deciduous/coniferous forest that would once have been prevalent on Montréal Island. Birchs, trembling aspens, maples, bog orchids, and much more serve as backdrops for such animals as beavers, lynx, and porcupines. The entire area is climate controlled; the plantings actually undergo seasons, just like outdoors, with temperatures remaining below freezing during the winter months. The best blooming is in March and April, as spring comes earlier indoors than out.

The *Marine Environment of the Saint Lawrence* is a mostly aquatic milieu, with only sparse vegetation around a 660,500-gallon (2.5-million-liter) saltwater basin, although some interesting salt-tolerant plants line the artificial granite that serves as a backdrop. There is even a "tide" (artificial, of course) that makes it possible to grow unique marginal plants, found only in the Saint Lawrence estuary in the wild, that need daily flooding to thrive.

The final ecosystem, the *Polar World*, is strictly without vegetation, but presents birdlife from both the Arctic and Antarctic . . . and who doesn't get a kick out of penguins?

It is possible to purchase tickets to see both the Montréal Biodôme and the Montréal Botanical Garden and Insectarium. A free shuttle bus leaves regularly from one site to the other.

OPPOSITE: *The size of the plants dwarfs visitors in the Tropical Forest.*

LEFT: *Looking down a tropical stream—in downtown Montréal.*

33

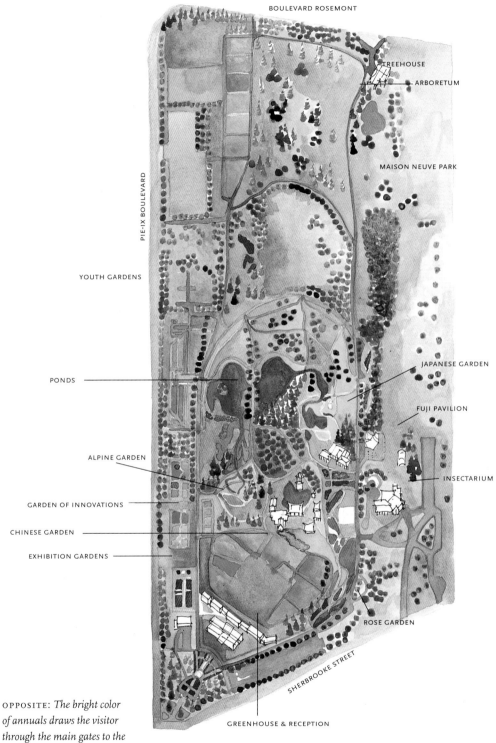

BOULEVARD ROSEMONT

TREEHOUSE

ARBORETUM

MAISON NEUVE PARK

PIE-IX BOULEVARD

YOUTH GARDENS

JAPANESE GARDEN

PONDS

FUJI PAVILION

ALPINE GARDEN

INSECTARIUM

GARDEN OF INNOVATIONS

CHINESE GARDEN

EXHIBITION GARDENS

ROSE GARDEN

SHERBROOKE STREET

GREENHOUSE & RECEPTION

OPPOSITE: *The bright color
of annuals draws the visitor
through the main gates to the
Reception Center.* Michel
Tremblay, Montréal
Botanical Garden

4 Montréal: Montréal Botanical Garden and Insectarium

LOCATION: IN MONTR AL, ON THE CORNER OF PIE IV BOULEVARD, NEAR THE PIE IX SUBWAY STATION

If any garden in Canada can be said to offer something for everyone, it is certainly the Montréal Botanical Garden. It is one of the largest botanical gardens in the world and includes what is by far the most complete plant collection in North America: some 21,000 species over 185 acres (75 hectares). In fact, it is generally ranked at second place among the world's botanic gardens—only England's Kew Gardens beats it. Even a full day's visit doesn't do it justice; botanists have been known to spend weeks there! It is also a primary tourist attraction for Montréal, drawing more than a million visitors per year.

Given the Montréal Botanic Garden's importance on the world scale, it is hard to imagine that it is still young as botanical gardens go. It was developed during the Great Depression of the 1930s, mostly as a make-work project to give gainful employment to the thousands of Montréalers who were out of a job. The man behind the garden was Brother Marie-Victorin, a teaching brother with a passion for botany. He had already founded the Botanical Institute of the Université de Montréal in 1920 and had drawn up plans for the Garden as early as 1925. An ardent lobbyist, he finally convinced the city to go ahead with the project in 1931. Additions and ameliorations are constantly being opened, so the garden is in constant evolution;

GARDEN OPEN: 9am to 5pm daily, September–May; 9am to 7pm, June–August.

ADMISSION: May–October: $9.50 adults, $7 seniors and students, $4.50 youths, free children 5 years and younger. November–May: $6.75 adults, $5.25 seniors and students, $3.50 youths, free children 5 years and younger.

FURTHER INFORMATION FROM:
Montréal Botanical Garden
4101 Sherbrooke Street East
Montréal, Québec H1X 2B2
(514) 872-1400
www.ville.Montréal.qc.ca/jardin

NEARBY SIGHTS OF INTEREST:
Montréal Biodôme, Montréal Olympic Tower and Olympic Park

scarcely a year goes by without some new project being unveiled.

Visitors with special interests should pick up a garden plan; collections are clearly marked and are therefore easy to locate. Those with more general interest might want to start out with a quick tour of the garden on one of the mini-trains that circulate throughout the opening hours. This will give you a brief general introduction to the garden and allow you to see where most of the gardens and collections are located. You can also use this means of locomotion to reach the farther-away parts of the garden, as the train makes regular stops to pick up and drop off passengers.

What you visit can also depend on the season. In winter and in inclement weather, the two top spots are the vast *greenhouse complex* and the Insectarium. The former includes ten public greenhouses, some housing plant collections, such as the fernery, the orchid and aroid greenhouse and the indoor bonsai display, others display greenhouses; the main greenhouse, for example, is always decorated with seasonal shows. The *Insectarium* is an offshoot of the Montréal Botanical Garden and acts as a living museum of insects. Visitors are expected not only to look, but to touch—and sometimes even to taste!—insects and arthropods of all sorts. There is also a butterfly shade house near the Insectarium, open in summer only.

TOP: *The Economic Plants Garden demonstrates well-known and little known vegetables, fruits, and textile plants.* Montréal Botanical Garden

BOTTOM: *The Chinese Garden, rising here from a bed of black-eyed Susans, is the only one of its kind in eastern Canada.* Montréal Botanical Garden

In spring, summer, and early fall, the outdoor gardens will likely be the main attraction. Two particularly interesting gardens are the *Japanese Garden* and the *Chinese Garden*, both authentic and built by artisans from their country of origin. The *Reception Garden*, with majestic fountains and broad flower beds, leads from the main entrance (corner of Sherbrooke Street and Pie IX Boulevard) to the Art Deco administration building, recently restored. The latter houses the garden's boutique. There is also a *Rose Garden* containing over 10,000 specimens, a shade garden, marsh and bog gardens, and a vast arboretum, with the "Tree House" (an exhibition devoted to trees) in one corner, which includes collections of just about every tree and shrub that can be grown in Québec.

Two very special gardens are the *Flowery Brook*, where a meandering brook wanders through a collection of perennials and bulbs, including irises, peonies, daylilies, and lilies, and

The Flowery Brook is very popular in early June.
Montréal Botanical Garden

the *Alpine Garden*, devoted to alpine and subalpine plants from around the world. Another "not to be missed" section is the *Exhibition Gardens*, which includes the Perennial Garden, the Annual Garden, the Economic Plant Garden (including useful plants, such as vegetables, fruits, and textile plants), the Medicinal Plant Garden, and a brand new Garden of Innovations where new plants are put on display.

For a more personalized visit, guided tours are offered daily except Wednesdays at 10:30am and 1:30pm, starting in the Reception Center. Groups can arrange tours at other times. Special shows, workshops, lectures, and other activities are held throughout the year; there is almost always some sort of special activity going on in the Montréal Botanical Garden.

It is possible to purchase tickets to see both the Montréal Botanical Gardens and Insectarium and the Montréal Biodôme and a free shuttle bus leaves regularly from one site to the other.

The above is only a brief summary of some of the main displays and activities in the Montréal Botanical Garden. Even casual garden visitors should allow a half day; serious gardeners will need a full day, or even two, to take in all the garden has to offer.

The Leslie-Hancock Garden features rhododendrons and azaleas.

GARDEN OPEN: 9am to 4pm daily, year-round. (Weekends, January and February, open to "Friends of the Arboretum" only.) **ADMISSION:** $5 adult, $3 senior, $2 children, $11 family.

FURTHER INFORMATION FROM:
Morgan Arboretum
150 Chemin des Pins,
C.P. 500
Macdonald Campus,
McGill University
Sainte Anne de Bellevue,
Québec H9X 3V9
(514) 398-7811
arbo@total.net
www.total.net/~arbo

NEARBY SIGHTS OF INTEREST:
Ecomuseum, Macdonald Farm, Sainte Anne de Bellevue

Wide paths take visitors deep into the virgin forest.

5 Montréal: Morgan Arboretum

LOCATION: ABOUT NINETEEN MILES (THIRTY KM) WEST OF MONTRÉAL. HIGHWAY 40 TO EXIT 41 (SAINTE ANNE DE BELLEVUE) AND FOLLOW SIGNS FOR CHEMIN STE-MARIE. LEFT AT STOP SIGN AT TOP OF HILL TO CHEMIN DES PINS AND FOLLOW SIGNS

The Morgan Arboretum is one of Canada's largest arboretums, covering some 605 acres (245 hectares) at the west end of Montréal Island. It came into being when the Morgan family donated the site to McGill University in 1945. They had already begun planting and maintaining a vast variety of trees, an effort that has since been accentuated.

The arboretum includes some of the oldest stands of trees remaining on Montréal Island, including a sugar maple forest nearly 200 years old. Most of the trees are natives and grow in typical environments for their type, but many introduced species also thrive. There are more than 150 species of trees, grouped in twenty different collections. There is also a collection of flowering shrubs in the "Blossom Corner" and also many exotic flowering trees, like tulip trees and magnolias. Most trees in the collections are labeled, as are many specimens along the numerous nature trails. Some thirty species of mammals and 200 species of birds also frequent the park and deer are frequently sighted, even in broad daylight. For the sake of the wildlife, please do not bring pets.

There are plenty of activities taking place in the arboretum throughout the year, including guided nature tours and bird-banding workshops, plus, in the winter, cross-country skiing. For information, contact the arboretum.

6 Montréal: Mount Royal Cemetery

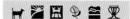

LOCATION: NORTHEAST SIDE OF MONT-ROYAL IN OUTREMONT (MONTRÉAL). FROM DOWNTOWN, DRIVE NORTH ALONG AVENUE DU PARC, LEFT ONTO CHEMIN CÔTE STE-CATHERINE TO REACH BOULEVARD MONT-ROYAL. LEFT AT CHEMIN DE LA FORÊT: THE GATES ARE AT THE END OF THE ROAD

Although some people may balk at the idea of calling a cemetery a garden, the Mount Royal Cemetery (Cimitière Mont-Royal) certainly is one. It was, in fact, designed from its very beginning to be a "garden cemetery." At the time of its founding, this was a revolutionary idea in cemeteries, very different from the typical churchyard interment sites with their straight rows and crowded tombs. It was based on North America's first garden cemetery, Mount Auburn, located in Cambridge, Massachusetts, and dating back to 1831. The idea that a cemetery could also be a beautiful garden where people could visit their loved ones in a healthier, more open atmosphere soon spread across North America.

Mount Royal Cemetery, first opened in 1847, followed the flowing contours of the mountain on which it was built, with curving paths, numerous tree plantings, lawns, flower beds, and much more. Today it covers 165 acres (68 hectares) on the north slope of Mount Royal. It contains many mature trees, including species rarely grown in Montréal, such as Kentucky coffee tree and Dawn redwood, and is a haven for over 145 species of birds. In May, the display of crabapples can be awesome, as can the lilac show that follows, and many flowering shrubs add further color into summer. By fall, fruit-bearing trees and shrubs with brilliant berries attract birds of all sorts while the late-blooming shrubs, like hydrangeas, add a last touch of color. The brilliant autumn reds of the maples and other trees and shrubs often makes the mountain seem ablaze with color. And under a layer of white snow, the conifers suddenly stand out and become the stars of the garden.

Obviously, history buffs will also enjoy a visit; many people in Montréal's history, mostly of Protestant background (the cemetery accepts all denominations, but has largely been used so far by Protestants, Jews, and certain ethnic groups), are buried here, including Ernest "Chinese" Wilson, the famous plant collector, and Henry Teuscher, first curator of the Montréal Botanical Garden.

Maps to major tree collections, historical graves, and good sites for bird watching are available at the gate.

GARDEN OPEN: 8am to 7pm Monday–Friday, 8am to 5pm weekends, mid-May–Labor Day; 8am to 4:30 pm Monday–Friday, 8am to 4pm weekends, Labor Day–mid-May. **ADMISSION:** free.

FURTHER INFORMATION FROM: Mount Royal Cemetery 1297 Chemin de la Fôret Outremont, Québec H2V 2P9 (514) 279-7358 www.mountroyalcem.com

NEARBY SIGHTS OF INTEREST: Montréal Botanical Garden, Montréal Biodôme

There's always something in bloom: here, lilacs blossom in late May. Mount Royal Commemorative Service

GARDEN OPEN: 8am to 10pm
daily, year-round.
ADMISSION: free.

FURTHER INFORMATION FROM:
Centre de la Nature de Laval
901, avenue du Parc
Laval, Québec H7E 2T7
(450) 662-4942
a.santerre@ville.laval.qc.ca

NEARBY SIGHTS OF INTEREST:
Cosmodôme

7 Laval: Centre de la Nature de Laval

LOCATION: **901** AVENUE DU PARC, LAVAL; JUST NORTH OF MONTRÉAL, WELL
SIGNPOSTED FROM MAJOR ROADS

There are several gardens to see within the Montréal region, and this is one of the largest ones. The Centre de la Nature is a vast city park of some fifty hectares. Located on the Laval Island, directly to the north of Montréal, it was designed by the City of Laval as a major project to make use of the city's worst eyesore; the gaping hole in the ground left by an abandoned quarry. Although originally considered as the future site of a garbage dump or landfill area, the quarry was located right in an area destined for suburban development and thus not particularly conducive to truck traffic. The city's planners instead came up with the idea of converting this giant hole in the ground into something much more attractive. Although there have been similar projects since elsewhere in Canada, in the 1970s, when the Centre de la Nature was planned, the concept was revolutionary. Thousands of truckloads of soil were carted in, trees were planted, gardens were prepared and today there is almost no sign of the park's origins.

Think of the Centre de la Nature as a vast urban park with plenty of recreation facilities such as playing fields, a swimming pool, an artificial lake with a beach, all making it very popular with the local population, especially in the summer months; it hosts more than a million visitors annually. There is even a working farm, although on a small scale, to introduce local children to agriculture. Horticulture, however, has been a major priority ever since the beginning of the project and the site is dotted with gardens designed to harmonize with the recreational activities. There are perennial and annual beds, of course, but also water gardens, a native plant garden, a medicinal garden, a sculpture garden, a recreated bog, and a conservatory displaying seasonal and tropical plants. The latter is open year-round, adding a bit of welcome horticulture interest to the winter landscape—at that season, visitors often show up on cross-country skis!

Although there is no fee charged for visiting the Centre de la Nature de Laval, there is a small fee for use of the parking lot that is applied on weekends and holidays.

It is astonishing to realize that this modern green park was once a hideous open hole.

8 Saint Eustache: Maison Chénier-Sauvé

LOCATION: FROM MONTRÉAL, HIGHWAY 13 TO EXIT 11, THEN WEST ON HIGH-WAY 640. EXIT AT ARTHUR SAUVÉ BOULEVARD AND HEAD SOUTH TO ST. LOUIS ROAD; RIGHT ON ST. LOUIS AND LEFT ON CHÉNIER

GARDEN OPEN: 2pm to sunset Tuesdays and Saturdays, mid-May to mid-October.
ADMISSION: $5.

FURTHER INFORMATION FROM:
Fondation Maison et Jardins Chénier-Sauvé
83, rue Chénier
Saint Eustache, Québec J7R 1W9
(450) 473-0149
romert@globetrotter.net

NEARBY SIGHTS OF INTEREST:
Centre de la Nature de Laval, Cosmodôme

The Maison Chénier-Sauvé draws its name after two famous families that have lived there over the years. Located in historic Old Saint Eustache, at the confluent of the Du Chêne and Thousand Islands Rivers and across from the town's historic church, the house has been, practically since its construction, inhabited by notables of all sorts, including no less than five provincial members of parliament and even one premier, Paul Sauvé! The current house was built in the late nineteenth century on the ruins of the original, destroyed by fire. It has been considerably enlarged over the years by the various families that inhabited it. At the time of writing, plans were being made to open the house as well as the gardens to visitors, but it would be best to phone ahead to check on this possibility.

Little is known of the original gardens, although some plantings, including some semi-wild shrub roses, survive from at least the mid-1800s. The current owner, Thérèse Romer, a well-known Québec garden writer, purchased the house in 1972 and slowly converted the vast lawns into flowerbeds. Her goal was to create a flower garden requiring only a minimum of care and no chemical pesticides or fertilizers. As a result, flowers mingle joyously in the vast borders and under the ancient trees in the forested sections. The garden is especially rich in shrubs, perennials, and bulbs, plus low-care roses and self-seeding biennials and annuals. Many of the plants are old varieties found on the site and since multiplied by Ms. Romer. There is something for every season, from the early bulbs first thing in spring to iris, peonies, daylilies, and other perennials as the season advances, and finishing with the fall crocus, autumn colors of trees, and the colorful berries of shrubs that attract birds right through the winter.

*Petals fall like confetti from a colewort (*Crambe cordifolia*) in the white perennial border.*

Workshops and lectures are given in the house and on the grounds during the summer; phone ahead for details. Admission is in the form of a donation to the Fondation Maison et Jardins Chénier-Sauvé.

Stanbridge East: À Fleur d'Eau Floral Park

LOCATION: ABOUT ONE HOUR FROM MONTRÉAL, NEAR THE AMERICAN BORDER, OFF ROUTE 202 BETWEEN BEDFORD AND DUNHAM

GARDEN OPEN: 9am to 4pm daily, mid-May–mid-June; 9am to 6pm daily, mid-June–mid-October.

ADMISSION: $7 adults, $5 seniors and youths, free for children 11 years and younger.

FURTHER INFORMATION FROM:
Parc Floral À Fleur d'Eau
140 Route 202
Stanbridge East, Québec J0J 2H0
(450) 248-7008
fleurdo@netc.net

NEARBY SIGHTS OF INTEREST:
Local vineyards (Domaine des Côtes d'Ardoise, L'Orpailleur, La Bauge), Missisquoi Museum, Les Caprices du Pré Soap and Cheese Factory

Many Canadian gardens feature water gardens, but only one is entirely dedicated to them. The Parc Floral À Fleur d'Eau (not to be confused with the Parc Botanique "À Fleur d'Eau" Inc., described on page 71) originally began in 1987 as Québec's first aquatic plant nursery, selling both wholesale and retail to gardeners throughout Québec. Even from the beginning, though, demonstration water gardens were a feature of the enterprise, but the lack of space at the original site meant they had to be very limited in size. The owners decided to look for a larger site and, in 1992, moved to the current one. Since then, they have spent much of their efforts in creating a park entirely devoted to water gardening.

Officially opened in 1997, the park now includes ponds and lakes, streams and waterfalls, and presents literally hundreds of aquatic plants, notably vast collections of water lilies and lotus. Some of the water features are quite formal, others more natural. One of the lakes, for example, is devoted to native aquatic and marsh plants. The naturally wooded site has been

Native and cultivated plants mingle on the border of this water garden. À Fleur d'Eau Floral Park

used to full advantage and, among other activities, there is a one-mile (two-kilometer) nature walk. There is also a butterfly garden and a garden of medicinal plants plus a picnic area. Naturally, the commercial end of the enterprise, the aquatic plant nursery, is also of great interest.

Note that many water lilies close in late afternoon, so it is best to visit before then to take full advantage of the gardens.

10 Sherbrooke: Howard Gardens

LOCATION: TAKE EXIT 140 FROM HIGHWAYS 10 AND 55, THEN FOLLOW HIGH-
WAY 410 TO EXIT 2. THE GARDENS ARE JUST OFF DE PORTLAND BOULEVARD AT
THE CORNER OF DE VIMY STREET

Sherbrooke is the "capital" of the Eastern Townships, actually in south*western* Québec (the townships got their name because they were east of Ontario), originally settled by United Empire Loyalists, although now mostly French-speaking. The city is known throughout Québec for the intricate carpet bedding that lines King Street, but the best displays are at Howard Gardens (Domaine Howard), known to locals as the "city greenhouses" or "serres municipales," depending on the language they speak.

Senator Charles Benjamin Howard donated the greenhouse on the corner of his immense estate to the city of Sherbrooke in 1940. The 1926 structure was first used by the city to produce annuals for their flower beds, but gradually developed a more public vocation as the lawns near the greenhouse became display gardens for the now almost forgotten art of carpet bedding, still their specialty to this day. The greenhouses, called the *Carl–Camirand Municipal Greenhouses* and now double the size of the original, today house collections of exotic plants, including a huge specimen of Queen of the Night cactus, *Selenicereus grandiflorus*, but are still used for producing annuals. Each fall, at the end of October and in early November, they host a highly popular chrysanthemum festival. Besides the annual beds, there are beautiful perennial borders, a Japanese garden, and collections of unusual shrubs.

Senator Howard finally donated the rest of his estate, a total of six acres (three hectares), to the city in 1962. Besides the three magnificent Anglo-Norman style homes dating to 1920 that serve various municipal functions, the grounds include flower beds, forest, parkland, picnic areas, and a large pond used as a beach in the summer and for skating in the winter. The site is often used for concerts, sports events, and other outdoor activities.

The gardens are open year-round, but are most interesting for their flowers from May to October. The greenhouses, closed in December, are usually free, but there are admission fees during the chrysanthemum festival and other special events.

GARDEN OPEN: dawn to dusk daily, year-round; greenhouse open 8am to 4pm daily, January–November.
ADMISSION: free.

FURTHER INFORMATION FROM:
Les Jardins du Domaine
Howard
1350, boulevard de Portland
Sherbrooke, Québec J1J 1S3
(819) 821-1919 or
(800) 561-8331
tourisme@sders.com
www.sders.com/tourisme

NEARBY SIGHTS OF INTEREST:
Seminary Museum of Natural History, King Street carpet bedding

Common annuals in complex patterns ensure summer-long color.

GARDEN OPEN: 11am to
6:30pm daily, mid-June–Labor
Day; by reservation only,
May–mid-June and
September–October.
ADMISSION: $5 adult, $3 stu-
dent, free children.

FURTHER INFORMATION FROM:
Jardin Daniel A. Séguin
3230 Sicotte Street
Saint-Hyacinthe, Québec J2S
7B3
(450) 778-6504 x209
www.ita.qc.ca/jardindas

NEARBY SIGHTS OF INTEREST:
ITA (Institute of Agricultural
Technology), Faculty of
Veterinary Medicine

11   # Saint-Hyacinthe: Jardin Daniel A. Séguin

LOCATION: ABOUT TWENTY MINUTES FROM MONTRÉAL. TAKE HIGHWAY 20 TO
EXIT 130, THEN FOLLOW SIGNS TOWARDS DOWNTOWN SAINT-HYACINTHE.
TURN RIGHT ONTO SICOTTE STREET

The Daniel A. Séguin Gardens are part of the campus of the
Institute of Agricultural Technology (ITA) and were originally founded in 1975 as a teaching garden for the students
in the school's horticultural program. From the beginning,
the gardens have been used for student training and appren-
ticeships, and most of the school's horticulture students
work in them at some point during their studies, helping
notably in planning, multiplication, and planting. The gardens have always been unofficially open to the public, but
their public nature was confirmed in 1995 when they were
inaugurated under the name of a retired professor, and one
of the founders of the original teaching garden, Daniel A.
Séguin.

   Today the gardens have become a very condensed botanical garden, including some 2,000 species of trees and flowers and over 350 annuals. The eleven-acre (4.5-hectare)
gardens are fully landscaped and include eleven different

thematic gardens: a formal French garden, a medicinal plant and vegetable garden, a Japanese garden including a Zen garden, a French-Canadian garden, a water garden, a herb garden, a shade garden, a rock garden, a composting demonstration site, and collections of shrubs and ornamental grasses. The test garden for annuals in the French garden is particularly interesting, always including the latest in annuals as well old-fashioned varieties that are rarely seen in modern gardens.

The extensive water garden offers lots of space to showcase marginal and aquatic plants.

12 Saint Charles de Mandeville: Jardin Forestier

LOCATION: FROM MONTRÉAL, TAKE HIGHWAY 40 TO EXIT 144, THEN FOLLOW HIGHWAY 347 TO SAINT GABRIEL. FROM THERE, FOLLOW THE SIGNS TO SAINT CHARLES DE MANDEVILLE

When Denis Lefrançois, inspired by pictures he had seen in a magazine, began pruning the conifers on his lot over thirty years ago, he certainly never imagined it would one day become a public garden. Yet his garden now receives thousands of visitors a year from all over the world and is the major tourist

GARDEN OPEN: 10am to 4pm daily, mid-June–Labor Day; open weekends in May and early June. ADMISSION: $6 adults, $5 seniors, $3 youths, free children 5 years and younger.

FURTHER INFORMATION FROM:
Jardin Forestier
547, 35th Avenue
Saint Charles de Mandeville,
Québec J0K 2N0
(450) 835-1377

NEARBY SIGHTS OF INTEREST:
Jardins du Grand-Portage,
Lake Maskinongé,
Mastigouche Nature Reserve

OPPOSITE: *The Japanese Garden is ideal for a relaxed stroll.* René Deschênes

LEFT: *Many of the topiary animals and forms were trimmed out of wild-growing conifers. Most took at least five years to form; taller ones required 15 years of pruning.* Jardin Forestier

45

attraction in tiny Saint Charles de Mandeville. The garden even received one of Québec's top awards for tourism when it opened in 1990.

Le Jardin Forestier (or Forestry Garden if you prefer a translation) is a simple one; there are no rare plants or vast borders and the only color comes from a few beds of common annuals. Instead, it is entirely devoted to topiary. There are over 700 pruned conifers on the site, mostly done in geometric forms, but there are also fifteen full-sized animals, including bears, an elephant, a snake, a peacock, and a giraffe. Mr. Lefrançois had to adapt the topiary styles he saw in books and magazines to local conditions; the boxwoods, privets, and yews usually used elsewhere simply won't grow in his yard—which is cut into the boreal forest, and cold even by Canadian standards. He's instead learned to use local species, mostly arborvitae, hemlock, and spruce. The majority of his topiaries were in fact not even planted; he simply pruned the evergreens where he found them. Their growth is painfully slow—it takes over five years to create a simple geometric shape, and up to twice as long for an animal one.

Although Denis Lefrançois still works in the garden, pruning leaves him little time for promotion or receiving visitors, and the garden is now administered by a profit-making organization. The site is wheelchair accessible and guided tours are offered.

GARDEN OPEN: 10am to 5pm daily, late June–late September. **ADMISSION:** $5 unguided visit, $9 guided tour.

FURTHER INFORMATION FROM:
Les Jardins du Grand-Portage
800 chemin du Portage
Saint Didace, Québec J0K 2G0
(450) 835-5813
colloidales@pandore.qc.ca
www.pandore.qc.ca/~colloidales/

NEARBY SIGHTS OF INTEREST:
Lake Maskinongé, Ste Ursule Waterfalls

13 Saint Didace: Jardins du Grand-Portage

LOCATION: EAST OF MONTRÉAL VIA HIGHWAY 20, EXIT 144 TO HIGHWAY 347 NORTH. HIGHWAY 348 EAST IN SAINT GABRIEL. AFTER PASSING THROUGH SAINT DIDACE, TAKE THE FIRST ROAD TO THE RIGHT, CHEMIN DU PORTAGE, ABOUT FOUR MILES (SIX KM) AFTER THE VILLAGE, AND FOLLOW SIGNS TO THE GARDEN

The Jardins du Grand-Portage are Québec's primary example of a organic vegetable garden that you can actually visit. Started over twenty years ago by Yves Gagnon and Diane Mackay, the gardens include not only a wide range of vegetables, herbs, and fruits—some of them, such as seed amaranthus, rare and unusual—but also plenty of ornamental plantings: perennials, annuals, shrubs, and trees. It is full of examples of using edible plants not only in the straight beds we think of when the word "vegetable garden" comes to mind, but in more ornamental ways, such as in containers, integrated into English borders, and even in formal knot gardens. All of this is done, of course, without the use of chemical pesticides and fertilizers. Even organic pesticides are used only very rarely.

A water garden waits around every turn.

The site includes vast flower borders, several gardens of oriental inspiration, including a *Zen Garden*—done in thyme rather than stone, and various water gardens. The gardens are home to many species of birds and butterflies while frogs regularly sing from the ponds. Starting from the entrance, you'll be invited to stroll down the main path through plantings of grapes, vegetables, green manures, and much more, so a visit does more than just appeal to the eye, it is a veritable learning experience at the same time. Guided tours, highly recommended, are available upon reservation . . . and yes, they do speak English! They cost a small additional fee over the usual admission price.

To fully enjoy the organic experience, reserve ahead and stay for lunch, offered in harvest season (August), as the Jardins du Grand-Portage are noted for their organic vegetarian cuisine. There is also a boutique selling local handicrafts and products of the farm plus refreshments. Books on organic gardening by the owner, Yves Gagnon, are also sold, although so far all are in French.

14 Shawinigan: Jardins de la Synérgie

LOCATION: NORTH SHORE OF SAINT LAWRENCE RIVER, HALF-WAY BETWEEN MONTRÉAL AND QUÉBEC, ABOUT FIFTEEN MILES (TWENTY-FIVE KM) FROM TROIS-RIVIÈRES VIA HIGHWAY 55 (EXIT 211). FOLLOW SIGNS TO THE CITÉ DE L'ÉNERGIE

GARDEN OPEN: dawn to dusk daily, year-round.

MUSEUM OPEN: 10am to 5pm Tuesday–Sunday in June; 10am to 8pm daily, late June–Labor Day; 10am to 5pm Tuesday–Sunday, early September–mid-October.

GARDEN ADMISSION: free.

MUSEUM ADMISSION: $14 adults, $13 seniors, $12 students, $8 children 6–12 years, free children 5 years and younger.

FURTHER INFORMATION FROM:
Cité de l'Énergie
1000 Avenue Melville
P.O. Box 156
Shawinigan, Québec G9N 6T9
(819) 536-8516
citedelenergie@qc.aira.com
www.citedelenergie.com

NEARBY SIGHTS OF INTEREST:
Cité de l'Énergie, La Mauricie National Park

The flowerbeds are always impeccably maintained. One features exotic cannas and Brazilian verbenas.

Melville Island hardly seems a likely spot for a garden. It sits in the middle of the Saint Maurice River, used both by smelly and polluting forestry and pulp and paper industries, and then later, starting in 1906, as a source of hydroelectric power for a burgeoning aluminum industry. And the town of Shawinigan was an industrial town, not a bucolic village. But that is now changing, and although the aluminum and forestry industries still remain, the Saint Maurice River is now pristine again, with clear water now flowing over its waterfalls, and the air is again pure. And, in an effort to revitalize the town, major investments were made in the 1980s and 1990s to convert the uninhabited island just across the river into a tourist attraction based on the area's industrial past. Today the site, now called the Cité de l'Énergie (City of Energy) includes a science center, an observation tower, a functioning hydroelectric power station and ruins of an abandoned one, a ferryboat, picnic areas, nature trails, and a deer enclosure. And also beautiful gardens.

Although the gardens were added on as an afterthought in an effort to make the site more congenial, they've become an attraction in their own right. Although admission is required for most of the activities of the Cité de l'Énergie (and a complete visit takes from three to six hours!), parking is free and there is unrestricted free access to the gardens, which now include over seventy impeccably maintained flower beds. Currently annuals dominate, but there is an increasingly vast choice of perennials, shrubs, and trees. And the gardens tend to specialize in lesser known plants. There is also a restored marsh that features native plants. Note that the gardens are spread over the entire site—that includes not only Melville Island and its science center, where most visitors arrive, but also the power station section across the river. Either take the ferryboat across from the docks or drive to the second section by car. There is a boutique and a cafe in the science center.

15 Kingsey-Falls: Parc Marie-Victorin

LOCATION: HALFWAY BETWEEN MONTRÉAL AND QUÉBEC, ON THE SOUTH SHORE. HIGHWAY 20, TO EXIT 185; FOLLOW HIGHWAY 255 TO KINGSEY-FALLS AND THE PARK

Brother Marie-Victorin (1885–1944) is a legendary figure throughout Québec. Founder of the Montréal Botanical Garden, ardent proponent of the teaching of botany and horti-culture in public schools, author of the province's most impor-tant book on botany, he, probably more than any other, contributed to awakening Québecers to the beauties of nature at a time when such things were still taken for granted. Brother Marie-Victorin was born in the tiny village of Kingsey-Falls and, in 1985, in commemoration of the 100th anniversary of his birth, a park was opened in his honor. Thanks to massive con-tributions by the multinational paper company, Groupe Cascades, Inc., which also got its start in Kingsey-Falls, what could simply have been a small town green space has rapidly grown into a vast and very colorful garden.

The twenty-nine-acre (twelve-hectare) park is built along the Nicolet River, and a natural stream runs through it. The developers have taken advantage of that to create a vast marsh garden of both native and cultivated species. Since no chemical fertilizers, pesticides, or herbicides are used in the park, the waters are home to birdlife, fish, and amphibians of all sorts. The main pavilion—providing space not only for administrative offices, but also for workshops, lectures, and other events—is built on higher ground, as are the other gardens. They include a flowering meadow, collections of trees, shrubs, conifers, and perennials, a garden of useful plants (herbs, vegetables, fruit trees), and a garden designed specifically to attract birds. The garden has developed a tradition of presenting amusing three-dimensional mosaic sculptures (plant-filled forms) of people and annuals. These change yearly and are highly popular with the younger set, and equally fascinating to adults.

A little over one mile (two kilometers) of easily accessible paths leads to all the sites and activities. Guided tours of the garden as well as one of the factories of Groupe Cascades Inc. are offered for a slightly higher fee; they leave daily at 10am, 11am, 1pm, 2pm, 3pm, and 4pm. It is recommended to phone ahead for an English language visit.

GARDEN OPEN: 9:30am to 5:30pm Sunday–Tuesday, 9:30am to 7:30pm Wednesday–Saturday, mid-June–mid-September; 9:30am to 5pm Monday–Friday, October–May. ADMISSION: $5.95 adults, $4.95 seniors, $3.95 students, $17 family.

FURTHER INFORMATION FROM:
Parc Marie-Victorin
385, Marie-Victorin
P.O. Box 356
Kingsey-Falls, Québec J0A 1B0
(819) 363-2528
parcm.victorin@ivic.qc.ca
www.ivic.cq.ca/mv

NEARBY SIGHTS OF INTEREST:
Laurier Museum

The Park has become a leader in Québec for three-dimensional carpet bedding.

GARDEN OPEN: 10am to 6pm weekends, mid-May–mid-June; 10am to 6pm daily, mid-June–Labor Day; 10am to 5pm weekends, Labor Day–mid-October; house open during garden hours.
ADMISSION: $8 adults, $7 seniors, $5 students, free for children 6 years and younger.

FURTHER INFORMATION FROM:
Domaine Joly-De Lotbinière
Route de Pointe-Platon
C.P. 669
Sainte-Croix, Québec G0S 2H0
(418) 926-2462
domnjoly@globetrotter.net

NEARBY SIGHTS OF INTEREST:
Québec City, Jardins Roger-Van den Hende

16 Sainte-Croix: Domaine Joly-De Lotbinière

LOCATION: SOME THIRTY MILES (FIFTY KM) FROM QUÉBEC CITY; TAKE HIGHWAY 20 TO EXIT 278, THEN HIGHWAY 271 TO SAINTE-CROIX. FROM THERE, TAKE HIGHWAY 132 WEST TO ROUTE DE POINTE-PLATON. THE GARDEN IS WELL SIGNED

Few gardens in Canada have a longer horticultural tradition than Domaine Joly-De Lotbinière. Practically from the time of its founding in 1828, as a summer residence for daughter of the seignior of Lotbinière, Julie Christine Chartier de Lotbinière, and her new husband, French champagne merchant, Pierre-Gustave Joly, the site became known for its gardens. Their son, Sir Henri-Gustave Joly-De Lotbinière, was especially passionate about forestry and horticulture. Although he is best known in Québec as a politician—he served as a deputy for both provincial and federal governments and was Québec's first premier—he was passionate about trees and, after he inherited the estate in 1860, planted dozens of varieties on the property to test their potential for wood production. Some of these, now midway through their second century, still stand, including a spectacular specimen of Norway spruce (*Picea abies*) that has self-layered. Likewise, although he was told that black walnut (*Juglans nigra*) could never grow so far north, he planted 10,000 seeds obtained from the northernmost locales where the tree grew at that time; most indeed did not survive the first few winters, but today over 250 centenarians remain, and seedlings derived from them are found in gardens throughout Québec. He planted oak and beech avenues and forests of red oak and sugar maple, which are presently being restored. He also helped established Arbor Day in Québec, where students got a day off each year to study and plant trees.

Alain, Henri-Gustave's grandson, inherited his grandfather's passion for forestry and horticulture and set out, from 1908 on, to make the estate the foremost private garden between Québec City and Montréal. Lawns and gardens were set out in the picturesque style. Formal French gardens were filled with exotic vegetables, such as blue potatoes, that Alain loved to test under the region's harsh climate. An orchard of now rare fruit trees was put in place, greenhouses were installed, and ponds and water features were added. By the 1960s, though, the family was finding their summer home too expensive to maintain, and it passed into the hands of the Québec government and went into a rapid decline. Fortunately a group of local residents formed a foundation to save the old estate and has been busily restoring both the house and the gardens since the early 1990s.

Today the estate has taken on the look it once had in its heyday, the mid-1930s, thanks greatly to the fact that the site's

Maple House was named for the ornate carvings of maple leaves that decorate the exterior.

last gardener, Toussaint-Emmanuel Le Pennec, now deceased, was still alive when the restoration began. Although over 90 years old at the time, he still vividly recalled the layout of the gardens and that plants that grew there. Thus the French style garden now contains, as it once did, a *potager*, a garden of curiosities, a white garden, a cut flower garden, and a garden of the senses. Rare apple trees are being grafted and replanted in the *Experimental Garden* and trees long dead have been replanted. The pond has been dredged and replanted and gazebos and fountains recalling the original ones have been installed. Likewise the rose garden and the original vast perennial borders have been re-established, including not only the plants traditionally grown by the Joly-De Lotbinières, but also new varieties, recalling the estate's long history as a testing ground for new plants. More recent additions include a small commercial nursery specializing in rare plants. Visitors should ask for the guidebook; it contains a map of the site including the placement of the estate's most remarkable trees. Plants in the formal gardens and perennial borders are identified by numbers keyed to a list of over 400 species also included in the guide. Although the guide is written in French, all plants are identified by botanical name.

The newly restored residence, called *Maple House* for the ornate carvings of maple leaves that decorate its exterior, is open again to visitors and includes period furniture, an art gallery, and a small boutique and cafe. Nature lovers will enjoy the estate's 1.5-mile (2.4-km) nature trail down to the river or a walk along the cliff top looking down over the Saint-Lawrence River. Bird-watchers should note that the site is renowned for the number of species that inhabit it or pass through during migration. There are two picnic areas for those who wish to stay for the day and also Sunday morning concerts. Guided tours of the house and gardens are likewise available.

GARDEN OPEN: 9am to 5pm daily, late June to mid-September, by reservation only. **ADMISSION:** $5 adults, $2 children.

FURTHER INFORMATION FROM:
Jardins Merle Bleu
708 Côteau des Roches
Notre-Dame de Portneuf,
Québec G0A 2Z0
(418) 286-3417
jmerlebleu@globetrotter.net

NEARBY SIGHTS OF INTEREST:
Old Deschambault
Presbytery, Moulin de la
Chevrotière, Portneuf Marina

17 Notre-Dame de Portneuf: Jardins Merle Bleu

LOCATION: THIRTY-ONE MILES (FIFTY KILOMETERS) EAST OF QUÉBEC VIA HIGHWAY 40. EXIT 251 ONTO ST. LOUIS ROAD, THEN ST. JACQUES ROAD, WHICH TURNS INTO CÔTEAU DES ROCHES ROAD

The name "merle bleu" means bluebird, after the eastern bluebird, a species that was considered endangered in Québec until a series of nesting box trails, set up in rural sites such as this garden, helped the species recover. The site was originally started as a bird sanctuary in 1980, and the ornamental gardens have been added gradually since then. They were opened to the public in 1993 and, in spite of a change in ownership (which has done in many "private gardens open to the public" in Québec), are still open daily, by reservation, during the summer months.

The seven-acre (three-hectare) site allows plenty of room for landscaping, and numerous paths lead into it over small bridges and streams, in to open and forested areas. The gardens are best seen as a series of often large garden rooms, including a formal French garden housing annuals and daylilies, a Baroque garden, a white garden, a shade garden, a secret garden, a fall garden, a rose garden, a crabapple garden, and much more. There is also a pergola near the largest lake that is open to picnickers.

Plant lovers will appreciate the vast collections of hostas, daylilies, bearded irises, and roses, most identified, while the younger set will enjoy the wildlife and the duck pond. The numerous bodies of water, including a natural stream, often plenty of opportunities for aquatic and marsh plants to show off. There are also thousands of spring bulbs—crocus, tulips, daffodils, —but special arrangements would have to be made to visit so early in the season. And in all seasons, don't forget to keep an eye open for the dozens of species of birds that make their home in this beautiful garden.

You can visit the gardens on your own, but guided visits are available to groups of ten or more. There is a boutique where local handicrafts are sold.

18 Québec: Domaine Cataraqui

LOCATION: FOUR MILES (SIX KILOMETERS) WEST OF QUÉBEC CITY VIA GRANDE-ALLÉE, TURN ONTO CHEMIN SAINT-LOUIS UNTIL NO. 2131

In the mid-1800s, Québec City was North America's largest metropolis and the major center of commerce between Great Britain and the New World. This prosperity attracted numerous merchants and businessman to the city. They inevitably built homes in the city for winter use, but also majestic summer residences on vast estates within carriage distance of the walls. Most of these estates were sold off and subdivided as the city's influence waned; the few that remain intact were purchased by religious orders for use as convents, monasteries, and private schools and are not open to the public. The only one that you can still visit and which has remained mostly intact is Cataraqui (see *Villa Bagatelle*, page 60, and *Parc du Bois-de-Coulonge*, page 61, are examples of two other now fragmented estates with a similar history). Inevitably, as was the case of Cataraqui, these estates were built high on the cliffs overlooking the Saint Lawrence River, affording an incredible view that still remains today.

The gardens of Domaine Cataraqui have undergone several modifications over their long history, starting with the building of the villa in 1850. At that time, the Scottish gardener Peter Lowe began landscaping the fields in front of the house and tracing paths through the woodlands of the site. Later efforts, such as those of Mary Stewart in 1929, one of the first North American women to work as a landscape designer, can be seen in the rock garden she created on a natural rock outcropping near the cliff edge. The site was nearly entirely redesigned by George Penny under the tutelage of its last owners, the influential artists Percyval Tudor-Hart and Catherine Rhodes, close friends of French artist Claude Monet. Today, the Fondation Bagatelle, with help from the Québec government, is working to restore the gardens to their former glory.

The site includes a small arboretum, a mixed border, the restored rock garden, and the vast, sloping lawn that the Tudor-Harts so loved. Many of the plants used in the restoration were recuperated from the property and multiplied on site, including the magnificent dutchman's pipe (*Aristolochia durior*) that covers the pillars on each side of the neoclassical villa's main porch. Work is being carried out on the greenhouses, once used to supply such exotic fare as oranges and figs to impress visitors, and the vast vegetable gardens, recalling the period when the landowners were so far from civilization, they had to grow their own produce. Most of the forest is still intact and gives an idea of the natural vegetation of this rather protected spot overlooking the Saint Lawrence.

The house has a two-fold function. On one hand, it is being used as a museum and small concert hall, with one

GARDEN OPEN: 9am until dusk daily, beginning of May to end of October; house open 10am to 7pm Tuesday–Sunday, March–December. **GARDEN ADMISSION:** free. **HOUSE ADMISSION:** $5 adults, $4 seniors and students, free children 12 years and younger.

FURTHER INFORMATION FROM: Domaine Cataraqui
2141 Chemin Saint-Louis
Sillery, Québec G1T 1P9
(418) 681-3010

NEARBY SIGHTS OF INTEREST: Villa Bagatelle, Maison des Jésuites

OPPOSITE: *Forest, shrubs, water, flowers, and open areas create a variety of environments to attract a great number of birds.* Les Jardins Merle Bleu

*Before restoration, magnificent specimens of Dutchman's pipe (*Aristolochia durior*) grew on either side of the main entrance. The younger plants found there today were taken as cuttings from the originals.*

section serving as a boutique. On the other, it is also the official residence of the Québec government, with the upper floor being used to host important visitors to the province. The winter garden, just off the main house, contains potted Victorian tropical plants as it once did. The other buildings, such as the workshop, the stables, and the servant's quarters, are in various stages of restoration; some are used as administration offices, others may be visited.

GARDEN OPEN: 8am to 9pm daily, year-round; house open 10am to 5pm daily, year-round. **ADMISSION:** free.

FURTHER INFORMATION FROM:
Domaine Maizerets
2000, boulevard
Montmorency
Québec City, Québec G1J 5E7
(418) 691-4872

NEARBY SIGHTS OF INTEREST:
Old City, Cartier-Brébeuf
National Historic Site, Île
d'Orléans

19 Québec: Domaine Maizerets

LOCATION: FROM THE AUTOROUTE DE LA CAPITALE NORTH OF QUÉBEC CITY,
TAKE HENRI-BOURASSA BOULEVARD SOUTH. TURN RIGHT ON MONTMORENCY
BOULEVARD TO NO. 2000

Surprising, isn't it, that a country retreat of sixty-seven acres (twenty-seven hectares) could survive so close to one of North America's most ancient cities? Yet that is the case with Domaine Maizerets, just outside of the Old City of Québec. Originally developed as a farm, it was purchased by the Séminaire de Québec in 1705 and used by it for almost three centuries, mostly as a farm to supply the tables of the seminary, a private Catholic school to which Laval University, the New World's oldest institution of higher education, traces its origin. As time went on, much of the land was returned to forest and it became a quiet country retreat—if such a term can be applied to an estate that has been surrounded by city for over two hundred years. Through part of the twentieth century, it even served as a summer camp, and indeed the swimming pool, play areas, and nature walks are still used by a local day camp during the summer months. Originally called *La Canardière* for the numerous ducks ("canards" in French) that Champlain harvested there to feed the newly founded capital of New France in the seventeenth century, it was renamed Domaine Maizerets in 1850 after the superior of the seminary, Louis Ango de Maizerets.

Although the Domaine has been a public park, operated by the City of Québec, since 1979, it still shows many traces of its past. The elliptical pond surrounding small Saint Hyacinth Island was built by the monks in 1859 to house a small oratorio, now gone and replaced by a gazebo. The main building, called the Château Ango-Des Maizerets, is built in the traditional Québécois style, with a high, pointed roof and thick stone walls. Originally a rather modest structure, it burnt down several times over the centuries, each time replaced by a longer and longer structure until it reached its present dimensions early in the twentieth century. It was restored in 1980 and is now used for several functions, including an exhibition relating the site's history. There are also lectures on nature and gardening as well as regular concerts during the summer months.

The city preserved the remaining forest and wetlands, and nature walks meander through them, taking visitors to, among other sites, the nesting area of the ducks that gave the estate its original name. About 180 other species of birds are also known to visit the site. A bicycle path also crosses the park and there is a swimming area. Of greater interest to gardeners are the various flowerbeds containing mostly perennials and the collections of hardy shrub roses and rhododendrons. There is even a pavilion with a roof covered in meadow flowers! The "new" section is a former snow dump which was incorporated when the city took over the park; it is now an arboretum of more then 1,000 trees and 15,000 shrubs, many of them identified, plus an observation tower and a maze.

The Château Ango-Des Maizerets, reflected in the elliptical pond, is built in the traditional Québécois style.
René Pronovost

GARDEN OPEN: 9am to 8pm daily, May 1–September 30. **ADMISSION:** free.

FURTHER INFORMATION FROM:
Société des Amis du Jardin
Université Laval
Pavillon de l'Envirotron
Sainte-Foy, Québec G1K 7P4
(418) 656-3410
patrice.belanger@crh.ulaval.ca
www.fsaa.ulaval.ca/

NEARBY SIGHTS OF INTEREST:
University Laval Campus, Old City

20 # Québec: Jardin Roger–Van den Hende

LOCATION: ON OUTSKIRTS OF QUÉBEC CITY, ABOUT ONE MILE (TWO KILOMETERS) FROM THE BRIDGES VIA BOULEVARD LAURIER, AT THE CORNER OF AUTOROUTE DU VALLON AND BOULEVARD HOCHELAGA

The Jardin Roger–Van den Hende is Québec City's botanical garden. It was originally founded in 1966 as a teaching garden by professor Roger Van den Hende for students studying horticulture at Laval University and is located to the extreme west of the university campus, cut off from the rest by Autoroute Du Vallon. The original garden is a series of rectangular beds called the *Herbacetum*, which contain over 1,200 species of herbaceous plants (perennials, annuals, biennials, bulbs, climbers), organized by family affinity. This gives a rather unique character to the garden, as useful plants such as herbs and vegetables mingle with strictly ornamental types—for example, potatoes and tomatoes are planted next to petunias, as all are in the same botanical family. This arrangement assures that even the casual visitor really does learn something from his or her visit—which is, after all, the goal of a teaching garden. Just about all the plants are clearly identified as to botanical name, and the signs are color-coded (red for annuals, gray for industrial, agricultural, and textile plants, white for herbs and vegetables, black and silver for winter hardy plants, and brown for half-hardy and greenhouse plants).

The garden has grown considerably since its inception, and an arboretum—a collection of trees and shrubs, in this case also arranged by botanical affinity—now covers the largest part of its surface. Considering the garden's northern location, it is particularly rich in "exotic" species, such as rhododendrons and magnolias, usually not considered hardy in cold climates. A windbreak does however offer some shelter from harsh winds, and Mr. Van den Hende specifically chose seeds of plants taken from the northernmost part of their zone to trial in the garden; many of his selections have since been distributed to commercial nurseries and have become the standard varieties for cold climate gardens around the world. The rhododendron/azalea collection, grouped together in a special *Ericacetum* at the back of the Herbacetum is particularly extensive and well worth a visit in May and June.

Recent years have seen a swing made from the rectilinear beds towards more decorative landscaping, including such additions as a large water garden, a rose garden, a pergola, hedges, an entry pavilion, several modern sculptures, a garden of new introductions, and several other features. One very colorful addition is the annual trial grounds, a test garden of over 400 annuals showing the current and future stars of many of

North America's most important seed companies. There is also a compost demonstration area and a modern research building, the *Envirotron*, which houses not only the garden's offices but also an atrium featuring tropical foliage plants. The numerous greenhouses on the site are not, however, open to the public.

Although there is no official charge for visiting the garden, a donation is suggested, and you'll have to pay for parking except on weekends.

21 Québec: Joan of Arc Garden

LOCATION: JUST OUTSIDE THE WALLS OF OLD QUÉBEC, WITHIN THE PLAINS OF ABRAHAM

Certainly the most visited of Québec City's gardens, the Joan of Arc Garden (Jardin Jeanne d'Arc) is located within the much larger, 264-acre (107-hectare) National Battlefields Park—better known to the locals as the Plains of Abraham (Plaines d'Abraham) after Abraham Martin, who originally farmed the land. It was the site of major battles between the English and French in the mid-1700s and was declared a national monument in 1908 during festivities marking the 300th anniversary of the founding of Québec. The *Plains of Abraham*, designed by American landscape architect Frederick G. Todd, are beautiful in their own right, with sweeping vistas overlooking the Saint Lawrence River and the Québec Citadel, vast open fields, munitions towers, and abundant trees, but are best considered an urban park more than a garden, as they are more green than colorful. There are however several floral enclaves in this vast green space, the major one being the Joan of Arc Garden.

This garden, designed in 1938 by Montréal landscape architect Louis Perron, came about after Anna Vaughn Hyatt Huntington, an American sculptress who had fallen in love with Québec City, donated her most celebrated work of art to the city: a beautiful bronze statue of Joan of Arc. After deciding to

GARDEN OPEN: dawn to dusk daily, May–October.
ADMISSION: free.

FURTHER INFORMATION FROM:
National Battlefields Commission
390 de Bernières Avenue
Québec, Québec G1R 2L7
(418) 648-4071
ccbn.mdld.pa@videotron.ca
www.ccbn-nbc.gc.ca

NEARBY SIGHTS OF INTEREST:
Plains of Abraham, Old City, Martello Tower, National Battlefields Park Interpretation Centre, Québec Citadel

ABOVE: *Perennial borders add color throughout most of the season.*

Located just outside the city walls, the gardens are a favorite of vacationers.

place it on the Plains of Abraham, authorities felt it was deserving of greater attention and that was how the idea of surrounding it with a garden came about. The style of the garden is very interesting; the statue is located at the axis of a large cross, in the precise center of the garden, very much in the classical French style. It is likewise always surrounded by intricate carpet bedding, recalling the knot gardens (*parterres de broderie*) developed in France in the late sixteenth century. However, the formality of the garden is softened by the sunken beds of perennials, annuals, bulbs, and perennials, very much British in concept, that surround the rectangular garden. This in turn is circled by a planting of mature American elms. The end result is a very unique garden that truly does seem to represent Québec's long history: distinctly French, but with a British overlay.

Many of the shrubs and perennials that line the extensive beds are the same cultivars planted in 1938, many times divided and moved, but still maintained year after year. New varieties are however constantly introduced, notably annuals that are used to ensure constant summer color, so the garden always has appeal to both people seeking historic interest and those who enjoy seeing the latest releases in plant material. All the plants are identified, although the labels can be hard to find.

GARDEN OPEN: 11am to 5pm daily, end of June to Labor Day. House open during garden hours, and also 1pm to 5pm Sunday, Labor Day to end of June. **ADMISSION:** $5 adults, $4 seniors, $3 students.

FURTHER INFORMATION FROM:
Maison Henry-Stuart
82 Grande Allée Ouest
Québec, Québec G1R 2G6
(418) 647-4347
cmsq@megaquébec.net
www.cmsq.qc.ca

NEARBY SIGHTS OF INTEREST:
National Battlefields Park, Québec Museum, Grande Allée, Cartier Avenue

22 Québec: Maison Henry-Stuart

LOCATION: IN QUÉBEC CITY, ONLY A SHORT DISTANCE FROM THE OLD TOWN, AT THE CORNER OF GRANDE ALLÉE AND CARTIER AVENUE

The Maison Henry-Stuart (Henry-Stuart House) is a rare pearl among Canadian gardens: a historic garden that has been maintained essentially as is. There are many recreations of older gardens or ancient gardens that have been restored to something close to their original state, but this one is authentic. It was designed and maintained by the same woman, the house's last owner, Adele Stuart, from 1918 to 1987. It is said she spent every morning in her garden, weeding and watering, until the very day of her death at the age of 98. She was helped by her faithful gardener, who was in his mid-eighties when Miss Stuart died.

This is a period garden, representing gardens of the English-speaking upper class in Québec City in the 1920s. By that time, the attraction of the fussy, detailed gardens of the Victorian era had waned and cottage gardens were all the rage. Miss Stuart followed that trend, notably after a visit to England where such gardens had already been popular for quite some time. She wanted a beautiful view all year long with plenty of cut flowers to bring indoors for arrangements. This style perfectly suited the colonial cottage house dating to 1849. It is worth noting that, at the time, the garden was located at the very edge of the city; the city has grown up around it and, with its relaxed country cottage style, the garden now looks somewhat out of place. The plants in the gardens were personally chosen by Miss Stuart and include scented shrub roses, goatsbeard, hardy clematis, peonies, and many self-sowing annuals and perennials. Many of the tools used by the owner and her gardener are still visible in the garden.

Admission to the garden includes a guided tour of the house (available in English or French, although it is preferable to reserve for an English-language visit), plus tea and pastries, as Miss Stuart was wont to serve guests. A visit is therefore very much like stepping back in time to the 1920s. The garden is the only one in Québec considered authentic enough to have merited the title of Historic Monument.

Shrub roses are among the many cut flowers Miss Stuart included in her garden.

GARDEN OPEN: dawn to dusk daily, early May to late October. House open 10am to 5pm Tuesday–Sunday, March–December.
ADMISSION: garden, free; museum, $3.

FURTHER INFORMATION FROM:
Villa Bagatelle-Musée Jardin
1563 Saint Louis Road
Sillery, Québec G1S 1G1
(418) 688-8074 or (418) 681-3010

NEARBY SIGHTS OF INTEREST:
Parc du Bois-de-Coulonge,
Old City

23 Québec: Villa Bagatelle-Musée Jardin

LOCATION: JUST OUTSIDE OF QUÉBEC CITY, INTERSECTION WHERE LAURIER BOULEVARD AND ST. LOUIS ROAD CONVERGE TO BECOME ST. LOUIS ROAD, NO. **1563** ST. LOUIS ROAD

The history of Villa Bagatelle is given in greater detail on pages 61–62, as it was originally part of Parc du Bois-de-Coulonge, formerly Spencer Wood. After a first subdivision, this part of the original estate became known as Spencer Grove, then after a second subdivision, during which the property took on its present 2.5-acre (one-hectare) outline, as Spencer Cottage. The original house, dating back to 1848, was destroyed in a fire in 1927, but the house today, a modified neo-Gothic cottage, was built according to the original plan. The house is noted historically as the residence of historian and author James MacPherson Lemoine.

Villa Bagatelle came very close to being demolished in the 1970s and early 1980s. It had already been abandoned for a number of years when the Fondation Bagatelle was formed to save the historic site and its gardens. In 1984, work began on renovating the dilapidated building and on restoring the gardens. Interestingly, many garden plants—vinca, autumn crocus, martagon lilies, *Anemone nemorosa*, *Mahonia aquifolia*—had not only survived decades of abandon, but had even proliferated. Today they still make up the backbone of the garden.

The original plans of the garden had been lost and no one recalled what the gardens had looked like in their heyday in the early twentieth century. The present style is therefore not historically accurate, but represents a typical upper class garden of the time, with a rose garden, a water garden, a cutting garden, and mixed borders. A lilac hedge now surrounds the property to keep out the sound of traffic at what has become a very busy

Villa Bagatelle is surrounded by shady nooks and perennial borders.

intersection. Much of the estate is now heavily wooded, so shade tolerant plants (ferns, hostas, wild ginger) are dominant. There are also shade-tolerant shrubs such as rhododendrons and numerous spring bulbs.

Although there is no cost for visiting the gardens, there is a suggested donation to visit the house, which serves as an art gallery and museum of natural sciences, with displays that change seasonally. Parking is extremely limited in the area and there is none in the garden itself. It is best to park at Parc du Bois-de-Coulonge, about one block away.

24 Québec: Parc du Bois de Coulonge

LOCATION: IN SILLERY, BETWEEN QUÉBEC AND SAINTE-FOY. FROM OLD QUÉBEC, SAINT LOUIS ROAD TO NO. 1215. FROM POINTS WEST OF QUÉBEC, TAKE BOULEVARD LAURIER WHICH TURNS INTO SAINT LOUIS ROAD ONE BLOCK FROM THE GARDEN

GARDEN OPEN: dawn to dusk daily, year-round.
ADMISSION: free.

FURTHER INFORMATION FROM:
Parcs de la Commission de la
Capitale Nationale
525, boul. René-Lévesque Est
Québec, Québec G1R 5S9
(800) 442-0773 or
(418) 528-0773
commission@capitale.
gouv.qc.ca
www.capitale.gouv.qc.ca

NEARBY SIGHTS OF INTEREST:
Villa Bagatelle, Old City, Joan
of Arc Garden

No other garden in Canada—and indeed, few in the New World!—has such a long history as an estate garden . . . nor has had as many name changes! First purchased in 1653 by the third Governor of New France, Louis d'Ailleboust, Sieur de Coulonge, it became the heart of the Châtellenie de Coulonge, an immense estate encompassing about half of the current city of Sillery. It later became the property of the Séminaire de Québec which sold it to an English officer, Henry Watson Powell, in 1780. He called it Powell Place, and built a villa and the site's first greenhouses, flowerbeds, and walkways. Under successive owners, it changed names several times, becoming eventually known as Spencer Wood. By 1833, it was under the ownership of Henry Atkinson, a prosperous wood merchant, who, with the help of his gardener, Peter Lowe, redesigned the paths and roads to and set about turning the estate into the best known showcase garden in North America. With its vast greenhouses of exotic plants, its arboretum, rose gardens, and English style flower beds, it attracted visitors from all over the continent.

The estate was subdivided in 1854, with the center part (the current park) being sold to the government of United Canada to become the governor-general's residence (Villa Bagatelle, page 60, was another part of the original Spencer Wood that would eventually become a public garden). The house burnt to the ground in 1863, and an even larger, more majestic home replaced it. Shortly after the new country of Canada was founded in 1867, the seat of government moved to Ottawa, as did the governor-general. In 1870, the Québec government bought the estate, which then served as residence for twenty-one successive lieutenant-governors. In 1950, the estate

Flower beds mark the site where the mansion once stood.

was renamed Bois-de-Coulonge in honor of the original founder of the estate. Then in 1966, Bois-de-Coulonge ended its long career as an official residence when the house again burned to the ground, this time tragically taking the life of the lieutenant-governor, Paul Comtois.

The cost of rebuilding the mansion was beyond what the Québec government could afford, and Bois-de-Coulonge was essentially abandoned until 1986 when a campaign to restore it for use as a public park began. Work is still ongoing, but the estate is slowly regaining its status as a major center of horticulture in the Québec City region.

Today's Bois-de-Coulonge covers fifty-nine acres (twenty-four hectares), about half of which is forested. A newly widened entrance leads to vast parking lot (although there is no charge for visiting the garden, there is a fee for parking during business hours). The guardian's cottage (now open to the public), near the original main entrance, is partly surrounded by a vast water garden. After a stroll through the sugar bush, the main garden area becomes visible. It includes collections of lilacs, rhododendrons, ground covers, climbing plants, roses, and perennials, a bowling green, a gazebo overlooking the Saint-Lawrence River, and a kitchen garden. There are also several outbuildings, not open to the public, that originally served as a barn, a chicken coop, an ice house, and a sugar shack. The most majestic structure on the site is one originally used as a stable and which now houses the administration offices and washrooms. From a large formal fountain at the base of a sweeping hill rises a majestic staircase bordered by shrub roses that leads to a formal annual bed that traces the foundation of the final mansion. There is no doubt that the estate really does lack the presence of a large house on this hill, but at least the flower beds do give an idea of their original dimensions. Plaques with photos give an idea of what the estate looked like with a house at its center.

Besides its horticultural interest, Bois-de-Coulonge remains a city park as well. There are play and picnic areas, lots of space for strolling and relaxing, and the park's steep hills are popular with sledders in winter.

25 Saint-Roch-des-Aulnaies: Aulnaies Manor

LOCATION: EASTERN QUÉBEC, JUST OFF HIGHWAY 20 AT SAINT-ROCH-DES-AULNAIES, AT 525 DE LA SEIGNEURIE BOULEVARD

Aulnaies Manor, better known as Seigneurie des Aulnaies, is not a garden per se, but a historical recreation that includes several gardens. It consists of a series of buildings and houses, including the more modern Victorian manor house, that were part of the original *seigneurie*, in the hands of the Dupuis family for many generations. Although many seigniorial homes remain in Québec, this is the only one that has been maintained with all the outbuildings that were part of the original site. Since the village of Saint-Roch-des-Aulnaies grew up around the *seigneurie*, the entire village will be of great interest to visitors interested in the nearly forgotten seigniorial past of the province. Of special interest is the gristmill dating to 1842 on the site of previous mills and restored in the 1970s; it is fully operational and still produces stone-ground flour used in baking the breads, cakes, and "galettes" (cookies) sold in the site's boutique. Check at the admissions desk to see what time the mill will be operating. Costumed guides are available for tours of the house and mill: English-language visits can be arranged.

The site includes nature walks through a sugar bush, visits of the manor, designed by renowned Québec architect Charles Baillargé, picnic areas, and paths along the ponds that serve as a reservoir for the mill's operations. Garden lovers will find the entire site of interest. It was redesigned as a private park in the mid-1800s in the Romantic style then in sway: vast lawns broken up by naturalistic plantings, ponds, brooks, and meandering paths, and a background of forest. There is also a formal

GARDEN OPEN: 9am to 6pm daily, end of May to mid-October; house open during garden hours. **ADMISSION:** $6 adults, $5.50 seniors and students, $3.50 children 6–12 years.

FURTHER INFORMATION FROM: Seigneurie des Aulnaies 525 Rue de la Seigneurie Saint-Roch-des-Aulnaies, Québec G0R 4E0 (418) 354-2800 and (877) 354-2800 www.laseigneuriedesaulnaies. qc.ca

NEARBY SIGHTS OF INTEREST: Bernier Maritime Museum, Domaine des Fleurs

Paths along the ponds display the reservoir for the historic gristmill's operations.

BELOW: *A field of tulips.*
Domaine des fleurs

ornamental garden displaying roses, shrubs, perennials, and annuals, although not necessarily varieties that would have been grown at the time. The vegetable garden as well is done in the French formal style, as would have been the case in mid-nineteenth-century Québec, the era to which the estate has been restored. There are also superb views of the rushing river below along some of the paths; a map is provided so you can find your way around. Make sure to visit the manor house, not only for the rooms restored with antique furniture to represent the lifestyle of one of the last of Québec's seigneurs, but also for some great views of the gardens. The site also includes several usual shrubs and trees reflecting the Dupuis family's long interest in horticulture. Some of the black locust trees (*Robinia pseudacacia*), which would have been a novelty at the time, are over 150 years old.

GARDEN OPEN: 10am to 5pm daily, June 23–Labor Day.
ADMISSION: $5 adults, free children 11 years and younger.

FURTHER INFORMATION FROM:
Domaine des Fleurs
24 Rue du Moulin
Saint-Pâcome (Kamouraska)
G0L 3X0
(418) 852-3409
dofleurs@globetrotter.net

NEARBY SIGHTS OF INTEREST:
Aulnaies Manor

26 Saint-Pâcome: Domaine des Fleurs

LOCATION: TAKE HIGHWAY **20** EAST OF QUÉBEC CITY, THEN EXIT **450** AT SAINT-PÂCOME. FOLLOW SIGNS FROM THERE

The King family built a sumptuous Victorian manor, one of the most remarkable homes in tiny Saint-Pâcome, near the sawmill they operated on the Ouelle River early in the twentieth century. The mill is long gone, but the residence has been maintained over the years and presently belongs to Diane Poirier and René Racine, who have renamed the site Domaine des Fleurs, a name that needs no translation. The house, now being reconquered by the Virginia creeper that once covered much of it, is not open to visitors, but the owners have been developing vast gardens on the twenty-six-acre (ten-hectare) site since 1986 and accept visitors throughout the summer.

Though the gardens are modern in origin, they use many plants that were found on the site or obtained from other local gardens: old-fashioned peonies, daylilies, lilies, iris, and dahlias. There are likewise old fruit trees still standing that were once part of an ancient orchard; they represent cultivars that are now rarely seen, but which represent the agricultural history of the Lower Saint Lawrence region.

There are presently nine gardens on the site, including a vegetable garden, a rose garden, a woodland garden, a flowering meadow, and a lupine meadow. The lupine meadow is perhaps the most remarkable; it is at its peak in late June when the garden opens to the public. Many plants are identified and there are considerable collections of peonies, daylilies, lilies, clematis, and roses as well as both modern and ancient perennials of all types. The owners enjoy natural-looking gardens and allow old-fashioned annuals and biennials such as poppies

and hollyhocks to self-seed practically at will, giving the entire site the look and feel of an old cottage garden.

The recently restored stables contain two displays, one recounting the history of the King family and its gardens, the other the story of the forestry industry in Kamouraska county. Access to the stables is included in the admission fee.

27 Cabano: Roseraie de Témiscouata

LOCATION: IN THE TOWN OF CABANO, IN EASTERN QUÉBEC, HALF-WAY BETWEEN RIVIÈRE-DU-LOUP AND EDMUNSTON, NEW BRUNSWICK, JUST OFF THE TRANS-CANADA HIGHWAY (185)

The Roseraie de Témiscouata (Témiscouata rose garden) is a relatively new garden in a very old site. It is located just outside the wooden barricades of Fort Ingall, a restored fort of the British period, built between 1839 and 1842 to protect the region from eventual American invaders. The admission price for the garden, in fact, also includes a visit to the fort (or, depending on your point of view, the cost of admission to the fort also includes a visit to the rose garden).

Although relatively small in size (about 1.2 acres or 5,000 square meters), the garden packs in a lot of flowers; there are 1,200 rose bushes of some 330 varieties, all identified. Given the region's harsh climate—winter temperatures drop to a bone-chilling −35 degrees Farenheit!—the roses chosen are all particularly hardy ones. The choice includes both old and modern roses and shrub and climbing roses, with an especially large delegation of the hardy Canadian hybrids, such as the Parkland, Explorer, and Morden series, known for their extra hardiness and repeat bloom. All are labeled. The area's cool summers mean the roses begin to bloom late in the season, usually around the beginning of July, but many continue flowering throughout the summer. Colors are particularly intense, strikingly so compared to those of roses in hotter climates.

The central part of the garden is quite classical in style. Four major beds, each featuring a different color of rose (red, pink, yellow, and white), surround a central fountain. Arches, pergolas, and trellises add architectural interest and give climbing roses support. There are also less formal beds, notably one of old-fashioned roses that leads towards the fort.

Before or after visiting the rose garden, Fort Ingall beckons and is worth at least an hour's visit.

GARDEN OPEN: 9:30am to 5pm daily, June–September. Fort open during garden hours. ADMISSSION: $7.

FURTHER INFORMATION FROM:
Roseraie de Témiscouata
81 Caldwell
Cabano, Québec G0L 1E0
(418) 854-2375
roseraie@transcom.qc.ca
www.roseraie.qc.ca

NEARBY SIGHTS OF INTEREST:
Fort Ingall, New Brunswick Botanical Garden

The blooming season for roses starts in July in this cool-summer climate.

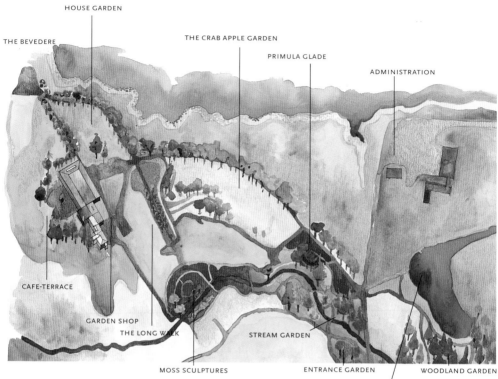

THE BEVEDERE

HOUSE GARDEN

THE CRAB APPLE GARDEN

PRIMULA GLADE

ADMINISTRATION

CAFE-TERRACE

GARDEN SHOP

THE LONG WALK

STREAM GARDEN

MOSS SCULPTURES

ENTRANCE GARDEN

THE POND

WOODLAND GARDEN

28 Grand-Métis: Reford Gardens

LOCATION: ABOUT FOUR HOURS EAST OF QUÉBEC CITY VIA
HIGHWAYS 20 AND 132

Probably no other Québec garden is as well known internationally as Reford Gardens, also called Métis Gardens (Jardins de Métis). It has been featured in gardening magazines throughout the United States and in Europe and is one of the major tourist attractions on the popular Gaspé Peninsula road tour. However, Reford Gardens would never have come into being had it not been for the decade's long effort of just one woman, Elsie Reford.

The Métis Beach area has long been popular as a summer retreat for wealthy English-speaking families from Montréal and Toronto. At the time it was developing in the mid-nineteenth century, it was especially noted for the fresh sea breezes that were considered essential for good health, but also for the abundant salmon fishing on the Mitis River. What was to be Reford Gardens started out as Estevan Lodge, a fishing camp built in 1887 by Lord Mount Stephen, founder of Canadian Pacific Railways, a train conglomerate. His niece, Elsie Reford, inherited it in 1918 and at first, she too intended to use it for fishing. An energetic woman with a great love of the outdoors, she excelled at salmon fishing, a sport rarely popular with women at that time. However, following a gall-bladder operation, she was advised by her doctors, appalled that a "woman her age" (she was in her mid-fifties) would even consider hoisting a fifty-pound (twenty-three-kilogram) salmon out of a raging river, suggested that it would be best if she took up a less strenuous hobby, such as gardening. She did, with a vengeance, and for the next thirty-three years, from 1926 to 1959, spent nearly all her boundless energy trying to make her gardens the very best in Québec.

Estevan Lodge was not an obvious place to begin a garden. The rocky shores of the Saint Lawrence River were mostly exposed rock and nearly devoid of soil, so she had truckloads of it carted in. And the climate was considered, at that time, improper for gardening; the winters were too long and cold, and the summers too short and cool. But Mrs. Reford remained undaunted, planting screens of conifers to keep out the wind and taking advantage of the site's natural layout that left much of it protected from the worst cold. There were, at that time, no garden centers or nurseries in the Gaspé Peninsula, so she sent for plants and seeds from around the world, and no books or magazines covered a climate even remotely similar to hers, so she experimented. She quickly found that, once good soil had been brought in, the local climate was actually excellent for gardening. Many plants that dislike hot summers actually thrive

GARDEN OPEN: 8:30am to 5pm daily, June and September–October; 8:30am to 6:30pm, July–August; the gardens close at 8pm.
ADMISSION: $12 adults, $11 seniors, $10 students, $3 children, free children 5 years and younger.

FURTHER INFORMATION FROM:
Reford Gardens
200, Route 132
Grand-Métis, Québec GoJ 1Zo
(418) 775-2221
reford@refordgardens.com
www.refordgardens.com

NEARBY SIGHTS OF INTEREST:
Gaspé Peninsula, Atlantic Salmon Interpretation Centre

OPPOSITE: *The Long Walk is lined with vast perennial beds, featuring spring flowers and peonies.*

there, the nearly mythic blue poppy (*Meconopsis betonicifolia*) among them. Although she had always claimed she couldn't tell a dandelion from a daisy when she started, she became such an expert at gardening that she even wrote articles for prestigious botanical journals later in life.

In declining health, she gave the garden to her son in the hopes he would discover the joys of gardening himself, but with little success. After her death, he considered abandoning the garden, but the Government of Québec, sensing its potential as a tourist attraction, stepped in and took over its administration. In 1994, the garden again came into the hands of the Reford family through a foundation that purchased the site and which is run by Alexander Reford, Elsie Reford's great grandson.

Today Reford gardens contains over 2,000 plant species and covers some forty-nine acres (twenty hectares), much still in native coniferous forest. Each visit begins with the *Entrance Garden*, surrounded by choice annuals, columbines, and lilies. There is a small boutique there where you can buy a few souvenirs, a snack, or film, then off along a meandering path through the *Stream Garden*, which, as the name suggests, crosses a babbling stream, not just once, in fact, but twice. Besides woodland plants, this section abounds in alpines, roses, and astilbes. The entrance into the most famous part of the gardens, the *Blue Poppy Glade*, is announced by the appearance of mixed plantings of rhododendrons and azaleas plus, of course, the blue poppies themselves, usually in bloom in late June. The eye is also taken in by the rock garden on the far side of the stream. Don't forget to take a quick look at a rather unusual living piece of art: the moss sculpture, at the tip of Blue Poppy Glade.

The path then leads upwards to the *Long Walk (Allée Royale)*, a vast and long rectilinear mixed border dominated by peonies, delphiniums, and lilies, depending on the season. Many of the plants are identified, but some older species and cultivars planted by Elsie Reford have still been maintained even though their labels have been lost over the decades. At the end of the walk, turn right to Reford Villa, surrounded by the *House Garden*. Besides the huge lilacs, shrub roses, and hanging baskets that dominate the house itself, the House Garden continues all around the building and

TOP: *Once a fishing lodge, Reford Villa now houses a restaurant and boutiques.*

BOTTOM: *In the foreground, roses will soon take over from the rhododendrons, azaleas, and crabapples that steal the scenes in late spring.*

includes hidden collections of interesting and often rare plants, plus a herb
garden supplying the villa's kitchen
with fresh herbs and edible flowers.
Reford Villa houses the main dining
room, a boutique of handicrafts, washrooms, a small museum, and, in an
extension of the main house, a gardening bookstore. Try to plan your visit in
order to dine at the villa—otherwise
there is a picnic area (and washrooms)
outside of the garden, beside the parking lot.

Beyond the villa, two rows of
carefully trimmed mugo pines lead
you to the *Belvedere*, offering an extraordinary view of the Saint Lawrence
River. On the walk back, a different set
of paths leads through the *Crabapple
Garden*, underplanted in alpine plants
and spring bulbs. It is at its best in
early June. The *Primula Garden* follows, with a vast collection of prim-
roses. Visitors from warmer climates
will be surprised to see that the primrose collection blooms well into July
because a long, cold spring delays
their blooming until well after their
usual flowering season elsewhere.
Continue the visit through the
Woodland Garden, a natural forest
filled with forest wild flowers, to the
pond, containing mostly native
aquatic and marsh plants, not to mention abundant birdlife.

Before leaving, don't miss Reford
Garden's latest development, the
International Garden Festival. At the
time of writing, this had only been
through its first year, but it is expected
to continue on as an annual event.
Each year garden designers from around the world will be
called upon to express their ideas of current trends by creating
small contemporary gardens in open spaces in the forest. Each
garden will be maintained for just one summer, to be replaced
by another the following year. Judging from the first year's displays, the Festival gardens will tend to be highly original and
very thought provoking.

A final note: since the garden is surrounded by coniferous
forest, insect spray may be handy, especially early in the season.

TOP: *A shady corner is
brightened up by tuberous
begonias.*

BOTTOM: *The blue poppy
(*Meconopsis betonicifolia*)
flourishes by the hundreds in
Blue Poppy Glade.*

69

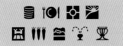

GARDEN OPEN: 9am to 6pm daily, June 24–Labor Day.

ADMISSION: $10 adults, $9 seniors and students, $5 youths, free children 7 years and younger.

FURTHER INFORMATION FROM:
Grands Jardins de
Normandin
1515 Avenue du Rocher,
C.P. 567
Normandin, Québec G8M
4S6
(418) 274-1993 or
(800) 920-1993
bg.jard@caramail.com
www.cigp.com/jardin.html

NEARBY SIGHTS OF INTEREST:
Saint-Félicien Zoological Park

Inspired by France's Villandry, this carpet bed is one of the most extensive gardens of its type in North America.

29 Normandin: Grands Jardins de Normandin

LOCATION: JUST OFF HIGHWAY 373, NEAR NORMANDIN, QUÉBEC, IN THE LAKE SAINT JOHN (LAC SAINT-JEAN) REGION; WELL SIGNPOSTED

If the Grands Jardins de Normandin are not the northernmost of Canada's public gardens—some of the gardens in Alberta are found at a higher latitude—they are certainly the one located in the most extreme climate. Winter temperatures can plunge to –49 degrees Farenheit, far too cold for most trees and shrubs as well as for many perennials. Snow is often still on the ground well into May, and winter has returned by November, plus few summers have more than 90 frost-free days. That hasn't stopped the gardens' organizers from creating one of the most unique gardens in Canada.

Visitors to this garden can't help but be surprised by the style of the gardens; formal French gardens are a rare thing these days, even in France, yet this garden is almost wholly based on them. Villandry, the famous French *potager*, and the intricate carpet bedding of the Victorian era are clearly the inspiration for this garden, where how the plants are placed is often far more important than what they are. Visitors can wander through the gardens at will but would be well advised to check whether a guide is available for a tour in English, as the gardens trace the history of gardening back some 4,000 years, something that may not be obvious to the casual visitor. Guided tours are included with admission, but depend on availability.

The long *Grande Allée* displays the coats of arms of the 61 municipalities of the Saguenay–Lake Saint John region, all intricately drawn in carpet bedding. There is a vast and extremely decorative formal *potager* including herbs, vegetables, edible flowers, and medicinal plants, then decorative French knot gardens of annuals. The tip of the site is devoted to a splendid recreation of the Arab gardens of yore, one of which floats on a basin of clear water like the floral carpet it was designed to be. There is lots of color, all that much more inspiring when you realize that the gardens can only be planted about two weeks before they open.

Besides the formal gardens that are the heart of the Grands Jardins, there is also a *natural forest* with an extensive series of nature trails, plus the beginnings of an *English garden*, one of the few spots in the Grands Jardins where you will see any perennials, and an *arboretum* of cold-hardy shrubs and trees is slowly being built up.

The Grands Jardins de Normandin were designed from the very beginning

as public gardens, a way to enticing tourists following the already popular Lake Saint-John circuit to head just a little further north than they usually would. That goal has been reached, as most guided tours and an increasing number of private vehicles now include the Grands Jardins on their itinerary as a matter of course.

30 Rouyn–Noranda: Parc Botanique 'À Fleur d'Eau' Inc.

LOCATION: IN NORTHWESTERN QUÉBEC, NORTH OF THE LA VERENDRYE RESERVE, NEAR THE ONTARIO BORDER. FROM ROUYN-NORANDA'S MAIN ROAD, GAMBLE STREET, TAKE PRINCIPALE STREET SOUTH TO NO. 325

It is hard to convince even Québecers that there could be such a beautiful garden in Rouyn-Noranda. It is in the heart of the Abitibi region of Northwestern Québec, known for mining and forestry, but too cold for almost any form of farming—even the tallest trees scarcely reach more than a story in height. Frost is common well into June and starts again by Labor Day. Plus Rouyn-Noranda *is* a mining town; no one thinks of going there to garden! However, such is man's nature that he wants to beautify his surroundings. The result is that the local horticultural society is very popular and, in spite of (or perhaps because of) the harsh climate, people do put in flower gardens and even grow their own vegetables (often in homemade greenhouses). And there is one major public garden, Parc Botanique 'À Fleur d'Eau' Inc.

Located practically in the heart of town, the park was developed by the local horticultural society with the help of the city, and is still run by volunteers. They chose a nine-acre (3.5-hectare) vacant lot, in fact, practically a dump, surrounding a small natural lake, Lake Edouard, and began a massive clean-up and planting program in 1989. Work continues to this day as the flower beds are gradually enlarged and new ones planted. The transformation has been quite incredible, as has the success the team has had with their plantings. The park now counts hundreds of species, both cold-hardy bulbs, perennials, shrubs, and trees, and fast-growing, frost-tolerant annuals.

Starting from the *Julienne Cliche Pavillon*, which serves as a reception area, boutique, and snack bar and also houses the restrooms, you can wander up the hill to the *Alpine Garden*, whose plants positively thrive in a climate very much like that of a mountain top. Or descend directly to the lake which is skirted by paths that take you through flower beds, a section of typical boreal forest, a water garden with aquatic and marginal plants, a compost demonstration site, a geological garden presenting rocks typical of the Abitibi, and community garden lots. There is even a rose garden . . . although it contains only the hardiest shrub roses.

GARDEN OPEN: 9am to 8pm daily, May–September; guided tours are available by reservation 24 hours in advance, (819) 762-3178. ADMISSION: $2.

FURTHER INFORMATION FROM:
Parc Botanique 'À Fleur d'Eau'
380, Richard Avenue, #200
Rouyn-Noranda, Québec J9X 4L3
(819) 762-3178
parcbotanique@cablevision.qc.ca
www.lino.com/~fleurdo/

NEARBY SIGHTS OF INTEREST:
Aiguebelle Provincial Park

Water gushes from a fountain in the center of the lake.

ONTARIO

43 44

40 41 42

35 36 37 38

8 15 16

13 23-34

6

1, 2, 3, 4, 5

17, 18, 19, 20, 21, 22

ONTARIO

Although Ontario is only Canada's second-largest province in area (1,058,582 square kilometers or 412, 582 square miles), it is largest in population: about eleven million. It is also home to about half the gardens in Canada that are open to the public, of which forty-four are described here.

As in Québec, much of Ontario lies within the Canadian Shield, a vast expanse of rolling pre-Cambrian rock nearly laid bare by glaciers during the last Ice Age. This region, which occupies all the northern part of the province and extends well into the south, is still largely uninhabited, a region of lakes, rivers, and coniferous forest better known for its recreational assets than for permanent settlements. Most inhabited areas of Northern Ontario are located towards the southern portion and even then are built up around mines or forestry.

Seven-eighths of Ontario's inhabitants live in Southern Ontario, a bird's-foot-like projection formed by four of the five Great Lakes: Lakes Ontario, Erie, Huron, and Superior to the south and west and by the Ottawa River (and Québec border) to the east. Although part of this is also Canadian Shield, with the same pattern of igneous rock covered by conifers forest, rivers, and lakes as the north, the southernmost part is covered in deep, rich soil and is prime farmland. Just about every food product adapted to temperate climates is grown or raised there, and food processing is a major industry. The climate is particularly clement and Southern Ontario reaches well down into the United States, much further south than any other part of Canada. Indeed, the southernmost tip of Ontario is at the same latitude as Northern California. The Niagara region, especially, is renowned for fruit production, including such

OPPOSITE: *Cullen Gardens and Miniature Village*

cold-intolerant crops as peaches and grapes, and its climate more closely resembles that of Virginia than the rest of Canada. The original vegetation of the Niagara Peninsula, now largely replaced by farmland, was Carolinian forest, represented by tall deciduous trees such as the tulip tree (*Liriodendron tulipifera*) and rampant liana-like climbers like Virginia creeper (*Parthenocissus quinquefolia*). The rest of Southern Ontario was originally mixed forest dominated by sugar maple (*Acer saccharum*), becoming gradually richer in conifers towards the north.

Ontario's richest farmland is now rapidly disappearing under urban sprawl. The western tip of Lake Ontario, from Toronto through Hamilton to Niagara Falls, for example, is almost entirely developed. Called the Golden Horseshoe because of its general crescent shape, it is the most densely inhabited area of Canada (and indeed, has few rivals in all North America) and is the home of much of its industry and business. Even so, Ontarians rarely have to go far to escape civilization; wilderness is never far away in any part of Canada.

Ontario may now be Canada's most populous province as well as the home to much of its industry, but the province's importance in modern times belies a

OPPOSITE: *Niagara Parks Butterfly Conservatory*

LEFT: *Allan Gardens*

slow start; although originally part of New France, along with what is now Québec, Ontario was never really settled by the French—they saw the huge area as merely a source of fur and trade with native Amerindians. They founded forts and missions (many of which, like Kingston, have since become major cities), but few permanent settlements.

The problem was that, in a period when water travel was vital, Ontario was virtually land-locked. Although the province touched salt water at Hudson Bay to the north, that route to Europe, essential for trade, was basically frozen and unnavigable much of the year, while rapids meant that the Saint Lawrence River was not navigable beyond Montréal. Not only were portages necessary to reach the Great Lakes system, but travel between the lowest of the Great Lakes, Lake Ontario, and the Upper Great Lakes, was also blocked by a huge drop in elevation over a very short distance, dramatically represented by the sheer cliffs of the Niagara Gorge. This has since been corrected, and canals began linking all the major water systems by the 1820s, opening the province to greater development, although it wasn't until the 1950s that the complete Great Lakes/Saint Lawrence Seaway system as we know it today allowed ocean-going vessels to travel from the

Atlantic Ocean to the northwestern tip of Lake Superior. Nowadays, of course, all of Southern Ontario is quickly reachable via highway and rail as well, although much of Northern Ontario remains very isolated.

European settlement really only began with the American Revolution, when United Empire Loyalists, no longer welcome in the new nation to the south, began to flood northward. Québec and the Atlantic Provinces were too crowded to handle the entire influx and the colonial government opened the lands between the Great Lakes and the Ottawa River to settlement. By 1791, the existence of the new territory was recognized when the British Parliament passed the Constitutional Act, creating French-speaking Lower Canada and largely English-speaking "Upper Canada," so-called because it was upriver of the French-settled areas.

Immigration came largely from Great Britain at first. When Upper Canada officially became part of the new nation Canada in 1867, under the name Ontario, immigration from other countries, notably in Europe, and then later in the twentieth century, from Asia and Africa, began to create the cultural melting pot that characterizes the province today. Ontario underwent rapid industrialization from the late 1800s through the mid-1900s, turning what had at first been a largely rural population into a mostly urban one. The province was rich in mineral resources and electricity and underwent the same twentieth-century boom as the United States to the south—and experienced also its crashes, such as the Great Depression of the 1930s. Ontario soon had its share of tycoons with money to burn and aspirations to match those of the even richer Americans to the south. They began to build stately homes and gardens to create comfort for their families and to display their wealth; several of Ontario's gardens owe their existence to this period in its history.

The latter part of the twentieth century and beginning of the twenty-first saw continued expansion of the cities and renewed emphasis on green spaces. New public gardens were created (and still are) practically overnight, often in run-down downtown areas as part of urban renewal projects.

Although there are gardens throughout Ontario, there are a few hot spots. Toronto, the provincial capital and, with a population of over three million (six million if you include the entire population basin), its largest city, obviously wins due to its dense population and huge area, as it takes people and space to make gardens. The Toronto Music Garden (page 112), Casa Loma (page 103), Parkwood Estate (page 115), and Cullen Gardens & Miniature Village (page 114) are just four of the gardens of the Toronto region that are not to be missed. Ottawa, though the capital of Canada, is a much smaller city but likewise has its attractive parks and gardens, especially Commissioners Park (page 119), which is home to Canada's foremost annual outdoor flower show, the Tulip Festival. The Royal Botanical Gardens (page 93), located smack in between the industrial cities of Burlington and Hamilton, is another absolute must and certainly the most complete botanical gardens in Ontario. Kudos, however, have to go to Niagara Falls (pages 96–101), certainly one of the most

Allan Gardens

beautifully landscaped cities in North America and the one investing the greatest proportion of public space in gardens, all under the auspices of the incredible Niagara Parks Commission.

GARDEN OPEN: dawn to dusk
daily, year-round.
ADMISSION: free.

FURTHER INFORMATION FROM:
Department of Parks and
Recreation
2450 McDougall Street
Windsor, Ontario N8X 3N6
(519) 253-2300
plewis@city.windsor.on.ca
www.city.windsor.on.ca/parkrec

NEARBY SIGHTS OF INTEREST:
Art Gallery of Windsor, Casino
Windsor, Dieppe Gardens,
Windsor Sculpture Garden,
Jackson Park

BELOW: *Coventry Gardens
looks across the Detroit River to
Detroit, Michigan in the U.S.*

OPPOSITE: *Colorful annual
display gardens, this one featuring a giant agave, dominate the park.*

Windsor: Coventry Gardens

LOCATION: ON WATERFRONT, ACROSS FROM DETROIT, ALONG RIVERSIDE DRIVE
EAST AT PILLETTE ROAD

Coventry Gardens, part of the vaster Reaume Park, gets its
name from Windsor's British sister city. The pleasant riverside
park of this border city looks across the Detroit River to the city
of Detroit, Michigan. It is a vast linear park, with wide, sloping
paths and brilliant green lawns. On both sides of the paths
meander broad beds of neatly trimmed shrubs and topiary
mingling with plantings of annuals and perennials, ensuring
color throughout the summer, while dwarf conifers and berried
shrubs maintain interest throughout the area's short winter.

The most striking feature of this garden is the huge floating *Peace Fountain*, a symbol of the City of Windsor's peaceful
ties to the neighboring United States. It sits directly on the
Detroit River, sending up a variety of water displays high into
the air, an open invitation to sit down on the grass or on one of
the numerous benches and pass a few hours watching the
changing spectacle.

2 Windsor: Dieppe Gardens

LOCATION: RIVERFRONT, ON NORTH SIDE OF RIVERSIDE DRIVE WEST, BELOW
OUELLETTE AVENUE

GARDEN OPEN: dawn to dusk
daily, year-round.
ADMISSION: free.

FURTHER INFORMATION FROM:
Department of Parks and
Recreation
2450 McDougall Street
Windsor, Ontario N8X 3N6
(519) 253-2300
plewis@city.windsor.on.ca
www.city.windsor.on.ca/parkrec

NEARBY SIGHTS OF INTEREST:
Art Gallery of Windsor, Casino
Windsor, Coventry Gardens,
Windsor Sculpture Garden,
Jackson Park

Windsor is located in one of the warmest parts of Canada and uses this mild climate to full advantage, with numerous parks and gardens, notably along the riverside, as is the case for Dieppe Gardens.

Windsor calls itself the "city of roses" and Dieppe Gardens are one reason why, as they contain a lovely rose garden. There are however several other gardens in this linear park, including a rock garden and beautiful displays of perennials and shrubs. The most remarkable part of the park, however, are the annual display gardens. These vary from year to year, but always include the massive use of annuals, both flowering and foliage types, in often intricate carpet bedding arrangements. Some surround the base of trees, others form their own beds. They're at their best from June to October.

The gardens provide a great view of ships from all over the world that sail through the Great Lakes system on their way either to the Upper Great Lakes or downstream, via the Saint Lawrence Seaway, towards the Atlantic Ocean. The park is named in memory of the many members of the Essex Kent Scottish Regiment who lost their lives during World War II.

3 Windsor: Jackson Park

LOCATION: DOWNTOWN, AT TECUMSEH AND OUELLETTE STREETS

GARDEN OPEN: 24 hours daily, year-round. **ADMISSION:** free.

FURTHER INFORMATION FROM:
Department of Parks and
Recreation
2450 McDougall Street
Windsor, Ontario N8X 3N6
(519) 253-2300
plewis@city.windsor.on.ca
www.city.windsor.on.ca/parkrec

NEARBY SIGHTS OF INTEREST:
Art Gallery of Windsor, Casino
Windsor, Coventry Gardens,
Windsor Sculpture Garden,
Dieppe Gardens

Jackson Park is first and foremost a city park with the usual picnic, sports, and playground areas. However this large sixty-four-acre (twenty-six-hectare) park also contains many ornamental elements, and notably one of Ontario's largest rose gardens. Built around a World War II airplane brought to Windsor in 1965, the *Lancaster Bomber Memorial Rose Garden* contains more than 12,500 roses of 450 different varieties. The compass-shaped garden is, due to its location in one of the warmest regions of the country, said to be the first rose garden in Canada to bloom, starting early in June. Of course, the flowering then continues for the rest of the summer, with some lingering bloom remaining until nearly Christmas.

Adjacent to the rose garden are the *Queen Elizabeth II Sunken Gardens*, a magnificent display of annuals and perennials built around a reflecting pool. Strategically placed lights make this part of the park as attractive at night as during the day. Some 25,000 tulips are likewise planted in the park, which also includes a good collection of trees and shrubs. The Jackson Park also contains a monument to Robbie Burns, a South African War Memorial, and a monument to the great Polish astronomer, Copernicus.

4 Toronto: James Gardens

LOCATION: WEST OF CENTRAL TORONTO, AT EDENBRIDGE DRIVE EAST OF
ROYAL YORK ROAD

James Park is a former estate garden of some ten acres (four hectares) located to the west of Toronto in the suburb of Etobicoke. Over time, it has taken on a rather formal appearance that is quite unique among Toronto's public gardens.

The vast beds are filled with thousand of tulips, narcissi, crocus, and other spring bulbs in bloom from March through late May. These are replaced by colorful and changing floral displays featuring mostly annuals during the summer months. The park also includes a network of spring-fed streams and pools crisscrossed by rustic bridges plus a wooded area that includes well-identified trees, some quite rare.

GARDEN OPEN: dawn to dusk daily, year-round.
ADMISSION: free.

FURTHER INFORMATION FROM:
City of Toronto Parks and
Recreation
21st Floor, East Tower
City Hall
100 Queen Street West
Toronto, Ontario M5H 2N2
(416) 392-8186
www.city.toronto.on.ca

NEARBY SIGHTS OF INTEREST:
High Park, Ontario Place

OPPOSITE, TOP: *Massive main gates welcome visitors.*
OPPOSITE, BOTTOM: *This fountain is the heart of the Queen Elizabeth II Sunken Garden.*

ABOVE: *Fall colors heighten the beauty of James Gardens.* City of Toronto Parks Department

Windsor: Windsor Sculpture Garden

GARDEN OPEN: dawn to dusk daily, year-round.
ADMISSION: free.

LOCATION: ALONG RIVERSIDE DRIVE, WEST FROM AMBASSADOR BRIDGE TO CURRY AVENUE

FURTHER INFORMATION FROM:
Department of Parks and
Recreation
2450 McDougall Street
Windsor, Ontario N8X 3N6
(519) 253-2300
plewis@city.windsor.on.ca
www.city.windsor.on.ca/parkrec

NEARBY SIGHTS OF INTEREST:
Art Gallery of Windsor, Casino
Windsor, Dieppe Gardens,
Coventry Garden, Jackson
Park

No one denies that gardens are living works of art. The Windsor Sculpture Garden sets out to reinforce that point by adding a wide variety of sculptures into an outdoor park setting. The Sculpture Garden unites two riverside parks, Assumption Park and Centennial Park, both verdant, tree-lined parks along the Detroit River. It is also part of the three-mile (five-kilometer) *Riverwalk* walking and cycling trail. And the view of the garden is a shared one, as it is clearly visible from Detroit, Michigan, a major American metropolis just across the Detroit River from Windsor.

The sculptures are contemporary, but the collection purposely does not conform to any one artistic vision. Instead, it is united by its very variety. Stark modern sculptures contrast with Indian totems, a realistic dancing polar bear with a vaguely technical Space Plow. Artists from across Canada and the world are featured, including Toni Putnam, Dame Elisabeth Frink, and Morton Katz.

Rinterzo, by Joseph DeAngelis, is built into a reflecting pool and overlooks Windsor's sister city of Detroit. Kevin Kavanaugh

6 Ridgetown: J. J. Neilson Arboretum

LOCATION: DOWNTOWN, NEAR CHATHAM, ONTARIO

The entire twenty-acre (eight-hectare) campus of Ridgetown College, an extension college of the University of Guelph, is officially an arboretum: the J. J. Neilson Arboretum. The campus is also beautifully landscaped, giving it a very park-like atmosphere. Trees and shrubs from around the world, with a special abundance of Carolinian species, are planted throughout the site and many are labeled as to common and botanical names. The mild climate in this Southern Ontario garden means too that many ornamental species can be grown there that it would not be possible to grow in most of the rest of Canada. There are plenty of paths linking the arboretum's collections as well as benches and quiet corners for relaxation.

The arboretum is practical as well as beautiful; it serves as an outdoor classroom for the college's Associate Diploma in Horticulture. Courses are likewise offered for horticulture industries and for the general public.

Although woody plants make up the better part of the arboretum's collection, it also contains several other gardens, with more being planned. There is a formal garden, a xeriscape garden, and also Canada's largest weed garden. Yes, you read correctly—a garden where plants commonly seen as weeds are identified and highlighted!

GARDEN OPEN: dawn to dusk daily, year-round.
ADMISSION: free.

FURTHER INFORMATION FROM:
J. J. Neilson Arboretum
Ridgetown College
University of Guelph
Ridgetown, Ontario NoP 2Co
(519) 674-1570
arboretum@ridgetownc.
uguelph.ca
www.ridgetownc.on.ca

NEARBY SIGHTS OF INTEREST:
Rondeau Provincial Park,
Chatham Cultural Centre

ABOVE: *The entire campus was designated an arboretum in 1997.* Ridgetown College

GARDEN OPEN: 12pm to 5pm
Tuesday–Sunday, year-round;
closed Christmas Day. House
open during garden hours.
ADMISSION: $6 adults, $2
seniors and students.

FURTHER INFORMATION FROM:
Eldon House
481 Ridout Street North
London, Ontario N6A 2P8
(519) 661-5169

NEARBY SIGHTS OF INTEREST:
Central London, Springbank
Park, London Museum of
Archaeology

BELOW: *The rock garden and
goldfish pond with a replica of
the Verrochio statue.* London
Regional Art and Historical
Museums

OPPOSITE: *The Springbank
Bridge takes visitors across
the Thames River.* Andrew
Macpherson

7 London: Eldon House

LOCATION: NO. 481 RIDOUT STREET NORTH

The oldest residence in London, Ontario is Eldon House, dating back to 1834. It has been restored to its nineteenth-century state, including furniture and decorations belonging to the original family. Gardeners, however, will most enjoy the gardens, which have been restored to their former Victorian splendor.

The front of the house contains the show garden, featuring mostly perennials and biennials that would have been popular in the late 1900s. Floral bouquets would have been an essential element of any Victorian decor, so there is the obligatory *cutting garden* out back, especially rich in annuals, bulbs, and perennials. There is also a *rose garden* that features old-fashioned roses, a *rock garden* with a goldfish pond, and magnolias, in full bloom in mid-spring, shade the back terrace.

From July through Labor Day, afternoon tea is served daily in the garden (indoors in case of rain) by staff in period costume; this is an event in itself. There are likewise special events and activities throughout the summer months; phone for specific dates.

GARDEN OPEN: dawn to dusk daily, year-round.
ADMISSION: free.

FURTHER INFORMATION FROM:
Parks Planning and Design
City of London
300, Dufferin Avenue
P.O. Box 5035
London, Ontario N6A 4L9
(519) 661-4980
www.city.london.on.ca

8 London: Springbank Park

LOCATION: OFF SPRINGBANK DRIVE

NEARBY SIGHTS OF INTEREST:
Eldon House, Central London, London Museum of Archaeology

When Springbank Park comes into discussion, Londoners mostly think of the park's children's theme park, *Storybook Gardens*, presenting storybook characters, amusements, a maze, a playground, and a small petting zoo, plus a miniature train. This enclave in the park (paid admission, open 10am to 8pm daily, early May to Labor Day, 10am to 5pm Labor Day to mid-October) is certainly nice enough for the families with small children and has some beautiful trees and flower beds, but the really attractive part of Springbank Park is *outside* the Storybook Gardens and is free of charge.

The Manness Conservatory insures interest in all seasons.
Andrew Macpherson

Springbank Park is a very large park covering some 281 acres (114 hectares) along the banks of the Thames River. There are plenty of green lawn, forests, and flower beds. Features include the *Rayner Rose Garden*, the *Curtis Perennial Garden*, the *Woodland Garden*, and *Manness Conservatory*, the latter with more limited opening hours (phone ahead). The park is wonderful for a long stroll and contains several rare and unusual specimen trees (labeled). There is also a large picnic area.

9 Sebringville: Brickman's Botanical Gardens

Unlike most botanical gardens, Brickman's Botanical Gardens
is not the work of a university or municipal government.
Rather it is the creation of one man, Gerald Brickman, who has
converted his own eleven-acre (4.5-hectare) property into a private botanical garden. Mr. Brickman specializes in testing
plants beyond their usual hardiness zone, and many of the
plants seen will seem surprising in such a cold climate; he's
even succeeded in overwintering agapanthus outdoors. There
are long English-style beds, separated by winding paths and
containing some 3,000 varieties of bulbs and perennials, plus
specialty gardens: an old rose garden, a Queen Mother's
Garden (filled with plants the Queen Mother is known to
favor), a biblical garden, a scree garden, a white garden, several
water gardens, a hosta bed, and a new formal garden.

The enterprise also includes a mini-zoo with rare breeds of
animals and birds, plus an English tea room and gift shop. Mr.
Brickman also runs a perennial nursery featuring many of the
same plants that can be seen in his gardens.

10 Stratford: Arthur Meighen Gardens

LOCATION: STRATFORD FESTIVAL GROUNDS

This garden is certainly better known under the name of the Stratford Festival Theatre Gardens, as it surrounds the main theater of the famous Stratford Festival, held annually over a twenty-six-week season. Considered to be among the three great English-language theatres in the world, it features not only the works of Shakespeare, but also of other great authors plus more contemporary drama and musical theater.

The sweeping green lawns of the theater, reaching down to the beautiful Avon River below, have been a feature of the Festival Theatre ever since the festival began in 1953, but they were restored and upgraded in 1997, with many added floral elements. Now named after Arthur Meighen, Canada's ninth prime minister, the new garden areas include thyme pathways, a pond, a native species section, and beds including more than 250 varieties of perennials. The gardens are well worth a visit whether or not you've come to see a show . . . but if you're in the neighborhood, it would be shame not to stop in for a bit of theatrical entertainment.

GARDEN OPEN: dawn to dusk daily, mid-March–mid-November. **ADMISSION:** free.

FURTHER INFORMATION FROM:
Head Gardener
Arthur Meighen Gardens
55 Queen Street
Stratford, Ontario N5A 6V2
(519) 271-4040
www.stratford-festival.on.ca

NEARBY SIGHTS OF INTEREST:
Avon River, Confederation Park, Shakespearean Garden

In the Elizabethan Gardens, the Renaissance is revived as a formal garden featuring heirloom plants of Shakespeare's era. Richard Bain

GARDEN OPEN: dawn to dusk daily, year-round.

ADMISSION: free.

FURTHER INFORMATION FROM:
Parks and Forestry Manager
27 Morenz Drive
PO Box 874
Stratford, Ontario N5A 6W3
(519) 271-0250, ext. 276
dmartin@city.stratford.ca
www.city.stratford.on.ca

NEARBY SIGHTS OF INTEREST:
Gallery Stratford, Millennium Park, Avon River, Festival Theatre

ABOVE: *This elegant park features beautiful borders and majestic trees along the Avon River.* City of Stratford

11 Stratford: Confederation Park

LOCATION: ROMEO STREET, BESIDE GALLERY STRATFORD

Stratford is renowned throughout Ontario for its parks and gardens. A winner of the 1997 Nations in Bloom worldwide competition, it features more than 1,000 acres (400 hectares) of parkland, among them the Shakespearean Gardens (below), the Stratford Festival Theatre Gardens (Arthur Meighen Gardens) (page 87), and Confederation Park (sometimes called Centennial Gardens), perhaps the jewel in the city's crown.

Located on the banks of the Avon River, where swans, ducks, and geese float lazily by, Confederation Park features flower gardens rich in annuals and perennials, stately fir trees planted by boy scouts in 1937, and a beautiful Japanese garden with a cascading waterfall and a restful pond. Nearby, a promising new park, Millennium Park, opened during the summer of 2000, acts as an addition to the original.

GARDEN OPEN: dawn to dusk daily, mid-April–late October.

ADMISSION: free.

FURTHER INFORMATION FROM:
Parks and Forestry Manager
27 Morenz Drive
PO Box 874
Stratford, Ontario N5A 6W3
(519) 271-0250, ext. 276
dmartin@city.stratford.ca
www.city.stratford.on.ca

NEARBY SIGHTS OF INTEREST:
Downtown Stratford, Avon River

12 Stratford: Shakespearean Gardens

LOCATION: OFF HURON STREET, BESIDE PERTH COUNTY COURT HOUSE

Yes, there really is a Stratford in Ontario and it *is* located on the Avon River. It took little more than that combination for the city to consider the idea of developing an Elizabethan garden, now called the Shakespearean Garden. Work began on the garden in 1926 on the suite of a burnt-out mill and it was opened in 1936. Today the garden still features the last remaining vestige of the mill, a brick chimney now topped by a twenty-four-suite purple martin house.

Today's garden has undergone many transformations over the years and is perhaps closer to the original 1926 plan than ever. The garden features paths winding through Elizabethan

cottage style plantings of herbs, perennial, shrubs, and trees featured in Shakespeare's plays and poems: thyme, lavender, marigold, daffodils, even onions and mustard. Flower-wreathed arbors, knot gardens bordered in boxwood, fountains, terraces, even a rose garden featuring, at its heart, a statue of Shakespeare, are part of the overall plan. Fragrance is a major factor in the gardens and visitors are encouraged to touch the plants to release the perfume of numerous herbs and medicinal plants as they stroll through the garden. Engraved plaques with quotes from Shakespeare recall the numerous associations he made between plants and the world of man.

Plants mentioned in Shakespeare's work are the basis of the Shakespearean Gardens. City of Stratford

GARDEN OPEN: dawn to dusk daily, year-round.
ADMISSION: free.

13 Brantford: Lorne Park

LOCATION: ON COLBORNE STREET WEST

Brantford has a well-deserved reputation of being one of Ontario's most beautiful cities and, especially, one of the most beautifully landscaped. There are several parks and public gardens of great interest, but perhaps the most beautiful is Lorne Park. It was even awarded a special award for "best planned garden" during the International Communities in Bloom competition in 1995.

The park consists of about five acres (two hectares) of green space along the banks of the Lorne River. There are beautiful trees and wonderful plantings of shrubs, perennials,

FURTHER INFORMATION FROM:
Parks, Recreation & Tourism
1 Sherwood Drive
Brantford, Ontario N3T 1N3
(519) 756-1500 or
(800) 265-6299
tourism@city.brantford.on.ca
www.city.brantford.on.ca

NEARBY SIGHTS OF INTEREST:
Bell Homestead National Historic Site, Glenhyrst Gardens and Art Gallery

ONTARIO

The Park's gazebo, here in daffodil season, is popular for wedding photographs. City of Brantford Parks, Recreation and Tourism

bulbs, and roses, but Lorne Park is especially renowned for its annual beds. Incredibly varied and extremely colorful, they represent perhaps the finest examples of carpet bedding in Ontario and are at their best from mid-June through September.

While visiting Brantford, don't miss the opportunity of seeing some of the city's other gardens, listed under *Nearby Sights of Interest* above.

GARDEN OPEN: dawn to dusk daily, year-round.
ADMISSION: free.

FURTHER INFORMATION FROM:
The Arboretum
University of Guelph
Guelph, Ontario N1G 2W1
(519) 824-4120, ext. 2113
arboretu@uoguelph.ca
www.uguelph.ca/~arboretu

NEARBY SIGHTS OF INTEREST:
University of Guelph

14 Guelph: University of Guelph Arboretum

LOCATION: ABOUT 62 MILES (100 KILOMETERS) WEST OF TORONTO; HIGHWAY 401 TO COUNTY ROAD 46, THEN NORTH ABOUT SIX MILES (TEN KILOMETERS) TO CAMPUS AND FOLLOW SIGNS

The Arboretum, as the locals call it, is a vast park of some 165 hectares (408 acres) on the University of Guelph campus. Founded in 1970, it includes not only forty collections of trees and shrubs from around the world, including groupings of dwarf conifers, lilacs, oaks, maples, roses, and rhododendrons, but also a forty-hectare (ninety-acre) nature reserve with a two-mile (three-kilometer) marked trail featuring a variety of habitats from an old-growth maple-beech forest to wetlands. There are also *ornamental gardens*, including recently completed Japanese and English gardens. Other ornamental gardens are planned and will open as funds permit.

One special section, called the *Gosling Wildlife Gardens*, consists of a series of small demonstration wildlife gardens for different types of conditions. They show visitors how they can turn their yards into habitats for birds, butterflies, and animals.

The *O.A.C. Centennial Arboretum Centre* is located near the middle of the arboretum and hosts a variety of workshops, lectures, plays, and plant sales throughout the year. Check with the arboretum staff for significant events of interest to gardeners, such as the Maple Sugar Days when trees are tapped and maple syrup is made on the site (March). Guided tours are available for groups upon reservation and on special occasions throughout the year.

The Japanese Garden provides a quiet corner for relaxation.

15 Hamilton: Gage Park

LOCATION: GAGE STREET AND MAIN STREET EAST

The City of Hamilton has many parks and gardens besides the jewel in its horticultural crown, the Royal Botanical Gardens—including Whitehern National Historic Site, Sam Lawrence Park, Bayfront Park, and Pier 4 Park, but Gage Park is perhaps the most spectacular.

Gage Park is a seventy-acre (twenty-eight-hectare) urban park with vast lawns, tall trees, and numerous walkways. However, it is best known for its *rose garden*. Literally hundreds of varieties of roses are on display, from Hybrid Teas to miniature roses to shrub roses, forming no less than 162 beds. It is at its most spectacular in June and early July, but bloom often continues right through until nearly Christmas.

For color year-round, Gage Park also has a public greenhouse featuring not only exotic plants, but seasonal shows. The best known is the fall Chrysanthemum Show, held each November (phone for details). It includes over 60,000 chrysanthemums of 125 different varieties.

There are also large perennial beds containing both common and lesser known perennials, as well as display gardens of bulbs and annuals.

GARDEN OPEN: 24 hours daily, year-round; greenhouse open during daylight hours.
ADMISSION: free.

FURTHER INFORMATION FROM:
Corporation of the City of Hamilton
Department of Public Works & Traffic - Parks Division
71 Main Street West
Hamilton, Ontario L8P 4Y5
(905) 546-2489
www.city.hamilton.on.ca/pw

NEARBY SIGHTS OF INTEREST:
Royal Botanical Gardens, Dunburn Castle

Formal carpet beds feature colorful annuals. City of Hamilton Department of Public Works and Traffic

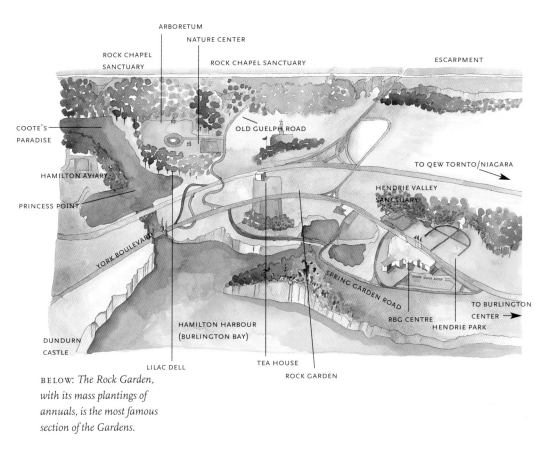

ARBORETUM

NATURE CENTER

ROCK CHAPEL
SANCTUARY

ROCK CHAPEL SANCTUARY

ESCARPMENT

COOTE'S
PARADISE

OLD GUELPH ROAD

TO QEW TORNTO/NIAGARA

HAMILTON AVIARY

HENDRIE VALLEY
SANCTUARY

PRINCESS POINT

YORK BOULEVARD

SPRING GARDEN ROAD

TO BURLINGTON
CENTER

RBG CENTRE

DUNDURN
CASTLE

HAMILTON HARBOUR
(BURLINGTON BAY)

Hendrie Park

LILAC DELL

TEA HOUSE

ROCK GARDEN

BELOW: *The Rock Garden,
with its mass plantings of
annuals, is the most famous
section of the Gardens.*

OPPOSITE: *The
Mediterranean Garden
includes a greenhouse on different levels.*

16 Hamilton: Royal Botanical Gardens

LOCATION: BETWEEN BURLINGTON AND HAMILTON, ABOUT ONE HOUR'S DRIVE
EAST OF TORONTO OR NORTH OF NIAGARA FALLS VIA HIGHWAY **403**, FOLLOW-
ING SIGNS TO THE GARDEN

The Royal Botanical Gardens is Canada's largest botanical garden in area and one of the most complete ones in North
America. It covers more than 2,700 acres (1,092 hectares) at
the westernmost tip of Lake Ontario and is in fact so vast that
you'll need a vehicle to get around it—a bicycle would do, but a
car would make for a faster visit!

The gardens began slowly, starting in the late 1920s when
the City of Hamilton began buying land to beautify its northwest entrance. In 1929, work began on converting an abandoned gravel pit into what would become the site's now
world-renowned Rock Garden. By 1930, regal permission had
been obtained to call the new garden the Royal Botanical
Gardens. More and more land was purchased until the late
1940s, when the gardens had reached their present dimensions. It was also at this time that the first formal plans for the
entire area were laid out. The plans have been gradually been
implemented until the gardens reached their present form,
although there is still more expansion to come.

One important factor to consider is that only a small portion (about 297 acres/120 hectares) of the Royal Botanical
Gardens is actually cultivated. The rest is a managed natural
area, including a vast fresh-water
marsh called *Coote's Paradise* that is
being restored to its original condition.
The developed gardens are located
here and there throughout the natural
reserves. There are over eighteen
miles (thirty km) of nature trails taking
visitors through marshland, woodland,
meadow, and even some rare virgin
Carolinian forest. Bird lovers will
enjoy a visit; nearly 300 species of
birds either live in the gardens or visit
during migration season.

There are parking lots located
near all the major trails and cultivated
sections. Pay admission to only one of
the gardens on any given day: the
receipt can be used as a pass to visit
the others. All the gardens offer
access to washrooms and drinking
fountains: some also have restaurant
services.

GARDEN OPEN: 9:30am to
dusk daily, year-round;
Mediterranean Greenhouse
open 9am to 6pm daily, year-
round. ADMISSION: $7 adults,
$6 seniors and youths 13–17
years, $2 children, free chiil-
dren under 5 years.

FURTHER INFORMATION FROM:
Royal Botanical Gardens
P.O. Box 399
680 Plains Road West
Hamilton, Ontario L8N 3H3
(905) 527-1158
www.rbg.ca

NEARBY SIGHTS OF INTEREST:
Art Gallery of Hamilton,
Dundurn Castle, Joseph Brant
Museum

The Rose Garden is a favorite with many visitors.

The greatest concentration of gardens is located near the RBG Centre, an administrative center that also houses the gardens' shop, a cafe, and special displays and collections. There are frequent lectures and workshops at this site throughout the season. *The Mediterranean Garden*, mostly under glass and, in the summer, extending to an outdoor terrace, is also part of this complex; it features subtropical plants and flowers as well as orchids and houseplants.

Adjacent to the RBG Centre is *Hendrie Park*, the floral heart of the park. Here is the *Rose Garden*, featuring nearly two acres (one hectare) of roses. Nearby is a tea house (open in summer) and the climbing plant collection. There is also a test garden for new annuals, a scented garden, a medicinal garden, water gardens, demonstration borders, and much more. If you only have time to visit one sector, the combination of the RBG Centre and Hendrie Park is probably the best choice.

About 2/3 mile (one km) from the RBG Centre is *Laking Garden*, the heart of the gardens' herbaceous plant collection. It is not be missed in June, as it includes a collection 250,000 irises in one of the world's largest iris gardens, plus an adjacent peony collection that is at its peak at about the same time.

The *Rock Garden*, about 1-1/3 miles (two kilometers) from the RBG Centre, is the oldest part of the garden and the best known to visitors. It particularly spectacular in the spring, when over 100,000 bulbs burst into bloom, but is nearly as attractive all summer, when 70,000 summer annuals come into bloom. Planted in 1929, many of the trees are now fully mature, and it is very hard to see in this beautiful sunken garden the ugly gravel pit that it originally housed. The Tea House offers snacks during the main season.

Nearby is the *arboretum*, some two miles (three kilometers) from the RBG Centre. It is home to collections of trees and shrubs, as well as the Nature Interpretive Centre that introduces the general public to the geology, history, wildlife, and restoration of the natural area. The arboretum is renowned for its collection of 800 lilacs, the largest collection in the world, which are at peak bloom in April. May is best for flowering trees, while June still sees many rhododendrons at their best.

Among the nature sanctuaries, *Coote's Paradise Marsh* is the best known, largest, and most varied, with several access points. Hendrie Valley, Rock Chapel (site of an 80 foot/25 m waterfall), and Berry Tract are others you might want to visit.

If you can do so, make sure you leave at least a full day to visit the Royal Botanical Gardens—it's worth at least that. If you live nearby, you'll find a membership (which allows unlimited free admission) to be the least expensive way of seeing this garden in all seasons.

The Mediterranean Garden brings together subtropical plants from around the world.

Laking Garden at the height of the iris season. Royal Botanical Gardens

GARDEN OPEN: dawn to dusk
daily, year-round.

ADMISSION: free.

FURTHER INFORMATION FROM:
Niagara Parks Commission
PO Box 150
Niagara Falls, Ontario
L2E 6T2
(905) 356-2241 or
(800) 877-NIAPARK
npinfo@niagaraparks.com
www.niagaraparks.com

NEARBY SIGHTS OF INTEREST:
Niagara Parks Botanical
Garden, Oakes Garden
Theatre, Queen Victoria Park,
Niagara Parks Commission
Greenhouse, Niagara Parks
Butterfly Conservatory

The Floral Clock carpet bedding is not only beautiful, it tells the exact time.

17 Niagara Falls: Floral Clock

LOCATION: ABOUT SIX MILES (TEN KILOMETERS) NORTH OF NIAGARA FALLS ON
RIVER ROAD, JUST PAST SIR ADAM BECK-NIAGARA GENERATING STATION

One of the most visited sites in Niagara Falls, Ontario—after
the falls themselves, that is—is the Floral Clock. This forty-foot
(twelve-meter) diameter clock, based on the original Floral
Clock in Edinburgh, Scotland, was built by Ontario Hydro in
1950. It is a true working clock with hands that tell the hour,
minute and second . . . and it chimes every quarter hour.

Designed, planted, and maintained by the Niagara Parks
Commission, the clock has floral displays that are in fact
changed twice each year. After the first hard fall frost, until May,
is the winter display of frost-hardy pansies, which add color
even when the ground is frozen. From May and through until
mid-fall, a much more intricate design, one whose pattern
changes every year, is put in place. It requires upwards of
16,000 carpet bedding plants; different cultivars of
Alternanthera in shades of yellow, green, red, and pink are used,
along with the green and gray forms of *Santolina*, plus a few
other low-growing plants.

A curved ten-foot (three-meter) wide pool curves along the
front edge of the clock, and the surrounding grounds feature
beautiful bedding displays. Just beyond the Floral Clock on a
ten-acre (four-hectare) site are the *Centennial Lilac Gardens*, a
collection of some 1,200 lilacs of over 200 species and cultivars, which is especially attractive in the latter part of May.

18 Niagara Falls: Niagara Parks Botanical Garden and School of Horticulture

LOCATION: ABOUT FIVE MILES (EIGHT KILOMETERS) NORTH OF NIAGARA FALLS, AT 2565 NIAGARA PARKWAY

Until 1990, this beautiful garden was simply called the Niagara School of Horticulture, but the grounds were renamed the Niagara Parks Botanical Garden in 1990 to better reflect its growing use by the public. The school still exists, though, and the gardens are maintained, planned, and operated largely by the students of the three-year program. Established in 1936, it is the only residential school for training horticultural students in Canada.

The 100 acres (forty hectares) of gardens include a bit of everything, from annual trial grounds to formal vegetable and herb gardens, a vast arboretum, perennial beds, intricate annual plantings, a shade garden, a rock garden, an ornamental grass collection, and numerous water elements. Many container gardens highlight the entrance and a large mosaic spells out the garden's name in brilliantly colored foliage plants. The annual beds are entirely replanted each winter and redone each spring by the students, so the garden is constantly changing. Finally, as one would expect from such a reputable school of horticulture, the plants are all carefully identified.

GARDEN OPEN: dawn to dusk daily, year-round.
ADMISSION: free.

FURTHER INFORMATION FROM:
Niagara Parks Commission
2565 Niagara Parkway North
PO Box 150
Niagara Falls, Ontario L2E 6T2
(905) 356-8554 or
(877) NIA-PARK
npinfo@niagaraparks.com
www.niagaraparks.com

NEARBY SIGHTS OF INTEREST:
Oakes Garden Theatre, Queen Victoria Park, Floral Clock, Niagara Parks Commission Greenhouse, Niagara Parks Butterfly Conservatory

ABOVE: *Ornamental carpet beds stretch out as far as the eye can see.*

GARDEN OPEN: 9am to 9pm daily, early June–Labor Day; 9am to 8pm daily, May 1–31 and Labor Day–mid-October; 9am to 6pm daily, mid-May–end of April; 9am to 5pm all other times.
ADMISSION: $6 adults, $3 youths 6–12 years, free children under 6 years.

FURTHER INFORMATION FROM:
Niagara Parks Butterfly
Conservatory
PO Box 150
Niagara Falls, Ontario L2E
6T2
(905) 356-8119
npinfo@niagaraparks.com
www.niagaraparks.com

NEARBY SIGHTS OF INTEREST:
Niagara Parks Botanical
Garden, Oakes Garden
Theatre, Queen Victoria Park,
Floral Clock, Niagara Parks
Commission Greenhouse

19 Niagara Falls: Niagara Parks Butterfly Conservatory

LOCATION: NIAGARA FALLS BOTANICAL GARDENS

There is now an extra reason to visit the Niagara Parks Botanical Garden (page 97); it is also home to one of Niagara's newest attractions, the Niagara Parks Butterfly Conservatory, one of North America's largest collections of free-flying butterflies. On any given day, some 2,000 butterflies belonging to over fifty species fly freely through the 11,000-square-foot (1,022-square-meter) conservatory, including the metallic blue morpho, the orange and black monarch, and dozens of tropical butterflies and moths of all sizes and shapes.

Don't however assume the greenhouse is devoid of horticultural interest. Besides the butterflies, the conservatory is packed full of tropical trees, shrubs, and vines that produce nectar for butterflies: lantanas, pentas, and passionflowers, among others. In fact, the whole habitat is designed to represent a lush, tropical rain forest. There are lianas, tall trees, cliffs, and waterfalls. A 600-foot (183-meter) network of pathways provides access for the physically challenged to the entire complex.

Besides the tropical habitat and its free-flying butterflies, visitors can look at a video about the lifestyle of butterflies and watch technicians as they scurry about in a glassed-in butterfly incubator. Chrysalis about to split open are constantly on view; it would be most surprising if you *didn't* see a butterfly emerging when you visit.

The great popularity of the Butterfly Conservatory and the limited number of people who can visit at any given time has meant that it has had to sell timed tickets, with admission only at a given hour. In some cases, you may find yourself showing up in the morning but only being able to get tickets for the afternoon. To avoid disappointment, therefore, it is best to reserve ahead, especially during peak hours (mid-morning to late afternoon).

RIGHT: *Butterflies gather at a feeding station.*

OPPOSITE: *There is carpet bedding even inside the greenhouse.*

20 Niagara Falls: Niagara Parks Commission Greenhouse and Fragrance Garden

LOCATION: ABOUT 1/4 MILE (500 METERS) SOUTH OF HORSESHOE FALLS

Originally, the Niagara Parks Commission built this greenhouse complex in 1945 as a working greenhouse. It has used it ever since to produce the over 150,000 bedding plants needed in the Parks Commission's gardens each year. Since 1980, however, there are also display greenhouses open to the general public plus a reception area housing a retail garden store selling plants, seeds, tools, and souvenirs.

The display greenhouses include a *Tropical House*, which features full-size specimens of many of our common houseplants, plus seasonal displays of flowering plants. Some seventy-five free-flying tropical birds live and nest in the greenhouse complex. Seven major shows are held annually: the Spring Show (mid-January to Easter), the Easter Display (two to three weeks at Easter), the Hydrangea Show (May), the Regal Geranium Show (June), the Summer Show (July to mid-September), the Begonia Show (mid-September to October), the Chrysanthemum Show (November) and the Christmas Light Show (December), the latter offering extended opening hours. Phone ahead to check for exact dates and specific hours, as they do vary from year to year.

Outdoors, the grounds surrounding the greenhouse feature a stunning statue/fountain in the hub of a water garden with floribunda roses in ring shaped beds surrounding it. A *Fragrance Garden* for the visually impaired was implanted nearby in 1985 in cooperation with the Canadian National Institute for the Blind. Many of the plants, some with fragrant foliage, others with sweetly scented flowers, are labeled with their common and scientific names in Braille as well as in regular script. In addition to this, a small native butterfly garden has been developed using common meadow plants that produce abundant nectar to attract wild butterflies.

GARDEN OPEN: 9:30am to dusk daily; closed December 24 and 25. ADMISSION: free.

FURTHER INFORMATION FROM: Niagara Parks Commission PO Box 150 Niagara Falls, Ontario L2E 6T2 (905) 371-0254 or (877) NIA-PARK npinfo@niagaraparks.com www.niagaraparks.com

NEARBY SIGHTS OF INTEREST: Niagara Parks Botanical Garden, Oakes Garden Theatre, Queen Victoria Park, Floral Clock, Niagara Parks Commission Greenhouse, Niagara Parks Butterfly Conservatory

21 Niagara Falls: Oakes Garden Theatre

GARDEN OPEN: 24 hours daily, year-round. **ADMISSION:** free.

FURTHER INFORMATION FROM:
Niagara Parks Commission
PO Box 150
Niagara Falls, Ontario L2E
6T2
(905) 356-2241 or
(877)-NIAPARK
npinfo@niagaraparks.com
www.niagaraparks.com

NEARBY SIGHTS OF INTEREST:
Niagara Parks Botanical
Garden, Queen Victoria Park,
Floral Clock, Niagara Parks
Commission Greenhouse,
Niagara Parks Butterfly
Conservatory

LOCATION: IN CENTER OF TOWN, AT FOOT OF CLIFTON HILL

One of the most striking Canadian examples of formal garden style is the Oakes Garden Theatre in downtown Niagara Falls. Originally constructed in 1936, the Greco-Roman amphitheater, with its limestone steps, ornamental iron gates, and massive stone balustrades, looks like something straight out of Italy. There is also a fan-shaped curved pergola with climbing plants and perfectly trimmed shrubs surrounding formal beds of annuals. The terraces and promenades provide a splendid view, as they directly overlook the American Falls.

Beyond the formality of the structure itself and its trimmed borders, there is also a beautiful rock garden of oriental inspiration, with a lily pond and fountains. The site plays host to numerous concerts throughout the year and provides an attractive formalized entrance statement to Queen Victoria Park.

22 Niagara Falls: Queen Victoria Park

LOCATION: JUST IN FRONT OF HORSESHOE FALLS

People who come to the Canadian side of Niagara Falls always come away at least as impressed by the beautiful, impeccably maintained park that surrounds the attraction as by the falls themselves. This is Queen Victoria Park, truly a royal gardening setting, named for Queen Victoria of Great Britain, the reigning monarch when the park was established in 1885.

Bounded by an escarpment, the Niagara Gorge, and the Niagara River, the park features a valuable collection of unique native and international plant material. Near the falls, the park is a vast green space peppered with mature trees, most identified by common and botanical name. Towards the cliff, there are more colorful floral features, such as a large pond with numerous naturalized perennials, a major rock garden, and a beautiful rose garden, likewise with perennial beds. There are also brilliantly colored carpet-bedding displays here and there while numerous park benches and beautiful lawns provide a pleasant opportunity for relaxation.

Queen Victoria Park is not only striking in summer, but in all seasons. Fall sees chrysanthemums and flowering cabbages mixing with the brilliant fall colors of the trees and shrubs. Although the latter give way to bare branches in winter, trees near the falls are regularly drenched in water vapor that freezes into ice, transforming them into living candelabras that sparkle like a million jewels. In spring, the park is home to over 500,000 naturalized daffodils that flow through open woodlands of the park. Magnolias, flowering cherries, and beds of brilliant tulips complete the spring parade. And the park's interest is maintained even at night, as it is fully illuminated by carefully placed landscape lighting.

GARDEN OPEN: 24 hours daily, year-round. **ADMISSION:** free.

FURTHER INFORMATION FROM:
Niagara Parks Commission
PO Box 150
Niagara Falls, Ontario L2E 6T2
(905) 356-2241
or 877-NIAPARK
npinfo@niagaraparks.com
www.niagaraparks.com

NEARBY SIGHTS OF INTEREST:
Niagara Parks Botanical Garden, Oakes Garden Theatre, Floral Clock, Niagara Parks Commission Greenhouse, Niagara Parks Butterfly Conservatory

OPPOSITE: *The mansion remains much as the family left it.*

LEFT: *Victoria Park, the gateway to the Canadian side of Niagara Falls, features flower beds throughout the vast green space.*

LOCATION: DOWNTOWN, BETWEEN GERRARD, JARVIS, SHERBROOKE,
AND CARLTON STREETS

GARDEN OPEN: 9am to 4pm
Monday–Friday, 10am to 5pm
weekends, year-round.
ADMISSION: free.

FURTHER INFORMATION FROM:
City of Toronto Parks and
Recreation
1st Floor, East Tower
City Hall
100 Queen Street West
Toronto, Ontario M5H 2N2
(416) 392-7288
www.city.toronto.on.ca

NEARBY SIGHTS OF INTEREST:
Yonge Street, Mount Pleasant
Cemetery

During the Victorian era, most of North America's cities had large conservatories, which were used not only to present exotic new plants to a people fascinated by horticultural novelties, but also as a site for gala balls, concerts, conventions, and flower shows. Toronto is one of the rare cities that has been able to maintain its public glasshouses over the years; there has been a conservatory on this site since 1879. The current palm house, the oldest part of the present greenhouse, was built in 1909 to replace a previous structure damaged by fire.

Today, the Allan Gardens conservatory's six greenhouses cover over 16,000 square feet (4,875 square meters). You enter through the largest and oldest of all, the *Palm House*, with its beautiful domed roof. It hosts a collection of palms, bananas, and tropical vines, many reaching nearly to the roof, plus seasonal flowering plants for added color. To the right, the *Tropical Landscape House* offers a colorful mixture of lush exotics, as well as a few plants of economic importance, such as tropical fruit trees, and next to it is the *Arid House* with its cactus and agaves. On the opposite side of the Palm House is the *Cool Temperate House*, a favorite with kids because of its koi-filled water garden. It contains plants that need a cool but frost-free environment, such as camellias and jasmines. The last two greenhouses, called the *Tropical Houses*, shelter collections of orchids, bromeliads, begonias, and gesneriads, ensuring year-round bloom.

Four major displays are organized each year. The Spring Display, from late January to late April, the Easter Show, the Fall Flower show, featuring chrysanthemums of all sizes, shapes, and colors, from late October to late November, and finally the popular of them all, the Victorian Christmas Show, in early December to early January.

The park outside the conservatory consists of lawns with massive oaks, sycamores, and other full-grown trees. The vast flower beds that fronted the conservatory into the 1960s had, however, gone into decline and, as this book was being written, the entire sector was in the process of being completely restored.

RIGHT: *The Palm House, recently restored, is the oldest section of the conservatory, dating back to 1909.*

OPPOSITE: *Casa Loma rises from a base of impeccably maintained gardens.*

24 Toronto: Casa Loma

LOCATION: JUST OUTSIDE OF DOWNTOWN, NEAR SPADINA AND ROADS, AT NO. 1 AUSTIN TERRACE

Casa Loma is one of Toronto's top tourist attractions. Almost all city tours at least pass by to let visitors take a quick look and most include a visit to Casa Loma as part of their regular tour. It is a 98-room medieval-style castle, built from 1911 to 1914 by financier Sir Henry Pellatt, with the help of 300 men and $3.5 million, by far the costliest private home in Ontario at that time. Unfortunately, Pellatt's fortune couldn't support the upkeep of the residence, and he had to abandon it before it was entirely furnished. It lay abandoned for years, known as Pellatt's Folly, until its value as a tourist attraction was recognized. Today thousands of people armed with self-guided audio tours visit it daily, and the house more than pays for itself.

Although the house was originally landscaped as an English gentleman's garden, with a series of *parterres*, a greenhouse, vegetable gardens, and the like, they were all abandoned when Pellatt's fortune collapsed and most of the original estate was sold off. The remaining five-acre (two-hectare) estate was then pretty much abandoned and the back slope especially turned into a tangled wilderness. It wasn't until 1987 that the Kiwanis Club of Casa Loma approached the Garden Club of Toronto with the idea of renovating the remaining grounds of the estate. A fund-raising project brought in $1.5 million and, in 1990, the gardens were officially re-opened.

GARDEN OPEN: 9:30am to 4pm daily, May–October (Tuesdays open late).
HOUSE OPEN: 9:30am to 4pm daily, year-round, close at 1pm on January 1, December 24 and 25. ADMISSION: $10 adults, $6.50 seniors and youths, $6 children 4–13 years.

FURTHER INFORMATION FROM:
Casa Loma
1 Austin Terrace
Toronto, Ontario M5R 1X8
(416) 923-1171
info@casaloma.org
www.casaloma.org

NEARBY SIGHTS OF INTEREST:
Spadina House and Garden, Toronto Music Garden

Today's gardens are not necessarily replicas of the original ones, but rather a reflection on how they might have evolved over time. The new garden has been designed as a series of specialty gardens, the most striking of which is the *Lower Terrace*, whose formal design surrounding a dancing fountain is equally attractive when seen from the turrets of the castle above or when strolling in the garden below. The Terrace gardens are filled with colorful annuals, perennials, bulbs, shrubs, and roses, ensuring color throughout the season. Other interesting gardens include the *Secret Garden*, with old-fashioned roses and specimen trees, *Rhododendron Dell*, at its best in mid to late spring, the *Woodland Walk*, with shade-tolerant ornamentals, and the *Spring Woodland Garden*, chock full of mostly spring-blooming shade perennials and bulbs.

A visit to the garden is included with admission to the house. Parking is extra. It is also possible to visit the gardens only for free on Tuesdays after 4pm from May through October. As you visit the house, make sure to take the underground passage to the vast "potting shed," which includes not only tools and instruments used by the original gardeners, but also a display that chronicles the original garden.

25 Toronto: Centennial Park Conservatory

LOCATION: WEST SIDE OF CENTENNIAL PARK, ON WESTERN EDGE OF TORONTO; 151 ELMCREST ROAD, JUST OFF RATHBURN ROAD

GARDEN OPEN: 10am to 5pm daily, year-round.
ADMISSION: free.

FURTHER INFORMATION FROM:
City of Toronto Parks and Recreation
21st Floor, East Tower
City Hall
100 Queen Street West
Toronto, Ontario M5H 2N2
(416) 394-8543
www.city.toronto.on.ca

NEARBY SIGHTS OF INTEREST:
James Gardens, Ontario Place

Centennial Park is Etobicoke's main park. Back when the suburb was still a borough, largely independent of Toronto, it was run as a showcase park for Etobicoke. However, it and the other boroughs surrounding Toronto were forced to merge in the 1990s, and the park has since lost some of its influence. It is now run by the City of Toronto Parks and Recreation Department, which only just seems to be realizing what a jewel it has inherited. The 260-acre (105-hectare) park features considerable forested areas and several picnic sites, but is mostly used for sporting activities, with a stadium, a skating pond, a toboggan hill, several playing fields, and even a ski hill. Garden lovers have not, however, been totally neglected, as off in the southwest corner, there is also a public garden: the Centennial Park Conservatory.

The conservatory features 12,000 square feet (1,115 square meters) of public greenhouse, plus production greenhouses used to produce annuals and containers for the city's other gardens. The *Main Greenhouse* features a tropical plant display including many exotic fruits: bananas, figs, pomegranates and

The Tropical Greenhouse is filled with exotic plants. Centennial Botanical Conservatory

even coffee plants, plus both common and little known house-plants. It is kept warm and humid throughout the year. The *South Wing* is home to a collection of arid climate plants, including full-size cactus and such giant succulents as agaves. The final wing, the *North Wing*, is the display greenhouse, with a regularly changing display of flowering plants. The "Christmas at the Conservatory" annual event, often featuring local choirs, is especially popular, as is the Easter display.

The beauty of the conservatory doesn't stop at its walls, though. The area around the greenhouse and the valley beyond it have been attractively landscaped and include a rock garden, perennial and shrub borders, ponds, and bridges, plus massive displays of annuals during the summer months.

26 Toronto: Edwards Gardens and Civic Garden Centre

LOCATION: NORTH OF DOWNTOWN TORONTO. EXIT 373 OFF HIGHWAY 401 TO CORNER OF LESLIE STREET AND LAWRENCE AVENUE EAST

GARDEN OPEN: dawn to dusk daily. **ADMISSION:** free.

FURTHER INFORMATION FROM:
Parks and Recreation
21st Floor, East Tower
City Hall
100 Queen Street West
Toronto, Ontario M5H 2N2
(416) 397-8186
www.city.toronto.on.ca

Rupert Edwards bought the site of the present garden in 1944, when it was a nearly abandoned farm. For the next ten years, he worked on transforming it into a country garden, with vast lawns, a huge rock garden, and breathtaking views of the deep ravine below. Fearing that his garden would disappear under urban sprawl after his death, he sold the property to the municipal government in 1955 at much less than its real value in return for it being maintained as a public garden. Mr. Edwards died in 1967, proud of having managed to ensure his garden would outlive him.

Today the thirty-four-acre (fourteen-hectare) garden is somewhat larger than in Mr. Edwards' time (the city bought adjacent land for use as a parking lot and for the construction of the Civic Garden Centre, described below), but is otherwise intact. Formal beds at the entrance of the garden display thousands of spring bulbs, followed by summer annuals and finally fall chrysanthemums. A verdant green lawn crisscrossed with paths and dotted with trees reaches down into the ravine where Wilket Creek has been dammed and remodeled into a series of pools and waterfalls. On the far side of the stream is a collection of over 200 varieties of rhododendrons and azaleas and a vast rockery. At the top of the slope to the west are flower beds filled with roses, peonies, lilies, and lilacs, surrounding a broad green lawn. Other features include bridges, fountains, a water wheel, a bog garden, native plants, and a teaching garden.

Edwards Garden shares its site with the Civic Garden Centre, not a nursery as the name might suggest, but rather a multipurpose building acting as a warehouse for horticultural activities from across Toronto. It includes a horticultural bookstore, a library, and meeting rooms where many plant clubs meet or hold their annual shows. There are regular lectures and workshops on all aspects of horticulture: for information, call (416) 397-1340.

A bridge crosses placid Willet Creek in the heart of the gardens.

27 Toronto: Guild Inn Sculpture Garden

LOCATION: THIRTEEN MILES (TWENTY-ONE KILOMETERS) EAST OF TORONTO VIA KINGSTON ROAD AND GUILDWOOD PARKWAY

The Guild Inn Gardens, certainly one of the most unusual gardens in Ontario, have a long and fascinating history. The main building, built in 1914, was originally the country home of General Harold C. Bickford. In 1932, Spencer and Rosa Clark purchased the house and forty acres of land surrounding it to create the Guild of All Arts, which became a thriving artists' colony. They eventually turned the main house into an inn to accommodate visitors to the artists' workshops, adding another building, The Studio, as a workshop for the artists. After a lull during the World War II, when the property was requisitioned as a military training base and hospital, the Guild Inn became a major landmark in the area, hosting important receptions and receiving prominent guests. Its influence was so great that when the surrounding area was developed as one of the early suburbs east of Toronto in the 1950s, it was called Guildwood Village, a name that remains to this day.

By the 1960s, the site had become famous as a public park and sculpture garden, and Spencer Clark began adding his most famous elements: architectural fragments salvaged from more than fifty buildings—facades, columns, entrances—demolished in downtown Toronto as it underwent a major urban make-over to its present skyscraper-covered silhouette. They remain the main elements of the garden today: a stroll through the architectural history of a city that grew a bit too fast.

The Guild Inn Gardens are now a public park operated by the City of Toronto, and the Inn and restaurant are being maintained for visitors' use. Overlooking the scenic Scarborough Bluffs and Lake Ontario, the park allows visitors to wander through green spaces and forest, flower gardens and wildflowers while admiring bits of Toronto's history. It is also a haven for wildlife, birds, and butterflies. Due to its architectural features, the garden is of interest in all seasons, even winter, although the restaurant is closed during the off-season. Tours can be arranged by appointment.

GARDEN OPEN: 24 hours daily, year-round.
HOUSE OPEN: 24 hours daily, Easter–New Year's Day.
ADMISSION: free.

FURTHER INFORMATION FROM:
The Guild Inn Gardens
191-201 Guildwood Parkway
Scarborough, Ontario M1E 1P5
(416) 266-4449
www.city.toronto.on.ca/parks

NEARBY SIGHTS OF INTEREST:
Scarborough Bluffs, Toronto Zoo, University of Toronto at Scarborough

Corinthian columns reassembled to form a Greek theater came originally from the Bank of Toronto in downtown. Guild Inn Gardens

West Toronto: High Park

LOCATION: BLOOR STREET WEST AND PARKSIDE DRIVE

GARDEN OPEN: dawn to dusk daily, year-round.
ADMISSION: free.

FURTHER INFORMATION FROM:
City of Toronto Parks and Recreation
21st Floor, East Tower
City Hall
100 Queen Street West
Toronto, Ontario M5H 2N2
(416) 392-6599
www.city.toronto.on.ca

NEARBY SIGHTS OF INTEREST:
Ontario Place, James Gardens

High Park is a former estate of some 400 acres (160 hectares) to the west of downtown Toronto. It features *Colborne Lodge*, the former residence of the original owners of the land that makes up most of the park, the *Animal Paddocks*, a small zoo featuring domestic and exotic species such as sheep, buffalo, and llamas, and beautiful *Grenadier Pond*, one of the most picturesque areas in the park, used for recreational activities (fishing, ice skating, and so forth) year-round, and also just as a quiet spot to sit and watch the waterfowl. And as with other municipal parks of any size, High Park has a picnic area, a playground, swimming and wading pools, a snack bar, and even an open-air theater operating in the summer months. There are also oak woodlands and nature trails, plus a self-guided walking tour.

Within this vast green space, definitely more park than garden, there are also true flower gardens, grouped together on the west side of the park. Although there are actually three different gardens, they are usually collectively referred to as *Hillside Gardens*. They include the true Hillside Garden (the more formal of the three), the Hanging Gardens (offering a wide variety of hanging baskets and container plants), and the Sunken Gardens. The three feature a wide range of shrubs, roses, annuals, and perennials and are in brilliant color from early spring right through fall.

Grenadier Pond is an oasis of peace and calm in the center of a bustling metropolis. City of Toronto Parks Department

29 Toronto: Humber Arboretum

LOCATION: NORTHWESTERN TORONTO. HIGHWAY **27** TO **205** HUMBER
COLLEGE BOULEVARD; TURN BEHIND COLLEGE FACILITIES TO NATURE
ORIENTATION CENTRE

GARDEN OPEN: dawn to dusk
daily, year-round.
ADMISSION: free.

The Humber Arboretum is located on 250 acres (100 hectares)
of green space on the West Branch of the Humber River, just
behind the north campus of Humber College. At the time this
book was written, the arboretum's location was not clearly
signed, so follow the directions above carefully; after passing
behind the campus, the wooded park to the right of the university buildings is the arboretum, even if no sign says so.

The Humber Arboretum begins with ornamental gardens
of shrubs, bulbs, annuals, and perennials displayed at the base
of the Nature Orientation Centre, overlooking the river valley.
Around these more formally landscaped gardens there is an
extensive collective of trees and shrubs, both species and
hybrids, set into lawns or grouped together into beds. A network of paths then leads down into the valley into natural forest, meadows, and marshland. Several well-marked nature
trails take visitors into different environments.

A whole section of flatter land on the valley floor is
presently under development and will further extend the
arboretum's collection of woody plants.

FURTHER INFORMATION FROM:
Humber Arboretum
205 Humber College Blvd.
Toronto, Ontario M9W 5L7
(416) 675-6622 ext. 4661
bodsworth@admin.
humberc.on.ca
www.humberc.on.ca

NEARBY SIGHTS OF INTEREST:
Centennial Park Conservatory

ABOVE: *Vast flower borders*
entice visitors to come into the
gardens.

GARDEN OPEN: 8 am to dusk
daily, year-round.
ADMISSION: free.

FURTHER INFORMATION FROM:
Property Manager
Mount Pleasant Cemetery
375 Mount Pleasant Road
P.O. Box 152, STN Q
Toronto, Ontario M4T 2M1
(416) 485-9129

NEARBY SIGHTS OF INTEREST:
Allan Gardens, Toronto Music
Gardens, Casa Loma,
Spadina House and Gardens

30 Toronto: Mount Pleasant Cemetery

LOCATION: NORTH OF ST. CLAIR AVENUE, SOUTH OF DAVISVILLE, FROM YONGE
STREET TO BAYVIEW. MOUNT PLEASANT ROAD BISECTS THE CEMETERY

Toronto's most varied arboretum is a cemetery! Mount Pleasant
Cemetery contains no less than 1,000 species and cultivars of
trees and shrubs in 200 genera, making it not only Toronto's
most important arboretum, but also one of the most complete
in North America. The cemetery office will even supply a list of
names along with their location.

This garden cemetery, opened in 1876 just outside the city,
now covers 200 acres (83 hectares) of rolling land and, thanks
to urban development, is now well within the city limits. It originally started out as a private farm, but was purchased in 1873
as a nonsectarian, nonprofit place for burial that would meet
the needs of an increasingly multicultural city. That the cemetery was intended from the beginning to be as much a park as a
garden is shown in the fact its original trustees hired Henry
Engelhardt, a landscape architect who had notably worked on
New York's Central Park, to lay out plans for the site and to
begin transforming it into a garden a full three years before it
officially opened for its first burials.

Today's Mount Pleasant Cemetery is a beautiful park of
statues and gardens, ponds and fountains, lawns and trees, and
is an urban haven for birds, animals, and butterflies. Of course,
historians will enjoy reading the inscriptions on tombstones,
memorials, and private mausoleums, which tell the stories of
the more than 180,000 people buried there—including many
notable Canadians, like Frederick Banting and Charles Best,
the discovers of insulin, and pianist Glenn Gould.

*The Niche Conservatory con-
tains a unique collection ivies.*
Mount Pleasant Cemetery

The cemetery's trees are impeccably maintained and are as
attractive in their stark winter silhouettes as when they are in
full bloom in spring, dressed in green in summer, or clothed in

gold and scarlet in fall. There are
numerous flower beds featuring brilliant annuals, perennials, and bulbs
and there are benches, planters, and
water features galore, notably at the
relatively new *Crematorium Garden*, a
masterpiece of modern landscaping
located just behind on the main office.
Remember that the cemetery is nearly
cut in half by Mount Pleasant Avenue,
so just when you think you've managed to see it all, you've only in fact
seen half of it.

31 Toronto: Spadina Historic House and Gardens

LOCATION: NEXT DOOR TO CASA LOMA, AT 285 SPADINA ROAD, SOUTH OF ST. CLAIR WEST

Spadina House (pronounced "spa-DEE-na" even though the street name is pronounced "spa-DYE-na") is just next door to the already very popular Casa Loma (page 103–104) and shares a common (paid) parking lot. The present house was built in 1866 and belonged to the Austin family until 1980. Fortunately they left the house intact with all its furnishings, including art and artifacts belonging to the family. It has been completely and beautifully restored and is open to guided visits, although on a limited schedule. There is an admission fee.

There is no admission charge for the gardens, however, and they are open throughout the summer over a longer schedule than the house. They have been restored to their approximate state in the early 1900s by the Garden Club of Toronto and the Toronto Historic Board.

The beds around the house and the stepped terraces have been planted with old roses as they would have been at the turn of the century. To one side of the house and to the back there is a vast lawn planted with beds of shrubs and mature trees. Called the *Pleasure Garden*, it would have been the most ornamental of the gardens of the time. There are formal flower beds here and there and lots of ornamental planters. The slope down at the base of the lawn had never been cultivated and remains forested.

To the other side of the house is a more utilitarian area, starting with a potting shed, a heated frame, the gardener's quarters, and a greenhouse. Not originally intended for public viewing, this section remains among the most fascinating for modern gardeners, as it gives an idea how an upper class family would have gardened at the time. The back quarter of the lot is mix of vegetable and herb gardens, some of them quite formal in outline, with a cutting garden and the remains of a small orchard. All the plants chosen were known to have been grown in Toronto in 1915.

Besides free visits of the garden, there are also guided tours on Sundays and Wednesdays during the summer. Call ahead to reserve.

GARDEN OPEN: 9am to 4:15 pm Monday–Friday; 9am to 5:15pm weekends, May–October. HOUSE OPEN: 12pm to 4pm Tuesday–Friday, 12pm to 5pm weekends, April–November; call for winter schedule. ADMISSION: free. HOUSE ADMISSION: $5 adults, $3.25 seniors and youths, $3 children 12 years and younger.

FURTHER INFORMATION FROM: Spadina Historic House and Garden
285 Spadina Road
Toronto, Ontario M5R 2V5
(416) 392-6910
www.city.toronto.on.ca

NEARBY SIGHTS OF INTEREST: Casa Loma, Toronto Music Garden

Flower beds provide plenty of material for cutting.

The Gigue is a series of giant grass steps.

GARDEN OPEN: dawn to dusk daily, year-round.
ADMISSION: free.

FURTHER INFORMATION FROM:
City of Toronto Parks and
Recreation
21st Floor, East Tower
Toronto, Ontario M5H 2N2
(416) 392-1111

NEARBY SIGHTS OF INTEREST:
Harbourfront Centre, Artists'
Gardens, CN Tower

32 Toronto: Toronto Music Garden

LOCATION: WATERFRONT, AT QUEEN S QUAY BETWEEN SPADINA AND BATHURST

The Toronto Music Garden, one of Toronto's newest gardens, has been getting rave reviews from visitors. Built directly on the waterfront in Toronto's inner harbor, the two-acre (one-hectare) park springs from the imagination of renowned cellist Yo-Yo Ma and Boston landscape designer Julie Moire Messervy. Yo-Yo Ma contacted her about the idea of planning a garden based on Bach's First Suite for Unaccompanied Cello; the site was intended to be Boston, Massachusetts. The plan was well underway when Boston dropped out and a new site had to be found. The City of Toronto, working a long-term revitalization plant for the harborfront, stepped in . . . and the rest is history.

The result is a garden made up of six "movements," whose form and feeling correspond to that suggested by the music. Each garden is named after an individual dance (Prelude, Allemande, Courante, Sarabande, Menuett, and Gigue) and flows according to how Ms. Messervy has interpreted the music. "Prelude," for example, seemed to her an undulating riverscape with curves and bends, while "Menuett" was a formal flower parterre, and "Gigue" inspired giant grass steps that dance downward. It's a very modern garden, including pathways, curving beds of shrubs, perennials, and grasses, play spaces for children, an open-air concert area for musical and theatrical events, and much more. Visitors can leave a deposit and borrow headphones to listen to the music as they visit, making for a unique garden that really has no comparison within Canada.

33 Toronto: Toronto Zoo

LOCATION: NORTHEASTERN LIMITS OF TORONTO. HIGHWAY 401 TO EXIT 389, THEN FOLLOW MEADOWVALE NORTH TO ENTRANCE

The Toronto Zoo (Metro Toronto Zoo) is an exciting, modern facility of some 710 acres (287 hectares) where animals roam relatively freely or, at least, with few visible barriers between them and their human visitors . . . and it is sometimes the latter who appear to be in cages! A special effort has been made to recreate the original environment of the some 5,000 animals from all around the world that live in the zoo, and that includes growing the appropriate vegetation. Which explains the inclusion of a zoo in a book on gardens—many parts of the zoo are beautifully landscaped with rare and exotic plants that are, furthermore, generally well identified.

The *Indo-Malaysia Pavilion*, for example, is basically a large, very stylized greenhouse that is home to both animals and hundreds of tropical plants, many rarely seen in culture. The *Americas Pavilion* is similar, including a South American Waterfall and simulated Mayan temple ruins overgrown with tropical vegetation. The *Africa Pavilion* and new *Gorilla Rainforest* likewise recreate tropical habitats indoors. Even the temperate outdoor exhibits feature plants indigenous to the region where possible. Native North American animals of forest origin, for example, have been integrated directly into the original hardwood forest of the Rouge Valley where the zoo is located.

It is worth noting that only a relatively small portion of the site has been developed as a zoo. Much of it remains a vast nature reserve, including natural wetlands, virgin forest, and beautiful butterfly meadows, accessible by numerous nature trails.

The zoo includes just about all imaginable services, from snack bars and restaurants to camel rides, animal demonstrations, and a zoomobile that takes visitors from one site to another on the zoo's vast territory. There are also beautiful planted gardens scattered here and there throughout the site, from the entrance to the picnic areas. If you love both animals and plants, make sure to allow at least a half day to visit this site.

GARDEN OPEN: year-round, hours vary according to season; phone ahead.

ADMISSION: $13 general admission, $10 seniors, $8 children 4–14 years, free children 3 years and younger.

FURTHER INFORMATION FROM:
Toronto Zoo
361A Old Finch Avenue
Scarborough, Ontario M1B 5K7
(416) 392-5900
torontozoo@zoo.metrotor.on.ca
www.torontozoo.com

NEARBY SIGHTS OF INTEREST:
Ontario Science Centre, Rouge Valley Park, Edwards Gardens

The zoo features many colorful annual borders.

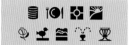

34 # Whitby: Cullen Gardens & Miniature Village

GARDEN OPEN: 10am to 5pm in spring; 9am to 8pm in summer; 10am to 5pm in fall; 10am to 10pm at Christmas. **ADMISSION:** $12 adults, $8.50 seniors and students, $5 children 3–12 years, $34.99 family.

FURTHER INFORMATION FROM:
Cullen Gardens & Miniature Village
300 Taunton Road West
Whitby, Ontario L1N 5R5
(905) 668-6606 or
(800) 461-1821
gardens@durham.net
www.cullengardens.com

NEARBY SIGHTS OF INTEREST:
Toronto Zoo, Guild Inn
Sculpture Garden

This typical Victorian style country home is actually a reduced model; the lawns and gardens are also to scale.

LOCATION: FIFTEEN MILES (THIRTY KILOMETERS) EAST OF TORONTO. HIGHWAY 401 TO HIGHWAY 12 EXIT; TURN NORTH TO TAUNTON ROAD WEST AND FOLLOW SIGNS

This privately owned garden is a major success story, having become one of the most popular gardens in Ontario—and one of the main tourist attractions east of Toronto—within only a few years of opening. Garden center owner Len Cullen had long had the desire to create a "dream garden" he could invite the world to visit. Work began on the dream garden in 1976, and by 1980 Cullen Gardens & Miniature Village had opened to the public. The Cullen family has never looked back since, and the gardens continue to grow almost yearly, with plentiful new additions. Today the site covers some thirty-eight acres (fifteen hectares) along and in a scenic river valley.

The main draw to the garden is the miniature village and the adjacent "Cottage Country," which feature 160 miniature buildings and homes built on a 1:12 scale. This section includes a miniature lake with speeding boats, a tiny super highway with moving cars, and many other amusing attractions. There is also a carnival with rides and music. Gardeners will be fascinated to discover that the lawns, landscapes, and flower beds surrounding the miniature homes are all done with live plants, trimmed to scale.

There are also beautiful plantings of annuals, perennials, and over 90,000 spring bulbs, plus stunning topiaries, many container gardens, and a giant peacock planted in annuals. A *wildflower garden* includes dozens of native flowers in woodland, meadow, and marsh settings and a new *Family Centre* provides, in season, swimming pools, a waterslide, miniature golf, and a playground. An entire pioneer village, made up of period houses brought onto the site, also seems to be developing. And the site is renowned for its special events: a tulip festival, a chrysanthemum festival, car shows, and, most especially, the Christmas Festival of Lights, held in November and December. There is also live entertainment, several restaurant possibilities, boutiques, and stores, plus exotic birds and animals. If any garden in Canada can be said to have "something for everyone," this is certainly it!

The greenhouse is open every season.

35 Oshawa: Parkwood Estate

LOCATION: EAST OF TORONTO VIA HIGHWAY **401**; EXIT **417** TO **270** SIMCOE ROAD; AT CORNER OF ALMA ROAD IN DOWNTOWN

The fifty-five-room Parkwood mansion is the former home of Canadian General Motors tycoon and philanthropist, Robert Samuel (Sam) McLaughlin and one of the rare surviving examples of an estate of the interwar years. It was first begun in 1915, with additions and alterations over subsequent years have resulted in the building's present form. It truly represents its time, as the McLaughlin family donated the home complete with period furniture, artwork, and even wallpaper and monogrammed linens. One almost gets the feeling the family still lives there.

If the house is a work of art, the same can also be said of the grounds. Unlike most former estates converted into public gardens, the twelve-acre (five-hectare) grounds are intact and maintain all the features of the McLaughlin period. They were designed by landscape architects H.B. and L. A. Dunington-Grub in the 1920s and feature perfect lawns, trimmed shrubs, tall trees, pavilions, garden paths, and strategically placed statues. The *Formal Garden* with its wide, elevated terrace, huge pool and illuminated fountains is as the family left it. The *Italian Garden* could have come straight from Tuscany, with a lily pool and elaborate trellises of climbing plants. There is also a shade garden, a white garden, a sundial garden, and a *Tea House* where lunch and afternoon tea are served in the summer. The greenhouse complex remains open year round so even winter visitors to the house can enjoy tropical plants it houses plus its indoor *Japanese garden*.

GARDEN OPEN: 10:30pm to 4pm Tuesday–Sunday, June 1–Labor Day. House open during garden hours in the summer, and 1:30pm to 4pm Tuesday–Sunday, Labor Day–May 31.
ADMISSION: $6 adults, $4.50 seniors and students, $14 family.

FURTHER INFORMATION FROM:
Parkwood
270 Simcoe Street North
Oshawa, Ontario L1G 4T5
(905) 433-4311

NEARBY SIGHTS OF INTEREST:
Cullen Gardens and Miniature Village, Toronto Zoo, Canadian Automotive Museum

LOCATION: HIGHWAY 7, TURN ONTO WILSON STREET, THEN TURN RIGHT AT FIRST TRAFFIC LIGHT ONTO SUNSET BOULEVARD. GARDENS LOCATED NEXT TO LANARK COUNTY ADMINISTRATION BUILDING

GARDEN OPEN: 24 hours daily, year-round. **ADMISSION:** free.

FURTHER INFORMATION FROM:
Teresa Weber
Round Garden for the Blind
R.R. #3
Perth, Ontario K7H 3C5
(613) 267-7464
weber@superaje.com

NEARBY SIGHTS OF INTEREST:
Historic Perth, Last Duel Park, Purdon Conservation Area

Raised beds provide easy-to-reach gardens for the blind to touch plants.

Forget those "Please keep off the grass" signs you see in so many other parks. The Round Garden for the Blind *wants* you to touch and feel. Designed for the enjoyment of handicapped people in general, and the blind in particular, it is a "hands-on" garden, designed to be felt. Fully wheelchair accessible, it features waist-high planter boxes (for easier access to the handicapped) filled with annuals, perennials, shrubs, bulbs, and herbs, all of which have some sensory attraction other than just sight. Some offer interesting textures, others have perfumed flowers, others still give off scents when stroked, and others yet were put there to be tasted! Most are identified with signs in English, French, and Braille. And to back up the sensory appeal of the plants, a splashing fountain charms the ear while birds sing on the trees and swallows twitter from a community nesting box. There are also plenty of benches, some shaded by a gazebo, for tired visitors.

The garden opened in 1983, the brainchild of Perth resident Joe Rawson, a retired teacher of mentally handicapped children, and was designed by his wife, Leah, based on a similar garden they had seen in Germany. It is run by a non-profit foundation and maintained largely by volunteers. Although both the garden and the parking area are free of charge, donations are graciously accepted. Guided tours by volunteers can be arranged by calling one week ahead.

Washroom facilities are available at the County Administration Building next door during regular business hours.

37 Morrisburg: Queen Elizabeth Gardens

LOCATION: NEAR KINGSTON. HIGHWAY 401 TO EXIT 750 OR 758; FOLLOW DIRECTIONS TO HIGHWAY 2. GARDENS ARE LOCATED JUST OUTSIDE UPPER CANADA VILLAGE, IN CRYSLER PARK

GARDEN OPEN: dawn to dusk daily, late May–late October.

ADMISSION: free.

Upper Canada Village is a major tourist attraction in southeastern Ontario; the recreated village represents life in a typical Ontario village in the 1860s and does include a few vegetable and flower gardens of interest. However, few visitors think to look at the far end of the parking lot, near the tourist information booth, where a beautiful public garden is open from spring through fall.

The garden is officially within *Crysler Park*, created to commemorate the soldiers who fought in the Battle of Crysler's Farm, in which a small contingent of Canadian and British soldiers fought back a much larger American force on November 11, 1813. The gardens were presented as a gift to Her Majesty Queen Elizabeth II by the Province of Ontario and the St. Lawrence Parks Commission during a visit to Canada in 1984.

The gardens include a sunken rose garden, a collection of antique roses, a wildflower garden, shrub collections, and plantings of annuals and perennials. There is also a large fountain and a water garden, plus verdant lawns. Although attractive spring through fall, the rose garden is perhaps the heart of the gardens and is at its best in late June and again towards the end of summer.

FURTHER INFORMATION FROM:
Saint Lawrence Parks
Commission
R.R. #1
Morrisburg, Ontario K0C 1X0
(613) 543-3704

NEARBY SIGHTS OF INTEREST:
Upper Canada Village

ABOVE: *Winding paths lead visits around the grounds.*

LOCATION: JUST OUTSIDE DOWNTOWN, AT MAPLE DRIVE

GARDEN OPEN: dawn to dusk daily, year-round; greenhouse open 9am to 4pm daily, year-round. **ADMISSION:** free.

FURTHER INFORMATION FROM:
Central Experimental Farm
Sir John Carling Building
930 Carling Avenue
Ottawa, Ontario K1A 0C5
(613) 759-1000

NEARBY SIGHTS OF INTEREST:
Commissioners Park,
Parliament Hill, Mackenzie
King Estate

The arboretum bursts into color with the first days of fall.
Friends of the Farm

How many North American cities have a working farm as part of their downtown core? Ottawa does: the Central Experimental Farm, a huge farming complex of 1,200 acres (500 hectares) dating back to 1886. It is the headquarters and main research station of Agriculture Canada and includes not only model barns and fields with cows, pigs, sheep, horses, and more, but also demonstration plots of about just about every crop grown in Canada and even also several ornamental gardens.

By far the most important of the gardens, both in size and in variety of plants, is the *Dominion Arboretum*. The eighty-five-acre (thirty-four-hectare) arboretum contains plantings dating back to 1889 and over 2,000 species and cultivars of trees and shrubs, including an important collection of lilacs and ornamental crabapples, at their best in May. It also offers a spectacular panoramic view of the city of Ottawa, notably of the parks around Dow's Lake and along the Rideau Canal. Some of the species are quite unusual for Ottawa's harsh climate, including dawn redwoods and wisterias. There are also two collections of trimmed hedges; the "Old Hedge Collection" dates to the 1890s, so it really does show how different species stand up to long term use!

The *Macoun Sunken Gardens* and the *Ornamental Gardens* along Prince of Wales Drive make up a fifteen-acre (four-hectare) enclave of flower gardens within the Experimental Farm. They contain annuals, perennials, shrubs, and bulbs, plus a rock garden and a demonstration vegetable garden. There is likewise a collection of hardy roses. The iris collection, at its peak in early June, is particularly interesting.

At the south end of the Arboretum is the *Fletcher Wildlife Garden*, an eighteen-acre (seven-hectare) section of wildflowers designed to attractive wildlife. It includes a butterfly meadow, a sedge pond, and a woodlot. And off Maple Drive, by the Observatory, there is a floral sundial; you can tell the time of day according to when various flowers open or close.

The Central Experimental Farm also includes a *tropical greenhouse*, located on Maple Drive. It houses some 500 different species of tropical plants, including orchids, cacti, and exotic fruit trees. It likewise hosts a series of seasonal plant shows, of which the fall Chrysanthemum Show and the winter Christmas Show are the most popular.

Of course, there is more to visit in the Central Experimental Farm than the gardens; there is an agriculture museum, sheep, cattle, horse, and swine barns, wagon rides, and seasonal demonstrations and displays, such as sheep-shearing. There are admission fees for some of the exhibits.

39 Ottawa: Commissioners Park and Tulip Festival

LOCATION: AT CARLING AVENUE AND PRESTON STREET

Commissioners Park is a lovely green park along the shores of the Rideau Canal, in front of Dow's Lake, and within easy walking distance of downtown Ottawa. In the summer, it is known for its trees, its lawns, and its annual flower beds. However, it is best known for its spring display, as it is the highlight of Canada's largest outdoor flower event, the Tulip Festival.

The Tulip Festival takes place in Ottawa every year from late April to late May (phone for exact dates). It began after World War II, when the Dutch royal family began sending tulip bulbs to the people of Canada to thank them for their help in hosting the family when they fled Holland after its fall to Germany. The 20,000 bulbs received annually were at first planted only in Commissioners Park, in a bed called the *Queen Juliana Gift Bed*. However, the tradition of planting tulips in Ottawa parks quickly led to the establishment of an entire Tulip

GARDEN OPEN: dawn to dusk daily, year-round.
ADMISSION: free.

FURTHER INFORMATION FROM:
National Capital Commission
202-40 Elgin Street
Ottawa, Ontario K1P 1C7
(613) 239-5000 or
(800) 465-1867
www.capcan.ca

NEARBY SIGHTS OF INTEREST:
Parliament Hill, Central Experimental Farm, Mackenzie King Estate

Mass plantings of lily flowered tulips fill Commissioner's Park during the Tulip Festival.

Festival, with over 600,000 tulips planted in sites throughout the National Capital Region: Ottawa and Hull, Québec.

The lion's share of the tulips are planted in Commissioners Park, about 290,000 of them, and it remains the highlight of the festivities. However, during festival time, there are vast beds of tulips planted throughout the region, from the Central Experimental Farm (page 118–119) to Ottawa Civic Hospital, along Colonel By Drive, Confederation Boulevard, Wellington Street, Sussex Drive, and Queen Elizabeth Driveway, on Parliament Hill, and in Jacques Cartier and Major's Parks. In Hull, look for major plantings on Laurier Street and at the Mackenzie King Estate.

Although most Tulip Festival events, including the parade, concerts, and sales areas are concentrated over a single week in mid to late May, the best period for blooming can be earlier or later. If you want to see the tulips at their best, but are not limited as to a date, it is worthwhile phoning ahead to see how the season is progressing before deciding exactly when to travel.

40 Ottawa: Rideau Hall

LOCATION: ABOUT TWO MILES (3.5 KILOMETERS) FROM PARLIAMENT HILL ALONG SUSSEX DRIVE

The grounds are open for free visits. Guided tours take visitors through the formal gardens bordering the house.

Rideau Hall, also called Government House, is the official residence of the Governor General of Canada, representative of Her Majesty Queen Elizabeth II. Royal visitors and foreign heads of state stay at Rideau Hall when they are in Ottawa. In spite of its official function, it is surprisingly readily open to the

public; in fact, it has been called the "world's most accessible official residence."

Part of the house can be visited with a guide (it's best to phone ahead to reserve). The house was originally built in 1838. Originally a rather simple two-story stone villa, it has been considerably enlarged since becoming an official residence and now boasts a ballroom and the Tent Room—once an indoor tennis court and now used for receptions. The present neoclassical stone facade bears a massive motif of the royal arms and is said to be the largest coat of arms in the world. Inside, the house is festooned with works of art, fine antiques, chandeliers, and other elegant decorative elements.

No reservation is needed, however, for a self-guided tour of the grounds. They cover 88 acres (65 hectares) and most of this area is open to the public. They feature vast lawns, forest, and walkways, as well as many trees planted by foreign dignitaries. Ask for information at the Visitor Center at the main gate. Many special events are held on the grounds, including an annual garden party to which everyone is invited and which attracts as many as 15,000 people. Special garden tours are also offered during the summer months, including visits of the extensive greenhouses and other parts of the grounds not usually open to the public. Phone for information, as dates change yearly.

Please note that, given Rideau Hall's regular use for official events and ceremonies, all visits and activities are subject to change without notice.

GARDEN OPEN: 10am to 4pm weekends, May–June; 10am to 4pm daily, July–August; 10am to 4pm weekends, September–October. **HOUSE OPEN:** 9am to one hour before sunset daily, year-round. **ADMISSION:** free.

FURTHER INFORMATION FROM:
Rideau Hall
1 Sussex Drive
Ottawa, Ontario K1A 0A1
(613) 998-7113 or
(800) 465-6890
www.gg.ca

NEARBY SIGHTS OF INTEREST:
Parliament Hill, National Museum of Science and Technology, Central Experimental Farm, Mackenzie King Estate

41 Thunder Bay: Centennial Botanical Conservatory

LOCATION: 1601 DEASE STREET, NEAR BALMORAL AVENUE

This beautiful conservatory, located in the port city of Thunder Bay, at the northwestern tip of Lake Superior, is Ontario's northernmost public greenhouse. The structure houses some 11,400 square feet (1,060 square meters) of viewing space and is divided into three main sections. The largest is the central one, called the *Tropical House*, which features plants native to humid tropical regions of the world and includes a delightful water garden: just the tropical paradise to escape to on a blustery, cold winter's day.

The *West Wing* houses a collection of plants native to arid regions, such as cactus and other succulents. The final section, the *East Wing*, is used for seasonal floral displays. There are also working greenhouses behind the main structure which are used to produce plants and flowers for the city's parks; they're

GARDEN OPEN: 1pm to 4pm daily, year-round; closed Good Friday and December 24 and 25. **ADMISSION:** free.

FURTHER INFORMATION FROM:
Botanical Conservatory
1601 Dease Street
Thunder Bay, Ontario P7C 5H7
(807) 622-7036

NEARBY SIGHTS OF INTEREST:
International Friendship Garden, Centennial Park

*A traveler's tree (*Ravenala madagascariensis*) raises its broad leaves to the sky in the Main Greenhouse.*

not officially open to the public . . . but no one will stop you from taking a peek. The botanically inclined will appreciate the fact that most plants in the greenhouses are identified by common and Latin name.

Although theoretically open only afternoons, special tours can be arranged for groups wishing to visit the conservatory at other times.

GARDEN OPEN: dawn to dusk daily, year-round.
ADMISSION: free.

FURTHER INFORMATION FROM:
Parks Division
City of Thunder Bay
111 South Syndicate Avenue
Thunder Bay, Ontario P7E 6S4
(807) 622-7036

NEARBY SIGHTS OF INTEREST:
Centennial Botanical
Conservatory, Centennial Park

42 Thunder Bay: International Friendship Garden

LOCATION: NORTHWESTERN TIP OF LAKE SUPERIOR, ON VICTORIA AVENUE BETWEEN TARBUTT AND WATERLOO STREETS

Located as it is only a short distance from the American border, it is perhaps not surprising that Thunder Bay should play host to a garden promoting friendship between nations. This garden first began to be developed in 1965 as a project for Canada's 1967 Centennial. Started by the city's Soroptimist International Club, the original garden, built around two artificial lakes, contained six gardens representing countries from around the world, each garden planned, designed, constructed, and financed by ethnic groups from the country represented. The garden has grown considerably since then and today there are seventeen gardens, representing such countries as diverse China, Canada, Holland, Italy, Slovenia, and the Philippine Islands. Soroptimist International Thunder Bay continues to act as a liaison between the city and the participating groups, ensuring that the gardens are always impeccably maintained.

Entrance to the gardens is through two arches provided by the Soroptimists. Each garden is quite unique, with elements as diverse as a functioning windmill in the Dutch garden, a pagoda guarded by two marble lions in the Chinese one, a cross of St. Andrew for Scotland, and various monuments and structures in the others. They are linked by paths that lead around the lakes and to each of the gardens.

One of the floral highlights are the 100 varieties of peonies in the *Ukrainian Garden*. Most of the other gardens feature annual plantings that change yearly, plus trees, shrubs, and other plants typical of the country the garden represents.

The windmill is part of the Dutch Community Bed.
David A. Reid

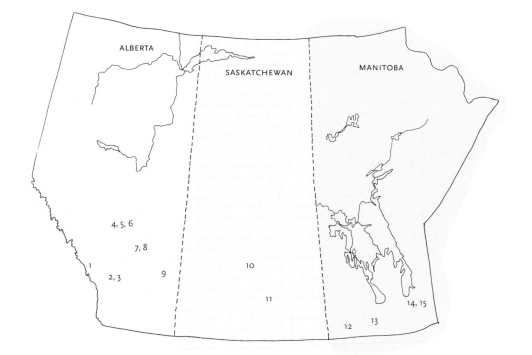

ALBERTA

SASKATCHEWAN

MANITOBA

4, 5, 6

7, 8

1

2, 3

9

10

11

12

13

14, 15

1 Banff: Cascade Gardens
2 Calgary: Devonian Gardens
3 Calgary: Dorothy Harvie Gardens
4 Edmonton: Muttart Conservatory
5 Edmonton: Saint Albert Botanic Park
6 Edmonton: University of Alberta
    Devonian Botanic Gardens

7 Trochu: Trochu Arboretum &
    Gardens
8 Lethbridge: Nikka Yuko Japanese
    Garden
9. Brooks: Crop Diversification Centre
    South
10 Saskatoon: Patterson Garden

11 Regina: Wascana Centre
12 Boissevain: International Peace
    Garden
13 Morden: Morden Research Centre
14 Winnipeg: Assiniboine Park
    Conservatory and Gardens
15 Winnipeg: Living Prairie Museum

PRAIRIE PROVINCES:

Alberta, Saskatchewan, Manitoba

Three provinces take up the entire center of Canada. Large in area, but rather low in population, these three, called the Prairie Provinces, are Manitoba, Saskatchewan, and Alberta. The name is somewhat of a misnomer, as the Prairies (from the French for "meadows," as the first French traders called the vast Western plains) actually only occupy about a third of the area of the three provinces—in their center, towards the south. Nevertheless, the Prairies, a large, often incredibly flat plain of rich, dark soil irregularly cut into by the broad valleys of meandering rivers, are the area's most striking characteristic. Called the "breadbasket of Canada," they supply much of its grain, including wheat, oats, rye, sunflowers, and buckwheat. In many areas, the land really is perfectly flat as far as the eye can see, with fields of wheat extending to the horizon, punctuated by the occasional farmhouse or grain elevator. Droughts are frequent, and most rivers and streams dry up to a trickle or disappear all together in the summer, and the winters are bitterly cold.

Other than the Prairies themselves, the Prairie Provinces are as diverse as any other area in Canada. Like most of the country, the northern part is covered in boreal forest and taiga, with numerous lakes (often called "sloughs") and rivers. To the east, too, forest predominates with plentiful lakes and rivers. Lake Winnipeg is one of Canada's largest lakes. The provinces' reputation as being very dry is actually therefore false; the south can indeed be dry, but water is rarely lacking in the north and in the Eastern Prairies. And the Prairies are not at all land-locked;

OPPOSITE: *Morden Research Centre, Manitoba*

125

much of the provinces' early development took place via Hudson's Bay in Northern Manitoba.

To the west, the Prairies rapidly give way to rolling foothills, then to the Rocky Mountains, a very tall, snow-capped mountain range that forms the border between Alberta and its neighbor to the west, British Columbia. Mountain lakes, dense forests, rushing rivers, and glaciers are part of the landscape.

European settlement of the Prairie Provinces was very slow at first. Native Amerindian tribes, such as the Cree, tended to be nomadic, following the vast herds of buffalo that once ranged the area. It was the fur trade that first stimulated Europeans to enter into this part of the world. From 1670 to the early 1700s, the fur trade, mostly in beaver pelts, was entirely controlled by the British, through the Hudson Bay Company, based at river mouths on the bay of the same name. Then French traders found a way to the Prairies via the Great Lakes and formed the North West Company. For the following 100 years, before the two merged, there were bitter rivalries between the two companies.

The fur trade brought Europeans into the Prairies, but led to the construction of forts, not settlements. It wasn't until the establishment of the first farming communities at the Red River Colony in Manitoba (in the early 1800s) that European habitation of the Prairies really began. Growth of the settlements was slow; unseasonable frosts, terrible floods, invasions of locusts, and long periods of drought were not conducive to rapid population growth. Besides, access to the Prairies was very limited—travel by water, either via Hudson Bay to the North or the Great Lakes to the east, took months.

It was the promise of law and order and schooling, plus a railroad, that brought the Prairie Provinces, at first called the Northwest Territories, into Canada. At the time of Confederation, in 1867, Canada lay strictly east of Manitoba. But ruthless whiskey traders moving up from the American territory of Montana were wreaking havoc on the native Amerindian populations and imposing their own violent laws, forcing the territorial government, run from Great Britain, to form the now world-famous Mounties—the North West Mounted Police—to bring law and order to the territories. At the same time, missionaries arrived and began to found the first schools. Then work on the Canadian Pacific Railway, designed to create a unified Canada from the Atlantic to the Pacific, began, and the vast Northwest Territories joined the new nation in 1870. The southern parts of the Northwest Territories weren't divided into the provinces we know today until 1882, as settlers began to rush in from eastern Canada, the United States, and Europe as the railroad, finally completed in 1885, pushed through from the east.

From the creation of the three provinces until World War I, immigration to the Prairies came in great waves, bringing people from across Europe—but notably from Germany, Russia, the Ukraine, and Iceland—to the Prairies, founding villages and towns as

Dorothy Harvie Gardens, Alberta

they came. But the immigrants didn't limit their activities to farming; forestry, mining, and industry followed. Then oil was discovered at Leduc, Alberta, in 1947 and brought greater prosperity than ever to the Prairie Provinces. Today on the Prairies, as in the rest of Canada, more people rely on industry and commerce for their wages than on farming. And immigration is ongoing, notably in oil-rich Alberta, whose cities are among the fastest growing in Canada.

As with most of Canada, the Prairies have developed mostly in the south; the north largely remains uninhabited, other than for a few mining towns. The area's gardens, obviously, follow the same pattern, and are generally located near the areas of greatest population, in the south. The local climate is generally colder and drier than that in other developed parts in Canada, and snow cover is variable, often disappearing entirely during periods of warm Chinook winds, blowing down from the Rocky Mountains. They can temporarily bring spring weather in mid-winter and push many plants to begin growing far too early in the season, only to be cut back harshly when temperatures again drop well below freezing. The combination of cold winters, mid-winter thaws, and dry summers means that many plants that are standards in temperate gardens around the world, even elsewhere in Canada, fail to thrive. Such problems, though, never stop Prairie gardeners, a hardy group if ever there was one, who have found lots of ways of compensating. They often grow Prairie-tested cultivars that are especially well adapted to their climate.

Alberta is most heavily populated of the Prairie Provinces, with some three million inhabitants. Relatively few people live in the Plains region itself, though; the two major population centers are Calgary, in the foothills region to the southwest, and Edmonton, the capital, closer to the center of the province and on the edge of the boreal forest. The Albertan section of the Prairies is particularly dry, and irrigation is often a necessity for crop production, but cattle raising on vast ranches is highly viable. Parts however are so dry as to be unfarmable, such as the badlands near Drumheller, known for its mushroom-shaped rock formations . . . and for its dinosaur skeleton discoveries!

Calgary is the largest city. Once known as "Cow Town," Calgary would be more appropriately named "Oil Town" today. The city's economy is closely linked to oil exploitation nearby, and booms and busts depend on world oil prices. In bad times and good, though, Calgary continues to grow, and its downtown, with its glittering skyscrapers and urban bustle, is a hub for much of the province's economy. The Calgary Stampede, a week-long summer rodeo that is the city's best known annual event, helps it maintain a distinctly "western" flavor. Among its "not to be missed" gardens are the Dorothy Harvie Gardens (page 134) and the unique downtown Devonian Gardens (page 133).

Edmonton is Calgary's rival, also a modern city, but with a more sedate atmosphere; there are more parks than superhighways, and green space seems to dominate rather than skyscrapers. Perhaps it is the city's role as provincial capital or its place as a university city that gives it a different ambiance from its more boisterous sister to the south, but, for whatever reason, there is a major differ-ence. Certainly it is as much an oil city as Calgary, as the entire city is ringed in oil wells. The city's best known garden is the Muttart Conservatory (page 135), a world-class public greenhouse complex, while the province's most important botanical garden, the University of Alberta Devonian Botanic Garden (page 138) is located not far from the city.

There are other Albertan gardens outside the two major urban centers, but the Nikka Yuko Japanese Garden (page 140), located in Lethbridge, is worth special mention as one of North America's most authentic Japanese gardens. If any Canadian province truly merits the name of Prairie Province or "bread basket of Canada," though, it is Saskatchewan. About two-thirds of its surface, including all of the southern part of the province, is prairie—and farming is still the province's major economic motor; sixty percent of all the wheat grown in the country comes from here, and cattle ranching is likewise very important. Oil, natural gas, and mining are among the primary natural resources, and industry is developing rapidly. In general, though, Saskatchewan remains a largely rural province with few truly large urban centers; Saskatoon, with a population of about 200,000, is the largest city, followed closely by Regina, the provincial capital. This lack of population concentration is reflected in the relatively few large public gardens of which Patterson Garden (page 143), in Saskatoon, and Wascana Centre (page 144), are the best known.

The easternmost of the Prairie Provinces—and the one with the least amount of actual prairie!—Manitoba is perhaps best seen as a province of forests and lakes, even low mountains, with just a southwestern corner of plains landscape. Most of the inhabitants don't live on the Prairies at all, but in the forested southeast corner, in the lower Red River Valley, near the great Manitoba lakes: Lake Winnipeg and Lake Manitoba.

Winnipeg is the capital of the province and the center of its population: over two-thirds of the province's population of about 1.1 million live in Winnipeg or in the surrounding area. Most of the province's major gardens are likewise in Winnipeg, such as Assiniboine Park and Conservatory (page 147), but there are gardens scattered over the southern part of the province. Perhaps most notable is the Morden Research Station (page 146), just north of the American border, renowned throughout Canada as the site of hybridization of hardy plants, notably the Morden series of roses.

The Far North

It is worth mentioning that Canada's ten provinces make up only the southern two-thirds of the country; three "territories"—Yukon, the Northwest Territories, and Nunavut, north of the Prairie Provinces and British Columbia—and largely wilderness although with scattered human populations occupy the country's far north. Mining, oil, gas, trapping, forestry, and hydroelectric power are either currently important or offer potential for future development. Native peoples, both Inuit and Amerindian, are in the majority throughout much of the Territories and many still make their living as hunters, as they have for thousands of years.

Devonian Botanic Gardens, University of Alberta

Without truly major urban centers and given a very cold, hostile climate, gardens in the territories are few and far between—even parks are rare. The Yukon Gardens, in Whitehorse, the capital of the Yukon, is under development, although not open to the public at the time this book was being written. Visitors could check on its status by contacting Tourism Yukon at (867) 667-5340.

Banff: Cascade Gardens

GARDEN OPEN: dawn to dusk daily, spring to fall.

ADMISSION: free.

FURTHER INFORMATION FROM:
Banff National Park
Box 900
Banff, Alberta ToL oCo
(403) 762-1550
www.worldweb.com/
ParksCanada-Banff/

NEARBY SIGHTS OF INTEREST:
Cave and Basin National
Historic Site, Icefields
Parkway, Lake Louise

LOCATION: IN THE TOWN OF BANFF, AT THE TIP OF BANFF AVENUE, AROUND THE BANFF NATIONAL PARK ADMINISTRATION OFFICES

Beautiful Banff National Park, located about 86 miles (138 km) west of Calgary, is perhaps the best known of all Canada's parks. It is 2,564 square miles (6,641 square kilometers) of snow-peaked mountains, vast icy glaciers, rushing rivers, thundering waterfalls, pure turquoise lakes, natural hot springs, and wildlife galore: a true wilderness experience. Plant lovers will enjoy not only the beautiful scenery, but numerous nature trails with identified trees, shrubs, and flowers, not to mention the natural alpine gardens—tiny, rock-hugging drabas, silenes, and campions—found on the mountains' upper slopes.

There is also a very beautiful ornamental garden right in the town of Banff. The Cascade Gardens, located around and behind the Park's Administrative Offices, were originally designed in 1933 as a geological garden, with the goal of teaching visitors about the different types of the rocks of the park as well as its geological history. The project was however never fully completed and the "Cascade of Time," as the rock garden linked by small streams and nine different cascades was to be called, was instead landscaped as a floral park and became the "Cascade Gardens."

Today, the gardens consist of a series of winding flagstone paths leading over rustic bridges, under groves of trees, and along sparking streams, with stops here and there for a view of the village of Banff and of the Bow River Valley below. Over 50,000 bedding plants of some 75 varieties are planted out each summer, usually in early June. All must be plants that can tolerate the Park's cool summers and short growing season, and browsing by the town's resident elk and deer! The gardens are at their best in July and August, but thanks to carefully planted conifers and shrubs, and the series of streams and cascades, they nevertheless hold interest from snow melt until late fall.

Beds of flowers surround the pavilion. Parks Canada, Jim Wiebe, 1999

There is no fee charged for visiting the Cascade Gardens, but there is an admission price per vehicle to get into Banff National Park itself.

2 Calgary: Devonian Gardens

LOCATION: DOWNTOWN CALGARY, AT 8TH AVENUE (STEPHEN AVENUE MALL) BETWEEN 2ND AND 3RD STREETS WEST, ON TOP OF TORONTO-DOMINION SQUARE

GARDEN OPEN: 9am to 9pm daily, year-round.
ADMISSION: free.

FURTHER INFORMATION FROM:
Calgary Parks & Recreation
Centre West Area, #88
P.O. Box 2100, Stn. M
Calgary, Alberta T2P 2M5
(403) 221-3782
dkroeker@gov.calgary
www.parks-rec.gov.
calgary.ab.ca

NEARBY SIGHTS OF INTEREST:
Downtown Calgary, Fort
Calgary Historic Park

The Devonian Gardens are certainly one of Canada's most unusual and delightful gardens, due to their unique location, directly downtown, on top of a shopping center and entirely surrounded by office complexes! Devonian Gardens is like a modern version of the Hanging Gardens of Babylon; it drips downward from the top level (fourth floor) to the second level of the Toronto Dominion Square complex in a series of hanging terraces, creating a beautiful green space in the middle of the province's most intensely developed city.

The mostly covered 2.5-acre (1.25-hectare) garden is open year round and filled with over 16,000 tropical plants, including not only foliage plants, but seasonal displays of flowering varieties. The glassed-in roof protects the plantations from the weather, although certain parts are either directly outdoors (the reflecting pool becomes an ice-skating rink in winter!) or exposed to outdoor conditions during the summer months thanks to movable glass panels.

The different garden areas include display areas, indoor ponds and fountains, a Quiet Garden, a Sun Garden, a Sculpture Creekbed, and even a play area for the younger set. There is likewise a stage where concerts, fashion shows, and other events are often held. The gardens are usually accessed via the shopping center escalators, but there are also glass elevators at the 7th Avenue and Stephen Avenue entrances for accessibility outside of business hours. All parts of the garden are wheelchair accessible. Since the site is sometimes rented out for private functions, it may be wise to call in advance before visiting.

The gardens were donated to the citizens of Calgary by the Devonian Group of Charitable Foundations and Calford Properties.

The Devonian Gardens are not to be confused with the University of Alberta's Devonian Botanic Gardens (page 138).

These children seem to be picnicking in tropical luxuriance.

3

Calgary: Dorothy Harvie Gardens

LOCATION: FROM CALGARY, TAKE DEERFOOT TRAIL TO MEMORIAL DRIVE WEST, THEN TURN ONTO SAINT GEORGE'S DRIVE. FOLLOW SIGNS FOR THE CALGARY ZOO

GARDEN OPEN: 9am to dusk (check for seasonal closing times) daily, year-round.

ADMISSION: $10 adults and seniors, $5 seniors Tuesday–Thursday, $5 children April through September; $8 adults, $4 seniors Tuesday–Thursday, $4 children October through March.

FURTHER INFORMATION FROM:
Dorothy Harvie Gardens
P.O. Box 3036, Stn B
Calgary, Alberta T2M 4R8
(403) 232-9306
oliviaj@calgaryzoo.ab.ca
www.calgaryzoo.ab.ca

NEARBY SIGHTS OF INTEREST:
Downtown Calgary, Fort Calgary Historic Park

Many zoos, through their efforts to reproduce habitats for their animals that resemble their natural ones, therefore including the vegetation indigenous to their homeland, are great sources of rare and unusual plants. Although this is also true of the Calgary Zoo, as can be notably seen in the African Bushveld and Prehistoric Park exhibits, plus the vast and varied Canadian Wilds display of native flora and fauna, it goes one better—it actually contains within its limits a full botanical garden: the Dorothy Harvie Gardens, better known locally under its old name, the Calgary Botanical Gardens.

The Dorothy Harvie Gardens is a formal garden of some 4,000 different ornamental plants, located in the center of Saint George's Island, surrounded by the zoo. It is of special interest for its outdoor gardens, at their best from April through October, as they include nearly the full range of plants that can be grown in Calgary's harsh climate. Starting early in the season with displays of tulips, crocuses, and other spring

Brilliant macaws live out their lives in a jungle environment.

bulbs, the show continues throughout the summer and into fall with large collections of perennials, shrubs, dwarf conifers, and trees. There is also a water garden, a water conservation garden, a woodland garden, and an alpine garden. Of special interest are the perennial and annual trial beds, where plants new to the Calgary area are put on trial.

To ensure interest year round, there is a large conservatory that doubles as a tropical aviary; exotic birds wander at will through the towering palms and thousands of colorful flowering and foliage plants. There is a large waterfall and goldfish pond in the conservatory, plus three gardens recreating distinct environments: the *Arid Garden*, including Old and New World cacti and succulents; the *Rainforest Garden*, focusing on tropical trees and ferns plus epiphytes such as orchids and bromeliads; and finally the *Butterfly Garden*, where butterflies flit about through a beautiful garden of nectar-rich flowers, like lantana, citrus, and passionflowers.

4 Edmonton: Muttart Conservatory

LOCATION: IN EDMONTON'S RIVER VALLEY, AT **9626–96A STREET**, EAST OF JAMES MACDONALD BRIDGE AND DIRECTLY ACROSS FROM CONVENTION CENTRE

The "Pyramids," as the locals call them, are located in a verdant green park along the Saskatchewan River, just across the river from Edmonton's downtown core. The striking pyramidal design of the four large greenhouses, accentuated by the way they seem to rise directly from a grassy slope, give the complex a very modern appearance; visitors will be surprised to realize the gardens are more than a quarter century old, having first opened in 1976. Those who hike up the slope outside the glasshouses—or who can see the greenhouses from a hotel room across the river—will discover that they are linked from above by a large reflecting pool and even, from certain angles, seem to be floating on water.

Access to the greenhouses is underground, through a Centre Court that links all four greenhouses. It is actually lit from above by a skylight in the same pyramidal shape as the display houses. The central space is used for activities of all sorts, including art shows, fashion shows, and several different flower shows and is decorated with a beautiful mural. Off the Centre Court is a gift shop and a cafe, plus washrooms. Many of the local horticultural societies, such as the orchid society and the African violet society, hold their annual shows here, so you may want to phone ahead to choose a date where you can take in a plant show as well as the greenhouses.

GARDEN OPEN: 9am to 6pm Monday–Friday, year-round; 11am to 6pm weekends and holidays; closed December. 25. ADMISSION: $4.50 adults, $3.50 seniors and students, $2.00 children 2–12 years, $12.50 family.

FURTHER INFORMATION FROM: Muttart Conservatory No. 9626–96A Street Edmonton, Alberta T6C 4L8 (780) 496-8755 muttart@gov.edmonton. ab.ca

NEARBY SIGHTS OF INTEREST: Alberta Legislature Building, Edmonton Art Gallery

Each of the four pyramids offers a radically different display. The *Show Pyramid* is, as the name implies, used for seasonal displays. The Christmas display gives way to the spring display, then others follow right through to the fall chrysanthemum display. There are ten seasonal displays in all. The *Temperate Pyramid* shows plants that are not hardy enough for Edmonton's brutal climate, but need distinct seasonal temperature changes. They include magnolias, Japanese maples, and even a mighty sequoia. In the *Tropical Pyramid* are found figs and palms, orchids and hibiscus, and many other plants that need warm temperatures year round. Finally, the *Arid Pyramid* features succulents, cacti, and other plants requiring low humidity and tolerating long periods of drought.

The area around Muttart Conservatory is an arboretum featuring hardy conifers, shrubs, and trees that leads to walking and nature trails along the river valley. There are also outdoor annual trial beds where the latest in annual flowers is displayed. There is likewise a picnic area. The park around the conservatory is open daily, dawn to dusk, and is free of charge.

BELOW: *The Conservatory's pyramids, dramatic against the Edmonton skyline, seem to float on the reflecting pool.* Muttart Conservatory

OPPOSITE: *The Cottage Garden features old-fashioned perennials and annuals.* St. Albert Botanic Park

5 Edmonton: Saint Albert Botanic Park

LOCATION: IN RED WILLOW PARK ALONG RIVER ON STURGEON ROAD, ONE-
HALF MILE (ONE KILOMETER) EAST OF BOUDREAU ROAD, IN SAINT ALBERT,
ALBERTA—ABOUT TEN MINUTES DRIVE FROM EDMONTON

GARDEN OPEN: dawn to dusk
daily, year-round.

ADMISSION: free.

The Saint Albert Botanic Park is a small but charming
enclave in Red Willow Park in Saint Albert, not far from
Edmonton. It is quite a young garden, dating only to 1994,
and is managed by a small group of volunteers whose enthu-
siasm shows in the wide variety of plantings, all adapted to
local growing conditions.

The beds include a perennial collection, a peony bed of
some fifty varieties, a daylily bed, an Asiatic lily bed, a dahlia
bed, a large rose garden of some 150 varieties of hardy shrub
roses, and a Sunflower Garden. There is likewise a demonstration vegetable garden, plus lots of trees and shrubs, mostly well
identified, including thirty-five varieties of lilac and many
crabapples. An iris garden is being planned for the near future.

The garden is attractive spring through fall, though is perhaps at its best when the lilacs and crabapples are in bloom in
late spring or during the annual rose show, held in mid-July.

FURTHER INFORMATION FROM:
Saint Albert Botanic Park
33 Ash Crescent
Saint Albert, Alberta T8N 3J6
(780) 458-1386
pmbell@home.com
www.geocities.com/
Heartland/Farm/1023

NEARBY SIGHTS OF INTEREST:
Hole's Greenhouses, Muttart
Conservatory, University of
Alberta Devonian Botanic
Garden

GARDEN OPEN: 10am to 4pm
daily, May 1–mid-May; 10am
to 7pm daily, mid-May–Labor
Day; 10am to 4pm daily,
Labor Day–mid-October;
11am to 4pm weekends, mid-
October–April 30.
ADMISSION: $5.75 adults,
$4.75 seniors, $3.50 youths,
free children 4 years and
younger, $17.50 family.

FURTHER INFORMATION FROM:
Devonian Botanic Garden
University of Alberta
Edmonton, Alberta T6G 2E1
(780) 987-3054
www.discoveredmonton.com
/Devonian/

NEARBY SIGHTS OF INTEREST:
Muttart Conservatory,
Provincial Museum of Alberta

6 Edmonton: University of Alberta Devonian Botanic Gardens

LOCATION: WEST OF EDMONTON, NEAR DEVON, ALBERTA. HIGHWAY 16 WEST,
THEN NINE MILES (FOURTEEN KILOMETERS) SOUTH ON HIGHWAY 60

The Devonian Botanic Garden, located within an attractive
rolling natural landscape of pine trees and wetlands, was established in 1959 by the University of Alberta, whose main campus is located in nearby Edmonton. It was designed as a garden
for research in horticulture—but also as a public garden. To
this day, the mixture of scientific rigor (the plants, for example,
are clearly labeled) and sound landscaping practices makes for
a particularly enjoyable visit.

The Botanic Garden itself covers some eighty acres (thirty-
two hectares) of landscaped area, while there is a further 110
acres (forty-five hectares) of natural forest and wetlands with
nature trails, as well as a picnic area and a wildlife refuge,
adjoining the developed section. Part of the research done in
the garden concerns plant hardiness. The fruits of this massive
testing can be seen directly; extra hardy clones and races of
many trees, shrubs, perennials, succulents, and bulbs that
would not normally be hardy this far north have been found or
developed and are being grown in the garden.

The numerous collections and gardens include the *Patrick
Seymour Alpine Garden*, the *Primula Glen*, the *Bulb and Shrub
Garden*, the *Iris Dell*, the *Peony Garden*, the *Beta Sigma Phi
Yellow Rose Garden* (where all roses are either yellow or shades
of yellow to orange), and the *Desert Garden*, featuring hardy

cacti and succulents, plus monochrome gardens in blue and white. There are also three greenhouses: a succulent and cactus house, an orchid house, and a butterfly greenhouse, plus several ponds. There are likewise more practical gardens: a vegetable garden, a herb garden, and the *Native People's Garden*, a fascinating look into healing plants used by local Amerindians. There is even a *Rhubarb Collection* featuring over fifty different cultivars and species of rhubarb and a berry patch where visitors are actually encouraged to pick and taste the fruit. For those who want to stay a bit longer, there is the Patio Cafe, plus the Shop-in-the-Garden where you can find garden supplies, books, and souvenirs.

As an added attraction, in the heart of the garden is the *Kurimoto Japanese Garden* with its authentic Japanese pavilion. This beautifully landscaped meditation garden makes a five-acre (two-hectare) enclave of peace and tranquility within the larger Botanic Garden.

OPPOSITE: *The Japanese Garden offers a quiet respite within the Botanic Gardens.*

7 Trochu: Trochu Arboretum & Gardens

LOCATION: FROM CALGARY, TAKE HIGHWAY 2 NORTH TO OLDS, THEN GO EAST ON HIGHWAY 27 TO HIGHWAY 21, THEN TWO MILES (THREE KILOMETERS) NORTH TO TROCHU

This arboretum northeast of Calgary is located in a most unlikely place: the dry prairie, certainly an area not known for the trees and shrubs one usually associates with an arboretum. However, successive owners of the farm where the arboretum is now located took a great deal of interest in trees, planting them first as shelter belts, then for their horticultural interest. The first trees were planted around 1918, and the tradition of adding new and usual trees has continued ever since, with each owner adding his or her own share. The Town of Trochu bought the land, by then already much admired as a prize-winning garden, in 1988, handing over direction of the future public garden to the newly formed Trochu and District Arboretum Society, which still operates the garden to this day, in 1989.

Today, the Arboretum consists mostly of a collection of some 1,000 trees of more than 100 species and cultivars. There is also an extensive collection of prairie-hardy shrubs, while beds of annuals and perennials are interspersed among the collections of woody plants. The former farmhouse is now used as an interpretive center and gift shop and also houses restrooms. The most recent addition to the arboretum is the Dr. Hay Water Garden, a pond surrounded by flower beds and planted with hardy aquatic plants.

GARDEN OPEN: 10am to 6pm daily, end of May–Labor Day; 10am to 6pm weekends, Labor Day–Canadian Thanksgiving Day.
ADMISSION: $2.

FURTHER INFORMATION FROM:
Trochu Arboretum and Gardens
Town of Trochu
Box 340
Trochu, Alberta T0M 2C0
(403) 442-2111 (summer)
trochutn@telusplanet.net

NEARBY SIGHTS OF INTEREST:
Saint Anne Ranch Provincial Historic Site, Dry Island Buffalo Jump Park

The arboretum rises like a beacon from the flat Prairies. Trochu Arboretum & Gardens

The entire garden is wheelchair accessible, and benches and tables make it a lovely spot for a summer picnic. Several special activities are held annually; phone for information.

GARDEN OPEN: 12pm to 5pm Thursday–Sunday, May 14–May 31; 9am to 5pm daily, June 1–June 11; 9am to 9pm daily, June 12–August 27; 9am to 5pm daily, August 28–September 10; 12pm to 5pm Thursday–Sunday, September 11–October 15.
ADMISSION: $4 adults, $3 seniors, $2 youths, free children 5 years and younger.

FURTHER INFORMATION FROM:
Nikka Yuko Japanese Garden
Box 751
Lethbridge, Alberta T1J 3Z6
(403) 328-3511

NEARBY SIGHTS OF INTEREST:
Henderson Lake Park, Fort Whoop-Up, Helen Shuler Coulee Centre

8 Lethbridge: Nikka Yuko Japanese Garden

LOCATION: IN LETHBRIDGE, ALBERTA, BESIDE HENDERSON LAKE AT 7TH STREET AND MAY MAGRATH DRIVE

Lethbridge, Alberta, hardly seems like a likely spot for a Japanese garden. For one, it is a relatively small city (population about 67,000); most public Japanese gardens on this continent are located only in the largest metropolises. Also, its south-central Alberta climate is too harsh for most traditional Japanese trees, plants, and shrubs. But there is a considerable local Japanese population interested in supporting the gardens, and ways have been found to use hardier, often local, plants to replace the original Japanese ones. Today, the garden is considered to be one of the most authentic Japanese gardens in North America.

The garden was planned starting in 1964 with Dr. Tadashi Kubo, who also designed the San Francisco's Japanese Garden, acting as the principal landscape architect. He not only chose the site and planned the garden, but oversaw the importation of the pavilion, shelter, bridges, and gates from Japan. The garden opened to the public in 1967 as a project for Canada's centennial celebrations. Its name comes from "ni" for "nihon" or Japan and "ka" for "Canada," while "yuko" means friendship.

Today visitors see a mature four-acre (1.6-hectare) garden providing a quiet, serene place for the appreciation of nature and the discovery of inner peace. Five traditional Japanese gardens are joined by a meandering path: the dry garden, the mountain and waterfall, the streams, the ponds and islands, and the flat prairie garden, the latter incorporating landscape from nearby Henderson Lake Park as *shakkei* (a borrowed view). Pruning techniques are authentically Japanese, although plants have had to be modified. Amur maples, for example, replace the traditional Japanese maple (*Acer palmatum*), while mugo and ponderosa pines have been trained to resemble Japanese red and black pines, and crabapples stand in for Japanese cherries. *The Pavilion*, made of rare Taiwanese cypress, acts as the center of the garden and also as a cultural center, with rooms for tea ceremonies and a moon-viewing verandah. Traditionally dressed hostesses act as interpretive guides to take you through it. Please remove your shoes before you enter!

The Nikka Yuko Japanese Garden is one of the most authentic Japanese gardens in North America.
Lethbridge and District Japanese Garden Society

GARDEN OPEN: dawn to dusk daily, June–September

ADMISSION: free.

FURTHER INFORMATION FROM:
Crop Diversification Centre
South SS 4
Brooks, Alberta T1R 1E6
(403) 362-1305
shelley.barkley@agric.gov.ab.ca
www.agric.gov.ab.ca/
ministry/pid/cdcs1.html

NEARBY SIGHTS OF INTEREST:
Dinosaur Provincial Park,
Aqueduct Historical Park

9 Brooks: Crop Diversification Centre South

LOCATION: FIVE KILOMETERS EAST OF BROOKS ON THE TRANS CANADA HIGHWAY, IN SOUTHEASTERN ALBERTA

The rather formidable name hides what used to be simply called the Alberta Horticultural Research Centre, and before even that (during the Great Depression), the Canadian Pacific Railway Demonstration Farm. The present role of the site is to test new crops for their capacity to adapt to Southern Alberta's harsh climate, but the term "crops" extends far beyond cereals and vegetables—it also includes ornamental plants. And the gardens, in their wide variety and beautiful color, are all that much more striking in that they are surrounded by pure, flat, golden Prairie as far as the eye can see.

There are several different ornamental collections in the gardens, of which the most colorful is perhaps the rose garden, which includes over 140 different prairie-hardy roses. The All America Selection flower trials, testing mostly annuals, are also striking. There is also the Golden Prairie Arboretum, with collections of trees and shrubs, including over 130 lilacs, plus the Forever Green Pinetum, a collection of over 120 coniferous trees and shrubs.

Of course, the Horticulture Unit, where new varieties of crop plants are tested, is also very interesting and can be just as colorful as the ornamental plants division. The fruit test plots, notably, are full of beautiful white and pink flowers in the spring followed by yellows, reds and purples when they ripen in mid to late summer.

Self-guided walking tours are available any time. A free guided tour, available weekdays from 9am to 11am and from 1pm to 3pm, can be arranged by appointment; please phone 24 hours ahead.

RIGHT: *Colorful flowerbeds are featured across the site.* Clive Schaupmeyer

OPPOSITE: *Patterson Garden features more than 500 varieties of prairie-hardy trees and shrubs.* Patterson Garden

10 Saskatoon: Patterson Garden

LOCATION: IN SASKATOON, THE SOUTHEAST CORNER OF COLLEGE DRIVE AND PRESTON DRIVE

Patterson Garden is part of the University of Saskatchewan, which is building a reputation for research and development in science, medicine, and agriculture. The garden is located within walking distance of the main campus and the scenic Saskatchewan River valley, both beautiful areas for a walking tour. Established in 1966, it was named in honor of the first and long-term head of the university's plant science department.

The five-acre (two-hectare) arboretum showcases more than 500 varieties of trees and shrubs in a beautiful, park-like atmosphere. There is a special emphasis on prairie-hardy species, and the arboretum is part of the Prairie Regional Trials of Woody Ornamentals working to test and develop hardier strains of trees and shrubs.

GARDEN OPEN: dawn to dusk daily, year-round.
ADMISSION: free.

FURTHER INFORMATION FROM:
Patterson Garden
Plant Science Department
University of Saskatchewan
51 Campus Drive
Saskatoon, Saskatchewan
S7N 5A8
(306) 966-5855

NEARBY SIGHTS OF INTEREST:
University of Saskatchewan campus, Wanuskewin Heritage Park, Forestry Farm Park and Zoo

11 Regina: Wascana Centre

LOCATION: DOWNTOWN REGINA, OFF ALBERT STREET

GARDEN OPEN: dawn to dusk, daily, year-round.
ADMISSION: free.

FURTHER INFORMATION FROM:
Wascana Centre Authority,
2900 Wascana Drive
P.O. Box 7111
Regina, Saskatchewan S4P 3S7
(306) 522-3661

NEARBY SIGHTS OF INTEREST:
Legislative Building,
MacKenzie Art Gallery, Royal
Saskatchewan Museum

Wascana Centre is Regina's major park, forming a ring around Wascana Lake. In fact, the 2,300-acre (930-hectare) park includes many of the city's important buildings: the Legislative Building, the MacKenzie Art Gallery, the Royal Saskatchewan Museum, and much more.

The park contains walkways and bicycle paths, forests and lawns, a huge lake and several ponds, and plenty of benches and picnic spaces. Among other sectors of interest is the *Wascana Waterfowl Park*, whose resident Canada geese and other waterfowl are so well fed they no longer even bother flying south for the winter!

There are numerous flower beds containing annuals, bulbs, and perennials, plus formal and informal shrub borders located here and therefore throughout the park. The *Legislative Flower Garden*, located on 100 acres (forty hectares) of landscaped grounds all around the Legislative Building, is especially rich in bloom. There are also massive beds of bedding plants around the *Wascana Centre Production Greenhouses*, with formal flower beds and collections of trees and shrubs.

The Legislature Building is surrounded by floral tapestries. Wascana Centre Authority

Boissevain: International Peace Garden

LOCATION: ON THE US/CANADA BORDER, SIXTEEN MILES (TWENTY-SIX KILOME-
TERS) SOUTH OF BOISSEVAIN, MANITOBA, ON HIGHWAY 10

There are other gardens in Canada and around the world dedicated to peaceful international relations, but few actually straddle two countries. The International Peace Garden is dedicated to the peaceful relationship between Canada and the United States and celebrates the longest unfortified border in the world. The garden is located midway between the Atlantic and Pacific Oceans, very close to the geographical center of North America, and consists of a vast park of 1,451 acres (586 hectares) in Canada (Manitoba) and an adjoining 888 acres (360 hectares) in the United States (North Dakota). Garden enthusiasts on both sides of the border founded it in 1932.

Formal flower beds filled with 150,000 annual flowers line the border itself, and there is also a sunken garden, a perennial garden, a wildflower garden, a field crop display, an All American Selection Display Garden, and much more. The biggest draw is a huge floral clock planted with carpet bedding in intricate patterns; its design changes yearly. A brochure for a self-guided walking and/or driving tour is available. The gardens are at their best from mid-July through August.

The International Peace Garden is much more than a floral park, though; there is an auditorium, a huge peace monument, a cairn bearing a pledge of peace, a chapel exactly half in Canada and half in the United States, and lots of facilities for camping, hiking, cross-country skiing, and other outdoor activities. The park is also the site of a music and fine arts camp and a sports camp.

GARDEN OPEN: 8am to 10pm daily, mid-May–mid-September; 8:30am to 4:30pm daily, fall through spring. ADMISSION: $10 per car.

FURTHER INFORMATION FROM:
International Peace Garden
P.O. Box 419
Boissevain, Manitoba R0K 0E0
(204) 534-2510
judi@peacegarden.com
www.peacegarden.com

NEARBY SIGHTS OF INTEREST:
Boissevain Murals, Turtle Mountain Provincial Park

ABOVE: *The lower terrace fountain in the Formal Garden Area.* International Peace Garden

145

GARDEN OPEN: 8am to
4:30pm daily, year-round.
ADMISSION: free.

FURTHER INFORMATION FROM:
Morden Research Centre
Unit 100-101, Route 100
Morden, Manitoba R6M 1Y5
(204) 822-7201
cdavidson@em.agr.ca
www.res.agr.ca/winn/
pagetwo.htm

NEARBY SIGHTS OF INTEREST:
Morden and District Museum

13 Morden: Morden Research Centre

LOCATION: ABOUT EIGHTY MILES (140 KILOMETERS) SOUTHWEST OF
WINNIPEG ON HIGHWAY 3

The name Morden is familiar to gardeners across Canada and
the northern United States. Since 1915, the Morden Research
Centre has been testing and developing field crops and ornamental plants for cold climate areas, and many of the plants
introduced by the Centre have gone on to become popular garden plants—including the Parkland and Morden series of
roses, the ultra-hardy Morden mums, and a series of disease-
resistant and dwarf monardas.

All told, the Morden Centre covers some 627 acres (254
hectares), with about twelve acres (five hectares) in gardens and
sixty (twenty-four hectares) in arboretum. The collections
include trees, conifers, and shrubs, notably a huge collection of
flowering crabapples (each spring, when they reach their peak
bloom, the Centre presents Blossom Week), field crop demonstrations, annual and perennial borders, a shade perennial border, a rock garden, a rose test garden, and demonstration
hedges, plus a garden featuring hardy roses hybridized in
Canada. One special display shows trees developed by the
Centre as alternatives to the American elm, a tree being
decimated by the deadly Dutch elm disease.

*The arboretum features col-
lections of Prairie-hardy trees.*
Morden Research Centre,
Agriculture Canada

The Park is filled with wooded groves and flowerbeds.
Assiniboine Park Conservatory

14 Winnipeg: Assiniboine Park Conservatory and Gardens

LOCATION: JUST OUTSIDE OF DOWNTOWN WINNIPEG, AT CORYDON AVE AND SHAFTSBURY ROAD

Winnipeg is Manitoba's largest city and also the location of most of its parks and gardens. In this city of parks, though, one reigns supreme: Assiniboine Park. This large park covers some 378 acres (153 hectares) along the Assiniboine River, just outside of downtown Winnipeg. Like most major urban parks, it features playgrounds, picnic areas, many sports facilities such as playing fields, a toboggan hill, and an ice-skating rink, and lots of walking trails and bike paths through green lawns dotted with tall trees. Winnipeg's zoo is likewise located in the park and there is a miniature train to delight the children. But the park is more than just a green space; it also features major garden elements, making the park a haven for all those who love flowers.

The most striking garden element of the park is the *Assiniboine Park Conservatory*. Dating to 1914 and renovated in 1969, it is one of only three public Victorian greenhouses still

GARDEN OPEN: dawn to dusk daily, year-round.
CONSERVATORY OPEN: 9am to 4:30pm daily, fall through spring, 9am to 8pm daily, summer. ADMISSION: free.

FURTHER INFORMATION FROM:
Assiniboine Park Conservatory
2355 Corydon Ave.
Winnipeg, Manitoba R3P 0R5
(204) 986-5537
lglowacki@city.winnipeg.
mb.ca

NEARBY SIGHTS OF INTEREST:
Assiniboine Park Zoo,
Manitoba Museum of Man and Nature, The Forks National Historic Site

in use in Canada. The core of the conservatory, the Palm House, features not only palms, but an entire tropical jungle. Visitors walk under a canopy of mature tropical trees on which grow beautiful epiphytic orchids. In the Floral Display Gallery, the conservatory offers ten different displays a year, including orchid and bonsai shows, plus the popular Holiday Lights Display. Also linked to the conservatory are the foyer, used for art shows, a gift shop, and the Garden Restaurant.

The staff of the conservatory are also in charge of other gardens scattered through the park. The oldest garden in the park, the *Formal Garden*, was designed by Frederick Todd in 1907 following the French formal style, with a precise geometric layout. The *English Garden* is reminiscent of an English cottage garden and is presently being entirely renovated to bring it closer to the original plan (the English Garden dates back to 1927) and to increase the range of plants. There is also an *Herb Garden* featuring a large variety of herbs in a round bed, and a unique *Garden of Life*, developed as a cooperative effort with the Manitoba Transplant Program. Its 3,000 flowers depict the shape, color, or care of the vital organs used in human transplantation. Finally, there is also the *Leo Mol Sculpture Garden* featuring sculptures, ceramics, paintings, and sketches by the famous Winnipeg artist, plus a reflecting pool and fountain.

The future holds even more promise for the gardens of Assiniboine Park; municipal authorities want to develop it as a botanical garden, adding more greenhouse space and an even wider array of gardens, so when you visit, you may find much more than is described above.

GARDEN OPEN: 10am to 5pm daily, July–August; 10am to 5pm Sunday only, June; off-season and weekdays in June: open for group hikes only.
ADMISSION: Nature Centre free; hiking $2.25 per person.

FURTHER INFORMATION FROM:
Living Prairie Museum
2795 Ness Avenue
Winnipeg, Manitoba R3J 3S4
(204) 832-0167
prairie@mbnet.mb.ca
www.city.winnipeg.mb.ca/city
/parks

NEARBY SIGHTS OF INTEREST:
Aviation Museum, Saint
James Museum

15 Winnipeg: Living Prairie Museum

LOCATION: IN THE CITY LIMITS OF WINNIPEG, IN THE SAINT JAMES DISTRICT, AT **2795** NESS AVENUE, ONE BLOCK NORTH OF PORTAGE AVE (HIGHWAY 1)

The Living Prairie Museum is certainly one of the most unique urban parks in North America. It is in fact a nature preserve within the city limits of Winnipeg, one that preserves one of the last vestiges of the tall grass prairie—once the dominant ecosystem in the more humid parts of the Great Plains, covering 385,000 square miles (one million square kilometers) from Texas to southern Manitoba, and now almost entirely lost due to agricultural development. This thirty-acre (twelve-hectare) preserve, set aside in 1968, is home to over 160 species of plants, many nearing extinction, and a great array of prairie wildlife as well.

The Nature Centre at the Living Prairie Museum shows displays about the Prairies, their history, and their ecology and there is a second floor observation deck offering an overall view of the prairie. Entrance to the Nature Centre is free, but there is a small fee for hiking into the *Tall Grass Prairie Reserve*. Plant lists and brochures for self-guiding tours are available. There is likewise a seed list offering seeds of native prairie plants; these are available at the Nature Centre and by mail.

Phone for information on special activities, workshops, and guided tours. One event worth seeking out is Crocus Weekend, in the latter part of April, when the Prairie crocus (*Anemone patens*) begins to bloom. The date varies from year to year.

Prairie sunflower and berg-amot thrive in the tall grass prairie. Living Prairie Museum

BRITISH COLUMBIA

11, 12, 13, 14, 15, 16,
17, 18, 19, 20, 21, 22

24 25 26
1
2–10 23

BRITISH COLUMBIA

Where climate is concerned, British Columbia has it all . . . or nearly so. It includes by far the widest range of climatic conditions in Canada, from glaciers and snow-capped mountains frozen year long to coastal areas that only rarely see snow. Although no part of the province is truly tropical, no where else in Canada boasts such warm winter temperatures as these coastal zones; gardeners can even grow such exotic plants as windmill palm, camellias, and gunnera outdoors. Where precipitation is concerned, the province likewise covers the whole gamut; both the rainiest and the driest climates in Canada—there is even a "pocket" desert!—are found in British Columbia. This diverse range of climates, and especially the possibility of truly temperate climates in coastal areas, has made British Columbia a haven for gardeners of all sorts and has consequently given it a range of public gardens quite out of proportion to the size of its population (about four million).

British Columbia is Canada's westernmost province; there is nothing but the vast Pacific Ocean between it and Japan. It is bordered by Alberta to the east and Alaska and the Yukon to the north, while the southern border, along the American states of Washington, Idaho, and Montana, forms the 49th parallel— although the southern tip of Vancouver Island does dip down below that.

Geographically, British Columbia is mostly a province of mountains. Other than a piece of northern Prairies to the northeast, it belongs to the North American Cordillera, a range of four nearly parallel mountain chains, generally extending north/south, the highest being the Rocky Mountains, along the Albertan border. The westernmost range, the Coast

OPPOSITE: *Butchart Gardens, Vancouver*

Mountains, sink into the sea along the Pacific coast, creating a complex series of fjords, inlets, and islands, the largest and best known of which is Vancouver Island, named after explorer George Vancouver.

There is more than mountainous terrain in British Columbia, though. The Central Plateau, a series of relatively flat glacial valleys, and including one of Canada's best-known wine and fruit-producing regions, the Okanagan Valley, forms a vital and populated corridor in the otherwise quite empty interior. The broad Fraser Valley, where the Fraser River meets the sea, is likewise an agriculture hot spot, among others for market gardening—and, with Vancouver at its mouth, home to more than half of the province's population. Elsewhere, ranching and grain production are the major agricultural activities.

The forestry industry reigns supreme in British Columbia, taking advantage of the stands of huge red cedars, western hemlocks, and Douglas firs that once covered all of the province's coastal areas—once virgin temperate rainforest. Tourism is the second most important industry, followed by fishing (the province's salmon fishing industry is legendary) and mining (copper, lead, zinc, silver, gold, and coal, among other products). Manufacturing is increasingly important, notably pulp and paper and aluminum smelting, due to the abundant supplies of raw materials and hydroelectricity.

Though currently a province that is growing rapidly in population, British Columbia was actually the last Canadian province to develop. The province was originally inhabited by Amerindians of various cultures, from the permanent settlements of coastal tribes living mostly off fishing—the ones famous for their totem poles—to the nomadic hunter/gatherers coming in from the Prairies; at the time of the arrival of Europeans they numbered some 80,000 people. Although there were no population statistics at the time, there were probably more Amerindians living in British Columbia at the time of European discovery than in all the rest of Canada put together.

Although Spanish explorers first sighted the shores of Vancouver Island in 1774, and Captain James Cook, renowned for his discovery of Hawaii, was the first Westerner to actually set foot on the island in 1778, Europeans only began settling British Columbia in large numbers around the early twentieth century. Until then, Europeans exploited the island almost uniquely for furs, sending pelts on months' long canoe trips through the mountain passes and across the Prairies to Hudson Bay. The few European "settlements" were actually forts, established to fend off possible American advances from across the border, to the south. It was the gold rush of the late 1850s that first opened the province to settlement. At the time British Columbia was a British crown colony. It had no specific links to the new country of Canada, just being formed. Its colonists seriously considered joining the United States to the south, to whom the citizens felt closer affinities than the far away administrators of Eastern Canada. It was the promise of a transcontinental rail link with the east, only finally completed in 1887, that swayed the colonists to join Canada.

Rapid development followed the arrival of the railroad and continues to this day. To the numerous inhabitants of European origin who still arrive from Eastern Canada and from Europe has been added considerable immigration from Asia, with the result that Vancouver has

OPPOSITE: *Bloedel Floral Conservatory*

BELOW: *Victoria Butterfly Gardens*

North America's second largest Chinese population, as well as important populations from the Indian subcontinent and from Japan. Immigrants from other ethnic groups from across the world continue to flock to British Columbia, drawn by its continually expanding industries and by its relatively mild climate. Interestingly, although British Columbia follows the same pattern of habitation as the rest of Canada, with the majority of the population clustered along its southern border, it is the only province in Canada that does have significant population developments right up to its northern border.

The relatively recent arrival of European and Asian immigration means that older gardens are nearly nonexistent and the term "historical garden" is applied to any green space over sixty years old. That doesn't mean there are no public gardens, though. To the contrary, the relatively mild climate, plus the influx of Canadians retiring to the province—and retirees are often major users and supporters of public gardens—means British Columbia has a proportionately greater share of gardens than anywhere else in Canada. Given the limited space in this book, the choice of which gardens to include and which to leave out was particularly difficult. I apologize to those who don't see a favorite garden included in this book: I had to leave out some very nice gardens indeed.

The capital of the province, Victoria, is found at the tip of Vancouver Island. Considered the most British of Canadian cities, it is renowned for its flower beds and its innumerable hanging baskets. Profiting from one of the mildest climates in Canada, it is home to several top gardens, not the least of which is Beacon Hill Park (page 157), Butchart Gardens (page 159), the most visited garden in Canada, and Crystal Garden (page 162).

Vancouver, with a metropolitan population approaching two million, is the province's metropolis as well as its main financial, industrial, shipping, and cultural center. (Since visitors always seem to get confused over this point, please note that Vancouver is *not* located on Vancouver Island, but on the mainland, across the Strait of Georgia. It is Victoria, the capital, that is located on the island.) Greater Vancouver is a very modern city largely built on the delta of the Fraser River, although extending up into the Coast Mountain Range, which provides a beautiful backdrop for the city. It is dotted with skyscrapers and bridges, yet is very much a garden city, pierced by inlets and beaches and peppered with beautiful parks and gardens. Among the major ones are the Dr. Sun Yat-Sen Classical Chinese Garden (page 171), Queen Elizabeth Park (page 173) with its Bloedel Conservatory (page 169), Stanley Park (page 174), the University of British Columbia Botanical Garden (page 176), and VanDusen Gardens (page 183).

Of course, gardens abound elsewhere in the province, as you will see in flipping through the upcoming pages. One of special note, though, is Minter Gardens (page 188) in Chillimack, well worth a special trip if you're in Vancouver and have a few hours to spare.

Minter Gardens, Chillimack

Ladysmith: Hazelwood Herb Farm

LOCATION: FIVE MILES (EIGHT KILOMETERS) SOUTH OF NANAIMO VIA
HIGHWAY 19 AND RR #1

GARDEN OPEN: 11am to 5pm daily, April–September; 11am to 5pm, Friday–Sunday, October–December.
ADMISSION: free.

FURTHER INFORMATION FROM:
Hazelwood Herb Farm
13576 Adshead Road
Ladysmith, British Columbia
V9G 1H6
(250) 245-8007
hazelwood@ultranet.ca
www.ultranet.ca/hazelwood

NEARBY SIGHTS OF INTEREST:
Black Nugget Museum,
Chemainus Festival of Murals

Hazel Herb Farm is first and foremost a specialty garden center selling herbs and herb products produced on site. However, it also includes quite extensive display gardens, again emphasizing herb culture. The owners, Jacynthe Dugas and Richard White, purchased the five-acre (two-hectare) property in 1985 and opened it for business the following year.

Located just behind the Nanaimo Airport, the farm is surrounded by woodland and meadow. There are two large gardens, one very formal, the other in a cottage garden style. They house a collection of some 500 herbs, all identified, plus trellised climbing roses, a gazebo, a pond, and much more.

Classes in soap-making, skin care, gardening, and cooking are also offered; phone for details.

BELOW: *Gravel paths provide easy access through herb beds.*

RIGHT: *Rough-hewn wood creates island beds of herbs.*

2 Victoria: Beacon Hill Park

LOCATION: JUST OUTSIDE OF DOWNTOWN VICTORIA, OFF DOUGLAS STREET

Beacon Hill Park, so named because two beacons were formerly located there, is British Columbia's oldest park and the largest public green space in Victoria. Just three years after founding of Fort Victoria by the Hudson's Bay Company in 1843, residents were already calling this area "The Park," and by 1850 it had been given its current name. The present layout of the park dates back to 1889, when Scottish landscape architect John Blare won a contest to landscape it. Some of the trees and rhododendrons planted at that time still survive.

Covering some 183 acres (74 hectares), Beacon Hill Park is a charming urban green space built on a rolling hill running down to the sea. It is likewise the site of Kilometer Zero of the 4,850-mile (7,760-kilometer) Trans-Canada Highway, which stretches from here all across Canada to Newfoundland. It contains the usual picnic areas, children's playground, and playing fields (including, in this most British of Canadian cities, a century-old cricket field), plus vast lawns, groves of ancient oaks and cedars, several lakes and ponds, a band shell where there are regular concerts, and even a small petting zoo. However, garden lovers will most enjoy the numerous flower beds and borders.

There are vast beds of colorful annuals here and there in the park, but notably just off Douglas Street along Bridge Way. There are also sumptuous shrub and perennial borders, plus rhododendron borders, mostly near Rose Lake, also the site of the formal Rose Garden. There is also a Fragrance Garden and a charming Alpine Garden maintained by the Victoria Alpine Club. Spring bulbs and notably daffodils have been naturalized throughout the park and, combined with a considerable collection of flowering cherries, dogwoods, and other spring-flowering trees, not to mention the rhododendrons, make the spring show particularly spectacular. But the summer show, with over 25,000 annuals, is almost as eye-catching.

GARDEN OPEN: dawn to dusk daily, year-round.
ADMISSION: free.

FURTHER INFORMATION FROM:
Beacon Hill Park
No. 1 Centennial Square
Victoria, British Columbia
V8W 1P6
(250) 361-0600
Gords@city.victoria.bc.ca

NEARBY SIGHTS OF INTEREST:
Inner Harbour, Parliament Buildings, Crystal Gardens, British Columbia Museum

Mixed perennial and annual borders are featured in the park.

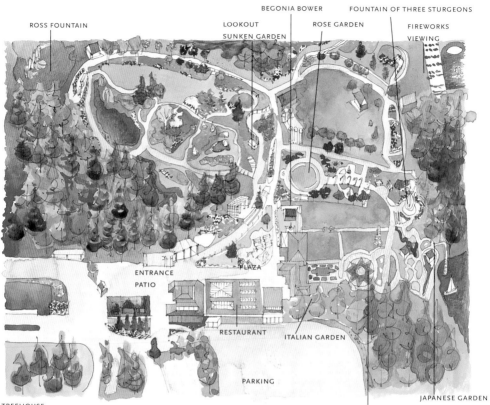

ROSS FOUNTAIN

BEGONIA BOWER

FOUNTAIN OF THREE STURGEONS

LOOKOUT
SUNKEN GARDEN

ROSE GARDEN

FIREWORKS
VIEWING

ENTRANCE
PATIO

PLAZA

RESTAURANT

ITALIAN GARDEN

PARKING

TREEHOUSE

STAR POND

JAPANESE GARDEN

3   Victoria: Butchart Gardens

LOCATION: ABOUT THIRTEEN MILES (TWENTY-ONE KM) NORTH OF VICTORIA.
TAKE HIGHWAY **17** TEN MILES (SIXTEEN KILOMETERS) TO BUTCHART-BRENT-
WOOD EXIT, TURNING LEFT ON KEATING ROAD AND CONTINUE ANOTHER FIVE
AND A HALF MILES (NINE KILOMETERS)

Butchart Gardens are Canada's best known and most visited
public gardens and, in fact, the major single tourist attraction
on Vancouver Island, with over one-quarter of a million visitors each year. Their popularity is such that even people who
never typically visit gardens come specifically to Victoria to
see them.

That the site would one day become Canada's most important display garden was in no way obvious when Robert Pim
Butchart and his wife Jennie bought the property at Todd Inlet,
just outside Victoria, in 1904. In fact, they chose the spot not
for the scenery, but because it was right next door to an open-pit
limestone quarry that Mr. Butchart was operating. Neither had
any gardening experience nor any true knowledge of gardening, but that changed as they settled in and Mrs. Butchart
began to look at beautifying her home and yard. She began to
design garden "rooms" around the house, based on ideas she
had seen during her travels and incorporating new plants she
was constantly bringing home. There was a Japanese Garden,
an Italian Garden, and much more. Mrs. Butchart loved to
receive visitors to her garden and everyone was welcome; she
even insisted on serving tea to one and all. After all, she is
quoted as saying, "I vowed that if ever I had a garden, less fortu-
nate people than myself should have the privilege of enjoying
it." The Butcharts called their estate Benvenuto, Italian for welcome. A sign of the family's openness, no "Do not . . ." sign was
ever allowed on the property.

It was when the limestone quarry ran out, though, that
she had the stroke of genius that would truly put her garden
on the map. She decided to turn the huge empty hole in the
ground into a Sunken Garden, and the rest is history. By 1912,
the effort was well underway; debris from the floor of the
quarry had been piled up to serve as the base of raised beds
and edging for flower beds, a lake with a waterfall and stream
was installed, a center column of rock was left as an observation deck, tons of topsoil were carted in, and the walls had
been planted in ivy. By 1915, the last year she served tea to all
visitors, 18,000 people visited the garden. By 1929, that was up
to 50,000 visitors a year. It wasn't until the war years, though,
that the by then elderly Butcharts finally had to begin charging
for each visit: 25 cents per person. Mr. Butchart died in 1943
and Mrs. Butchart seven years later; both had lived to be over
80 years old.

GARDEN OPEN: 9am to
10:30pm daily, June
15–September 1; earlier
closing hours September
2–June 14. ADMISSION: $18
peak season.

FURTHER INFORMATION FROM:
The Butchart Gardens
Box 4010
Victoria, British Columbia
V8XZ 3X3
(250) 652-4422
email@butchartgardens.com
www.butchartgardens.com

NEARBY SIGHTS OF INTEREST:
Victoria Butterfly Gardens,
Victoria's Inner Harbour,
Parliament Buildings, Crystal
Gardens, British Columbia
Museum

OPPOSITE: *Ross Fountains
are located in a naturally
landscaped part of the former
quarry.*

Flowers everywhere—even at the entrance to the dining room restaurant.

The family's descendants still manage the garden today. Some elements of the original garden remain, but many newer innovations have also been added; lighting, for example, was added for the convenience of nighttime visitors. As the estate stopped being used as a private home and became truly public, the home and outbuildings were converted to restaurant space, a gift shop, and service buildings.

Butchart Gardens is a display garden, not a botanical garden, and tries to maintain an image of the private garden it once was. Plants, for example, generally aren't labeled, although there is a plant identification center where you can ask for names. Massive use of 135,000 spring bulbs, blooming from February through May, and even greater numbers of summer annuals ensure color for much of the season. And the gardens are very popular during the Christmas holidays, when special seasonal lighting and the presence of choral groups create a wonderful Yuletide atmosphere.

Among the numerous highlights of the gardens is of course its famous *Sunken Garden*, where a spring-fed artificial lake is surrounded by gracious gardens dripping in bulbs and annuals. At the far end, a new section of the quarry has been converted into the *Ross Fountains*, where constantly changing jets of water, the center one reaching eighty feet (twenty-four meters) in height, ensure non-stop movement. The *Italian Garden*, with a classical pool and symmetrical flower beds, and the nearby *Star Pond*, with its star shape outlined in flowers, are the most formal of the gardens, while the *Rose Garden*, rich in color for months at a time, includes bowers of climbing roses, shrub roses, and a wide range of hybrid roses, not to mention beautiful perennial beds. A non-traditional *Japanese Garden*, started by Mrs. Butchart in 1906 with the help of Japanese landscaper Isaburo Kisheda, reaches down to a hidden wharf where the Butcharts used to keep their yacht. Close to the entrance is the *Begonia Bower*, a large pergola dripping in tuberous begonias and fuchsias. There is even the *Private Garden*, representing the smaller, intimate garden of the early years of the estate.

To all of this must be added the numerous statutes and fountains, some five miles (eight kilometers) of mostly wheelchair accessible walkways, and much more. Even mining carts from the original quarry have been turned into good use—as giant containers for plants!

The garden covers fifty acres (twenty hectares). It is open year round and is attractive in all seasons, even under the snow—although such an occasion is very rare in southern Vancouver Island's mild climate. And there is plenty to see; even casual visitors should allow three hours for a visit, while serious gardeners would probably do best to allow five hours. Since midday is very busy, especially on summer weekends, you might want to consider an early morning or late afternoon visit. The latter is especially interesting, as it would allow time to visit the gardens, take a leisurely meal at one of the site's fine restaurants, then take in the evening's entertainment at the concert lawn stage before coming back into the gardens after dark to enjoy their fully illuminated splendor. And to complete the evening, there is a fireworks display every Saturday in July and August.

ABOVE: *The Japanese Garden in autumn.*

BELOW: *Mass plantings of annuals, like these snapdragons, give Butchart Gardens rich color.*

Victoria: Crystal Garden

LOCATION: DOWNTOWN VICTORIA, BEHIND EMPRESS HOTEL

GARDEN OPEN: 8:30am to
8pm daily, July–August; 9am
to 6pm daily, April–June and
September–October; 10am to
4:30pm daily,
November–March.
ADMISSION: $7.50 adults,
$6.50 seniors, $4 children
5–16 years, $20 family.

FURTHER INFORMATION FROM:
Crystal Garden
713 Douglas Street
Victoria, British Columbia
V8W 2B4
(250) 953-8800
crystal@islandnet.com
www.bcpcc.com/crystal

NEARBY SIGHTS OF INTEREST:
Empress Hotel, Inner
Harbour, Royal British
Columbia Museum

When Crystal Garden opened in 1925, it was an amusement center that included the largest indoor saltwater swimming pool in the British empire. It was designed following the principles of the great public conservatories of the Victorian era, with a structure of brick and reinforced concrete and a steel and glass superstructure—and it included a ballroom, tea rooms, a promenade . . . and yes, some actual greenhouse space. By 1955, the salt water had taken its toll on the equipment, pipes, and machinery, and the pool was converted to fresh water. However, the pool's condition continued to decline and it was determined that little could be done to save it. It was closed in 1971 when a new Crystal Pool opened uptown.

Crystal Garden was abandoned after that and quickly became an eyesore. After some discussion about demolition, it was instead decided to entirely restore it—this time as a public greenhouse. This was done at a cost of $2.5 million and the new old Crystal Garden opened in 1981.

Crystal Garden is now one of Canada's most readily accessible public greenhouses, literally in the very heart of Victoria, a prime tourist city. It contains a recreation of a tropical rainforest, including palm trees, bamboos, anthuriums, cycads, bananas, orchids, and ferns, plus seasonal flower beds, a waterfall, a formal fountain and koi pond, and a butterfly greenhouse. There are also tropical animals and birds, including pink flamingos, fruit bats, lemurs, and the world's smallest monkeys: the golden lion tamarin. Most wildlife in the gardens consists of protected species being bred there in the hopes of returning them to the wild.

Plants are labeled by number; a corresponding identification listing, *Plant Highlights*, is available for a small fee.

Parrots, flamingos, and people cohabit in the tropical rainforest garden. Crystal Garden

5 Victoria: Government House Gardens

LOCATION: JUST OUTSIDE DOWNTOWN VICTORIA, AT 1401 ROCKLAND AVENUE

Government House is the residence of British Columbia's Lieutenant-Governor. The thirty-five-acre (fourteen-hectare) estate was first built in the 1850s as the private home of the province's first Attorney General, and then it served as the Colonial Governor's residence until British Columbia became a province. Some of the plantings date back at least that far, while others, including some 200- to 500-year-old Garry oaks (*Quercus garryana*), were already on the site before it was developed. The present residence (closed to the public) dates back only to 1957, being the third house on that spot (the two previous homes burned).

Tradition has it that each Lieutenant-Governor, or his or her spouse, adds a personal touch to some part of the grounds, and that has been generally respected. The result is the look of the present garden: a series of garden rooms dating to different periods. The rooms include a beautiful sunken rose garden, a newer Victorian rose garden, groves of rhododendrons, ponds, fountains, wrought-iron pergolas, a rock garden on natural stone outcrops, some exceptionally beautiful perennial borders, and lots of bulbs and annuals, not to mention many flowering trees. The garden is open year round and can be very interesting even in its skeletal winter garb, but is more attractive with some bloom, therefore from April through October.

GARDEN OPEN: dawn to dusk daily, year-round.
ADMISSION: free.

FURTHER INFORMATION FROM:
Government House Gardens
1401 Rockland Avenue
Victoria, British Columbia
V8S 1V9
(250) 387-2080

NEARBY SIGHTS OF INTEREST:
Craigdarroche Castle, Crystal Garden, Beacon Hill Park, Inner Harbour

ABOVE: *The formal rose garden is among Victoria's most beautiful.*

6 Victoria: Horticulture Centre of the Pacific

The Centre, founded by the city of Saanich in 1975 to promote a wetlands area, covers some 136 acres (fifty-five hectares) of mostly natural terrain. However, within this reserve, the members and volunteers of several Vancouver Island garden clubs have cleared six acres (2.5 hectares) for use as demonstration gardens. The gardens at the Horticulture Centre of the Pacific were designed as teaching gardens, and students taking horticulture courses offered by the non-profit organization use them as a living laboratory. The gardens are also open to the public.

The Horticulture Centre of the Pacific is a true plantsman's paradise. Meandering gravel paths lead to over 185 different perennials, mostly labeled, including collections of chrysanthemums, oriental poppies, ferns, and the largest collection of fall asters in British Columbia: over fifty cultivars. There is an *Annual Garden* and large selections of spring and summer bulbs, with notable collections of lilies and dahlias. The semicircular *Old Rose Garden* contains roses dating back as far as the 1500s, including the 'White Rose of York.' There are also beautiful displays of fuchsias and begonias, both in hanging baskets and in enormous wooden tubs. Also to be seen are the *Doris Page Winter Garden*, the *Rhododendron Garden*, the *Heather Garden*, the *Japanese Garden*, a *kiwi arbor*, and a *greenhouse*, plus a gift shop offering dried flowers and seeds from the garden.

The site is staffed by volunteers, and the students and instructors working there can also be very helpful in identifying plants or giving gardening advice. Phone for information on the various activities held regularly, including special days, lectures, and workshops.

BELOW: *Container plantings welcome visitors into the garden.* Horticulture Centre of the Pacific
OPPOSITE: *Point Ellice House gardens have changed little in 100 years.* Point Ellice House

7 Victoria: Point Ellice House

LOCATION: FIVE MINUTES FROM DOWNTOWN, NORTH ON GOVERNMENT
STREET, WEST ON BAY STREET, NORTH ON PLEASANT STREET

Point Ellice house was built in 1862 for Peter O'Reilly, a district magistrate, and remained in the same family until 1976 when it was taken over by the Government of British Columbia as a heritage property. The vast Italianate house has since been partially restored, using mostly the original furnishings and belongings of the family, and can now be visited. It contains the largest collection of Victoriana in British Columbia.

The gardens too were restored. The O'Reillys had the habit of never throwing anything out, so it was possible to trace down notes about the garden over the years, even such details as the date when particular seeds were sown, and what cultivars did well. This proved invaluable, as it was possible to retrace most of the plants formerly used in the garden. Some were found still alive in the jungle of the abandoned yard, others were retraced in specialist nurseries, and there were even a few cases where it turned out to be possible to germinate seeds that had been saved decades earlier. And as the "brush" was cleared, structures and patterns from the old garden were revealed, and many garden objects, like old tools, glass cloches, and lattice-work trellises were unearthed or found intact in long-forgotten storage areas. Even single-flowered hollyhocks dating from before 1920 magically sprouted anew from buried seed once the dense foliage that had smothered them was removed.

Today's garden is therefore a very close replica of the original one, which dated from circa 1889 to 1914. The garden

GARDEN OPEN: 10am to 5pm daily, May–September. Special openings at Halloween and Christmas; phone for details. House open during garden hours.
ADMISSION: $5 adults, $4 seniors and students, $2 children 6–12 years.

FURTHER INFORMATION FROM:
Point Ellice House
2616 Pleasant Street
Victoria, British Columbia
V8T 4V3
(250) 380-6506
www.tbc.gov.bc.ca/culture/
schoolnet/victoriana/

NEARBY SIGHTS OF INTEREST:
Crystal Gardens, Beacon Hill Park, Victoria's Inner Harbour, Parliament Buildings

Most plants are heritage varieties. Point Ellice House

today includes a restored croquet court, a small rose garden, a kitchen garden, shrub plantings including rhododendrons and hydrangeas, and mixed annual and perennials borders and the entire yard is surrounded, as was the tradition, by white picket fence.

The historic importance of this garden cannot be underestimated. Although there are plenty of cases of the vast estates of the rich and famous being preserved and restored, such as at Hatley Castle (below), very few gardens remain that tell the story of how the middle classes lived and gardened. Visiting Point Ellice House is therefore very much a look back in time at how such a family would have gardened, back at a time when land was cheap and even ordinary people could afford the luxury of beautifying their surroundings.

An audio-tape tour of the house and garden is available with the cost of ordinary admission, but it is also possible to pay more for the High Tea and House Tour, which allows you to partake in high tea on the house's lawn, served by costumed hostesses. Reserve ahead for this service, which is offered from May until mid-September. The gift shop offers, among other products, heritage seeds collected from the garden.

GARDEN OPEN: dawn to dusk daily, year-round; house open 10am to 4pm daily, summer months. **ADMISSION:** free.

FURTHER INFORMATION FROM:
Royal Roads Botanical
Garden and Hatley Park
2005 Sooke Road
Victoria, British Columbia
V9B 5Y2
(250) 391-2511
www.royalroads.ca

NEARBY SIGHTS OF INTEREST:
Fort Road Hill National
Historic Park, Galloping
Goose Trail

8   Victoria: Royal Roads Botanical Garden and Hatley Park

LOCATION: SIX MILES (TEN KILOMETERS) EAST OF VICTORIA VIA HIGHWAY 14

The beautiful grounds and spectacular Hatley Castle at Royal Roads were developed from 1908 to 1909 by James Dunsmuir, heir to a coal mining fortune left by his father, Robert, who had built a castle of his own, Craigdarroche Castle, in downtown Victoria. James Dunsmuir also had a parallel career in politics, first as Premier of British Columbia, then as Lieutenant-Governor. He built Hatley Castle so he and his wife could retire in luxury amidst beautiful gardens. No expense was spared in building the castle ("Money doesn't matter, build me what I want!" he has been quoted as saying), and much of the material used to furnish the twenty-two-bedroom structure with a eighty-two-foot (twenty-seven-meter) turret was imported, including stained glass windows, oak, and teak, although the stone was quarried from islands nearby.

The "money doesn't matter" attitude also reflected in the gardens. He went for the best, hiring the reputed firm of Brett and Hall from Boston as landscape architects. The stone wall that surrounds the 850-acre (344-hectare) estate alone was worth $75,000, a fortune at that time. The estate was laced with six miles (ten kilometers) of roads and required 80 to 120 workers to maintain. The greenhouse (still standing) was used to put fresh fruits and vegetables on the Dunsmuir table at all seasons, while the grandiose conservatory, now gone, marveled guests with its exotic palms, orchids, and tropical plants centered around a large banana tree.

After Dunsmuir's death in 1920, the house was inhabited by his wife and daughter and then sold to the Canadian federal government in 1940 for a mere $75,000—in a sense, the family's contribution to the war effort. The castle then became HMCS Royal Roads, an officer training establishment, and continued to play that role up until 1995. In 1996, it became Royal Roads University. Today, the gardens are open free of charge (although there is a fee for parking) while the castle, long closed to visitors except on special occasions, can now be visited on guided tours for a fee, at least while the university is on summer break.

The vast and spectacular grounds are largely made up of an *arboretum* characterized by mature well-spaced trees, often of species rarely grown in Canada, such as the monkey puzzle (*Araucaria araucana*). Some of the trees near the Neptune Steps, at the entrance to the grounds, are pollard-pruned, a technique rarely seen in the New World, and there are topiary yews near the castle.

The main gardens are the *Italian Garden*, filled with formal beds, reflecting ponds, and climbing roses and wisteria, the *Japanese Garden*, a quiet place with three lakes, a well, and a

The magnificent Hatley Castle and its spectacular gardens. Royal Road University

waterwheel, the *Rose Garden*, scattered rock and alpine gardens, a native plant woodland garden, and the Upper and Lower Lakes. The foundations of the old conservatory are still visible near the greenhouse. From the lakes, the garden sweeps down to the ocean, offering beautiful views of the Straits of Juan de Fuca and the Olympic Peninsula in the neighboring United States.

GARDEN OPEN: 9am to 5pm daily, March 1–October 31. **ADMISSION:** $8 adults, $7 seniors and students, $4.50 children 5–12 years.

FURTHER INFORMATION FROM:
Victoria Butterfly Gardens
1461 Benvenutto Avenue
P.O. Box 190
Brentwood Bay, British
Columbia V8M 1R3
(250) 652-3822 or
(877) 722-0272
butterfly@victoriabc.com
www.butterflygardens.com

NEARBY SIGHTS OF INTEREST:
Butchart Gardens

BELOW: *A tail jay butterfly stops for a sip of nectar at a cluster of lantana flowers.* Victoria Butterfly Gardens

OPPOSITE: *Palm trees strive to reach the top of the dome.*

9 Victoria: Victoria Butterfly Gardens

LOCATION: NEAR BUTCHART GARDENS, NINE MILES (FOURTEEN KILOMETERS) NORTH OF VICTORIA VIA HIGHWAY 17. CORNER OF WEST SAANICH ROAD AND KEATING X ROAD

There are several butterfly gardens throughout British Columbia, but this one is particularly attractive and is well situated from a garden-lover's point of view—being only three minutes away from Canada's most visited garden, Butchart Gardens. It is also one of the largest and most complete butterfly conservatories in Canada.

The Victoria Butterfly Gardens is an indoor tropical garden featuring about 600 free-flying butterflies at any one time, some produced at the facility, others imported from around the world. Its colorful butterflies and moths relish the warm, humid atmosphere of the conservatory, which is complete with winding cobblestone paths, a babbling brook, and waterfalls. Tall plants provide shelter for shade-loving butterflies, while others sun themselves on strategically placed rocks. Other butterflies will be seen sipping nectar from the numerous flowers, feeding on sweet fruits at a feeding station, or drinking at one of the shallow ponds. Attracted to brightly colored clothing, butterflies often land on visitors, much to their delight!

The gardens offer an introductory video session explaining the life cycle of butterflies or visitors can simply visit on their own. There is a restaurant and a delicatessen, plus the Nature Gift Shop for souvenirs . . . or more film! The entire garden is wheelchair accessible.

Vancouver: Bloedel Floral Conservatory

10

LOCATION: JUST OUTSIDE OF DOWNTOWN, IN QUEEN ELIZABETH PARK AT **33**RD
AVENUE AND CAMBIE STREET

This beautiful conservatory in the heart of Queen Elizabeth
Park is mostly the result of a $1.25 million gift from lumber
industrialist Peter Bloedel in 1971. The dynamic triodetic dome
of nearly 1,500 plexiglass bubbles is some forty-nine feet
(fifteen meters) tall and 141 feet (143 meters) in diameter. It covers three different indoor environments, the most spectacular
being the tropical zone, where palm trees, orchids, bromeliads,
and lianas share space with over thirty different types of free-
flying tropical birds: parrots, doves, Brazilian cardinals, and
many colorful finches. Free bird lists are available for those who
like to keep track. In the arid zone, cactus and succulents from
three continents bask in the sun. The temperate zone houses
seasonal displays of rhododendrons, azaleas, and flowering
bulbs, summer annuals, and fall chrysanthemums.

At the entrance to the conservatory is a lovely fountain
plaza with wading pools that is very much appreciated by the
local Chinese population for morning Tai Chi exercises. It is
surrounded by benches, trellises, hanging baskets, and container plantings, as well as trees and shrubs.

GARDEN OPEN: 9am to 8pm
Monday–Friday, 10am to 9pm
Saturday–Sunday, April
15–September 30; 10am to
5pm daily, October–April 14.
ADMISSION: $3.50 adults, $2
seniors, $1.65 youths, free
children 5 years and younger.

FURTHER INFORMATION FROM:
Vancouver Board of Parks &
Recreation
2099 Beach Avenue
Vancouver, British Columbia
V6G 1Z4
(604) 257-8570

NEARBY SIGHTS OF INTEREST:
Queen Elizabeth Park &
Sunken Gardens, Van Dusen
Botanical Gardens, University
of British Columbia Botanical
Gardens

GARDEN OPEN: 24 hours daily, year-round. **ADMISSION:** free.

FURTHER INFORMATION FROM:
City of Burnaby
Parks, Recreation and
Cultural Services
Suite 101—4946 Canada Way
Burnaby, BC V5G 4H7
(604) 294-7450
www.city.burnaby.bc.ca

NEARBY SIGHTS OF INTEREST:
Burnaby Art Gallery, Burnaby
Village Museum

Forget-me-nots and azaleas in spring. City of Burnaby Parks

11 Burnaby: Century Gardens

LOCATION: IN THE GREATER VANCOUVER AREA, AT **6450** DEER LAKE AVENUE (CORNER OF CANADA WAY)

This charming garden (about 3.7 acres/1.5 hectares) is a floral enclave within Deer Lake Park. The gardens were originally the grounds of an estate known as Fairacres, now the Burnaby Art Gallery, and surround the imposing Tudor mansion. The gardens, located on a sloping lawn overlooking Deer Lake, were entirely renovated in 1967 as a project for the Canadian Centennial. At that time, it was decided to dedicate them specifically to the culture of rhododendrons, and today the park contains some 200 different cultivars, including a hybrid created especially for the garden, "Burnaby Centennial." Consequently, the ideal season for visiting Gardens is when the rhododendrons are at their best, usually between April and June.

The gardens include circular pathways bordered by plantings of rhododendrons, azaleas, and, for summer color, roses and the site is surrounded by mature conifers. Each year, in early May, the site is used for the annual Burnaby Rhododendron Show. Phone the Burnaby Rhododendron Society at (604) 291-6864 for hours and dates. Curiously, the gardens have the reputation of being frequented by ghosts!

The Tudor-style art gallery/mansion in the center of the garden is also open to visitors for a small fee. It is open year round Tuesday to Friday from 9:30am to 4:40pm and Saturday, Sunday, and holidays from 12:30am to 4:30pm. For details, phone (604) 205-7332. Also, just next door is the Burnaby Village Museum, which re-creates the sights and sounds of an 1890 to 1925 village (604) 293-6500.

12 Vancouver: Dr. Sun Yat-Sen Classical Chinese Garden

LOCATION: IN THE HEART OF VANCOUVER'S CHINATOWN, MINUTES, AT
578 CARRALL STREET

The Dr. Sun Yat-Sen Classical Chinese Garden is the first authentic, full-scale Chinese garden built outside China. It contains quiet ponds, natural rock sculptures, courtyards, plants, and dozens of other elements that work together to create a garden typical of the private classical gardens developed in the city of Suzhou during the Ming Dynasty, 1368–1644. The garden was built in 1986 using materials brought in from China, including lattice windows, hand-fired roof tiles, and precious Taihu limestone rocks, and was reconstructed by fifty-two Chinese artisans using only traditional tools and methods. Not one nail was used in its construction!

Truly unique, the garden represents the Taoist philosophy of yin and yang; rugged and hard objects are balanced by those that are soft and flowing, and dark elements by light ones. Nothing is the fruit of hazard—everything in the garden, from tree to stone, has been purposely placed and carries a symbolic meaning. It is a place for a quiet stroll or tranquil meditation, not a collection of plants, as is the case in so many other public gardens. If possible, take one of the guided tours included in the cost of admission; they take about forty-five minutes and are almost essential to understanding the garden's philosophy. They take place several times a day, with hours varying according to season. Phone for details. Also included in the cost of admission is a complimentary cup of tea. There is a gift shop on the grounds.

There are many special activities taking place in the garden throughout the year: musical performances, art exhibits, horticultural displays, lectures, Chinese festivals, and much more, plus the Enchanted Evening series, a one hour program of Chinese music followed a stroll through the garden lit by lanterns. The latter takes place every Friday night from July through September. For other activities, phone for information.

GARDEN OPEN: 9:30am to 7pm daily, June 1–September; 10am to 4:30pm daily, October–May 31. ADMISSION: $7.50 adults, $6 seniors, $5 students, free children 5 years and younger, $18 family.

FURTHER INFORMATION FROM:
Dr. Sun Yat-Sen Classical Chinese Garden
578 Carrall Street
Vancouver, British Columbia
V6B 5K2
(604) 662-3207
Fax: (604) 682-4008
sunyatsen@telus.net
www.discovervancouver.com/sun

NEARBY SIGHTS OF INTEREST:
The Lookout! at Harbour Centre Tower, Science World, Chinatown

ABOVE: *Waterlilies float near the footbridge.*

13 Vancouver: Nitobe Memorial Garden

LOCATION: IN VANCOUVER, ON THE UNIVERSITY OF BRITISH COLUMBIA CAMPUS, AT TIP OF POINT GREY. NW MARINE DRIVE TO MUSEUM OF ANTHROPOLOGY. THE GARDEN IS ACROSS STREET

Canada has several Japanese gardens, but certainly none quite so restful as this one. Unlike the formal classical style of most others, this one is based on a more contemporary trend in Japan, the school of naturalistic landscape architecture. Other than the more formal Tea Garden, the rest of the garden, of the type known as a stroll garden, was designed using natural looking plantings, rocks, and ponds, the goal being to make you feel you are not in a garden, but in an idealized piece of nature. Natural scenery—waterfalls, rivers, forests, and islands—has been recreated, but on a smaller scale, so the eye can interpret each in its entirety. Even the paths are designed to slow the step, to force the visitor to become one with his surroundings, to meditate peacefully. Other than brief bursts of color in spring coming from Japanese iris, azaleas, and a few other plants, the garden is not a flower garden, but one of greens, browns, grays, and ochres, of mossy banks and sunlight filtering through foliage, of varying and contrasting textures. Small rustic bridges crisscross the streams and lakes, giving the visitor the impression of having left the hustle and bustle of the city far behind.

The plants used combine native North American species like salal, mahonias, and deer ferns with traditional Japanese plants like Japanese maples and flowering cherries. Each tree has been carefully trained to fit in with the scale of the garden and pruned to best reveal its trunk and branches.

The *Tea Garden* is a more formal section and includes a ceremonial Tea House (closed except on special occasions). The

The most restful Japanese garden in Canada.

path leading to it passes a hand basin for ceremonial cleansing before humbly entering the Tea House.

The garden, opened in 1960 and renovated in 1992, honors Professor Iznazo Nitobe (1862–1933), a Japanese philanthropist and advocate of world peace who wanted to be a "bridge across the Pacific." He died unexpectedly while on a trip to British Columbia.

Admission to the Nitobe Memorial Garden is free on Wednesday. On other days, a discount can be obtained on the price of a combined admission ticket to the University of British Columbia Botanical Garden. Participation in tea ceremonies (phone for reservations) is extra. Washrooms are available in adjacent university buildings.

Just across opposite the entry gate to Nitobe Memorial Garden is the *Asian Centre*, which also includes stunning samples of Japanese side gardens, including a Zen stone and gravel garden and a hillside garden.

14 Vancouver: Queen Elizabeth Park and Quarry Gardens

LOCATION: JUST OUTSIDE OF DOWNTOWN VANCOUVER, AT 33RD AVENUE AND CAMBIE STREET

GARDEN OPEN: dawn to dusk daily, year-round.

ADMISSION: free.

FURTHER INFORMATION FROM:
Vancouver Board of Parks & Recreation
2099 Beach Avenue
Vancouver, British Columbia
V6G 1Z4
(604) 257-8570

NEARBY SIGHTS OF INTEREST:
Bloedel Conservatory,
VanDusen Botanical Gardens,
University of British Columbia
Botanical Gardens

Right at the top of Little Mountain, at the geographical heart of Vancouver, is one of its most popular parks: Queen Elizabeth Park. The sunset garden at the top of the park offers a breathtaking, 180-degree view of the city and the mountains and inlet that surround it. Do an about-face and you'll see the geodetic dome of the Bloedel Floral Conservatory (described separately on page 169).

Today's park is in rather a surprising location, though; it is built on the land surrounding an abandoned quarry, which should typically look more like a lunar landscape than a verdant garden. The quarry dates to the early 1900s when it was used to supply crushed rock for the city's first roadways. Afterward, it was used for some time as a holding reservoir for the city's water supply. However, the gaping hole, plainly visible from much of the city, was an urban eyesore for decades. Then citizens groups, and notably the British Columbia Tulip Association, pressed the city to convert the quarry into a urban garden based on the quarry converted into sunken garden in the Butchart Gardens on Vancouver Island (page 159).

The Parks Department finally did the job in 1961, turning the 130-acre (52-hectare) eyesore into a beautiful, sloping park. The original quarry garden is still the most spectacular. Paths and streams meander and cross in a lush green valley set off by

The Quarry Gardens are a blaze of color throughout the summer.

brilliantly colored annual and perennial beds and giant, leafy gunneras. On Saturday afternoon the site is so popular with wedding parties that they often have to wait in line for a particularly choice spot! The second sunken garden, opened in another part of the quarry, represents a *xeriscape garden*: plants adapted to arid conditions. There is also a *rose garden* displaying seventy-five different cultivars, and the entire site is ringed with an *arboretum* made up of a wide variety of rare trees and shrubs, including species rarely seen in such a cold climate, like eucalyptus.

To complete the portrait of Queen Elizabeth Park, there is a driving range and tennis courts, plus a restaurant and washroom facilities.

GARDEN OPEN: 24 hours daily, year-round. **ADMISSION:** free.

FURTHER INFORMATION FROM:
Vancouver Board of Parks & Recreation
2099 Beach Avenue
Vancouver, British Columbia
V6G 1Z4
(604) 257-8400
www.city.vancouver.bc.ca/
parks/parks&gardens/
stanley.htm

NEARBY SIGHTS OF INTEREST:
Downtown Vancouver,
Vancouver Aquarium,
beaches, Prospect Point

15 Vancouver: Stanley Park

LOCATION: AT WEST END OF GEORGIA STREET, FIVE MINUTES DRIVE FROM DOWNTOWN VANCOUVER

Stanley Park is certainly one of the most celebrated and popular parks in Canada, with some eight million visitors each year. This huge urban green space, named for Lord Stanley, Governor General of Canada in 1888 when the park was officially opened, covers 1,000 acres (405 hectares): an entire peninsula just off downtown Vancouver. It includes sections of virgin rainforest with giant conifers, plus lakes and ponds, nature preserves rich in waterfowl, over fifty miles (eighty kilometers) of walking trails, and plenty of possibilities for sports of all kinds: tennis courts, beaches and a heated pool for swimming, and a pitch and putt golf course. For the kids, there are pony rides, a miniature steam railway, and a children's zoo, while adults will enjoy the concerts and open-air theatre during July and August. And for the whole family, there are picnic areas, restaurants and snack bars, a display of totem poles from across the province, and a large zoo, not to mention the very popular Vancouver Aquarium (paid admission), with more than

56,000 marine animals, including beluga whales, and performing dolphins, killer whales, and sea lions. For plant-lovers, the aquarium also has a very nice reconstituted rain forest.

Of course, Stanley Park also offers much more for the gardener than huge evergreens as a backdrop for rolling green lawns. The *Ted and Marion Greig Rhododendron Garden*, near Second Beach, contains over 8,000 rhododendrons and azaleas of all sizes, shapes, and colors, plus spring bulbs, magnolias, camellias, and much more. Because of the diversity of plants, it remains in bloom right through April and May.

The *Rose Garden* is located a just about the center of the park. Planted in 1920, the garden is surrounded by beautiful perennial borders and contains over 3,000 rose bushes of eighty varieties planted in rather informal beds. Its season of interest stretches from April until nearly Christmas. There are also other perennial and annual beds here and there throughout the park, notably at Prospect Point, where a carpet bedding display embellishes a beautiful place to stop and view one of the city's most celebrated panoramas: that of Lion's Gate Bridge stretching over Burrard Inlet to North Vancouver.

Access to Stanley Park is free, but you'll have to pay for parking. The main road is one way only, counterclockwise. Visiting the park by foot is not only feasible, but makes a lovely activity for the whole family. However, it will take a full day to get most of it in. Cycling and roller-blading are other—and faster—possibilities. There is also a shuttle bus disguised as an old-fashioned trolley that does the rounds daily, every twelve to fifteen minutes, during the summer months; tickets are inexpensive and you can get on and off as often as you like, making it one of the cheapest and most convenient ways of visiting the park.

A small stream cascades into one of Stanley Park's numerous ponds.

Vancouver: University of British Columbia Botanical Garden

GARDEN OPEN: 10am to 6pm daily, mid-March–early October; 10am to 2:30pm daily, early October–mid-March. **ADMISSION:** $4.50 adults, $2.25 seniors and students, $1.75 youths (grades 1–7), free children under 6 years.

FURTHER INFORMATION FROM:
University of British Columbia Botanical Garden
6804 Southwest Marine Drive
Vancouver, British Columbia
V6T 1Z4
(604) 822-9666
www.hedgerows.com

NEARBY SIGHTS OF INTEREST:
Museum of Anthropology, Nitobe Memorial Garden

LOCATION: ON UNIVERSITY OF BRITISH COLUMBIA CAMPUS. FROM DOWNTOWN, WEST ON W 4TH AVENUE AND W 16TH AVENUE TO THE UBC CAMPUS; FOLLOW SIGNS TO BOTANICAL GARDEN OFFICE

The beautiful UBC Botanical Garden has some of the finest collections of plants in Western Canada: over 10,000 species and cultivars. They thrive in its mild climate, as the Strait of Georgia, only 330 feet (100 meters) below moderates the climate and helps prevent extreme cold. The garden was founded by the university's first botany professor, John Davidson, in 1916 on the main campus, using plants taken from the garden's predecessor, Essondale Botanical Gardens in Port Moody (now Riverview Lands, page 187). The gardens have since expanded to cover seventy acres (twenty-eight hectares). And as is expected in a botanical garden, all plants are labeled.

One of the main collections is the thirty-five-acre (fifteen-hectare) *David C. Lam Asian Garden*, named after British Columbia's first Chinese-Canadian Lieutenant-Governor. It contains a collection of plants native to Asia under a canopy of native conifers, including the garden's famous rhododendron collection of some 400 different varieties, at its best in April and May. Equally prestigious is the 2.5-acre (one-hectare) *E. H. Lohbrunner Alpine Garden*, beautiful at any time of the year, a rock garden featuring alpine plants from around the world and certainly the most complete collection of this type in Canada.

Other featured gardens include the *Food Garden*, with vegetables, berries, grapes, and espaliered fruit trees, the *Arbor Garden*, a beautiful wood pergola dedicated to climbing plants, the *Physick Garden*, a circular area displaying medicinal plants, the eight-acre (three-hectare) *Native Garden*, featuring 1,500 species of plants native to British Columbia, the *Winter Garden*, with plants that bloom in fall and winter such as hazels,

The Food Garden present edible plants in an attractive layout.

heathers, and daphnes, and the *Evolutionary Garden*, which traces the history of plants from the most primitive forms to modern hybrids.

The UBC Botanical Garden also tests new plants and has a plant introduction program that has introduced many new varieties, some of which, like the Vancouver Jade bearberry (*Arctostaphylos* 'Vancouver Jade') and the Mandarin climbing honeysuckle (*Lonicera* 'Mandarin') have become staple in gardens throughout North America.

To complete the portrait, there is also a visitor's center and a gift shop complete with a small nursery that sells, among others, some of the Botanical Gardens introductions. The gardens are open free of charge on Wednesdays. On other days, a combined ticket is available that includes admission to the Nitobe Memorial Garden, nearby, and also managed by the staff of the UBC Botanical Garden.

BELOW: *The Bell Tower at the heart of the gardens.*

17 Vancouver: Fantasy Garden World

LOCATION: AT 10800 NO. 5 ROAD, IN RICHMOND. FROM DOWNTOWN VANCOUVER, HIGHWAY 99 SOUTH TO STEVESTON HIGHWAY EXIT, WEST AT END OF RAMP, THEN FOLLOW SIGNS

Fantasy Gardens is probably best described as a horticultural theme park or, if you prefer, a sort of Disney World of gardening. It starts off with a European Village, a maze of shops and restaurants with costumed clerks and waiters. There is no admission charge for this part of the visit.

Beyond the village are the gardens themselves, which do charge an admission fee. Founded by former British Columbia premier, Bill VanDerZalm, a former garden center owner and bulb producer, and his wife, they represent their idea of the perfect garden. A winding trails takes visitors through a series of gardens: water gardens, flower gardens, a Biblical Garden featuring scenes and plants from the Bible, a Japanese Garden, a hanging fuchsia garden, a formal rose garden, and a large conservatory. There is also a bell tower, aviaries, a petting zoo, a mini-train, and lots of other family activities. The gardens feature plenty of color; spring bulbs early in the season, then mainly annuals after that, although there are also plenty of trees, shrubs, and perennials, many of them identified.

GARDEN OPEN: 9am to dusk daily, year-round. **ADMISSION:** $3.50 adults, $2.50 seniors and students 13–17 years, $1 children 6–12 years, $7.50 family.

FURTHER INFORMATION FROM:
Fantasy World Garden
10800 No. 5 Road
Richmond, British Columbia
V7A 4E3
(604) 277-7777

NEARBY SIGHTS OF INTEREST:
Richmond Art Centre, Gallery, Museum and Archives

18 New Westminster: Japanese Friendship Garden

GARDEN OPEN: dawn to dusk daily, year-round.

ADMISSION: free.

FURTHER INFORMATION FROM:
Japanese Friendship Garden
511 Royal Avenue
New Westminster, British
Columbia V3L 1H9
(604) 527-4567
www.city.new-westminster.
bc.ca

NEARBY SIGHTS OF INTEREST:
Queens Park, Irving House
and New Westminster
Museum

Japanese cherry blossoms burst forth with the first days of spring. Claude E. LeDoux

LOCATION: IN CENTRAL NEW WESTMINSTER, PART OF THE GREATER VANCOUVER AREA. FROM DOWNTOWN VANCOUVER, KINGSWAY (HIGHWAY 1A/99A) EAST ABOUT SEVEN MILES (ELEVEN KILOMETERS) WHERE IT BECOMES 12TH STREET; DRIVE ONE MILE (1.5 KILOMETERS) AND TURN LEFT ONTO ROYAL AVENUE. THE PARK IS ABOUT 1/2 MILE (0.8 KILOMETERS) TO THE LEFT, AFTER NEW WESTMINSTER TOWN HALL

This intimate two-and-one-half-acre (one-hectare) garden is dedicated to New Westminster's sister city, Moriguchi, Japan. It is a sort of westernized version of a classical Japanese garden—and that is not intended as a negative comment, because it is a very beautiful garden indeed, successfully blending a bit of each style in one space.

The heart of the garden is a slope over which gently cascade four stream-fed waterfalls. Nearby are over 100 Yoshino cherry trees, a gift from Moriguchi, in full bloom in early spring. There is also a grove of black bamboo and a koi pond, over which droops the arching branches of a weeping willow and the giant leaves of a gunnera. The whole garden gives off a feeling of peace and tranquility: a quiet corner in the bustling city of Greater Vancouver.

A curving bridge in the Japanese Garden. Park and Tilford Gardens

While you're in the neighborhood, you may also want to visit Queen's Park, only three blocks away. A more traditional city park, it has the usual playing fields, picnic area, and playground, but also lots of lovely annual beds and a small botanical garden.

19 North Vancouver: Park and Tilford Gardens

LOCATION: AT 440–333 BROOKSBANK AVENUE IN NORTH VANCOUVER. FROM VANCOUVER, NORTH ON HIGHWAY 1 TO EXIT 23; TRAVEL WEST 3/4 MILE (1.2 KILOMETERS) ON MAIN STREET TO PARK AND TILFORD SHOPPING CENTRE

GARDEN OPEN: 9:30am to dusk daily, year-round.
ADMISSION: free.

FURTHER INFORMATION FROM:
Park & Tilford Gardens
No. 440–333 Brooksbank
Avenue
North Vancouver, British
Columbia V7J 2S8
(604) 984-8200

This two-and-one-half-acre (one-hectare) garden is an excellent example of how careful garden design can work miracles on a small lot. No less than eight different theme gardens are included in a space smaller than many gardens that only manage one theme—yet the results are more than satisfactory.

The gardens include the *Display Garden*, a seasonal garden were spring bulbs dominate early in the year to be followed by annuals in summer and early fall, and the *Native Garden*, where a footpath winds through a recreated forest of cedars, hemlock, ferns, and other plants indigenous to the Pacific coastal forest. There is an *Oriental Garden* with bonsai and bamboo; a *White Garden*, including careful arrangements of plants with white or silvery foliage or flowers; the *Rock Pool* with its lush vegetation and waterfall; the *Colonnade*, where a series of arches are decorated with vines and hanging baskets; the *Rose Garden*, with over 250 cultivars of rose; and finally the *Herb Garden*, whose softly scented plants release a potpourri of fragrances. During the special Christmas Lights Festival, the gardens are open after dark, until 9:30pm.

Park & Tilford Gardens, designed by landscape architects Justice and Webb, were originally sponsored by Park & Tilford Distilleries Ltd. as a community beautification project in 1967. They were an instant success, drawing up to 300,000 visitors a year, but the gardens closed nonetheless in 1984 when the distillery moved. The project was revived in 1988 by the Park & Tilford Shopping Centre at the southwest corner of the gardens, and the gardens reopened a year later. Park & Tilford Gardens have remained a private non-profit teaching and display garden, largely financed by the shopping center, ever since. The teaching aspect of the garden comes from the unique training program developed by the garden's staff and the horticulture instructors at nearby Capilano College. Students get hands-on training in the gardens; he best students are then hired to work in the garden over the summer.

There are no services within the gardens themselves, but restrooms, restaurants, and gift shops are available in the shopping center next door.

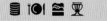

GARDEN OPEN: 8:30am to dusk daily, mid-May–September 30; 9am to 5pm daily, October–mid-May.
ADMISSION: free.

FURTHER INFORMATION FROM:
Capilano Suspension Bridge and Park
3735 Capilano Road
North Vancouver, British Columbia V7R 4J1
(206) 985-7474

20 North Vancouver: Capilano Suspension Bridge and Park

LOCATION: OFF HIGHWAY 1, EXIT 14, THEN 1.2 MILES (TWO KILOMETERS) NORTH ON CAPILANO ROAD

The major draw to this beautiful, forested, fifteen-acre (six-hectare) park is the narrow suspension bridge of wire rope and wood decking that crosses the 455-foot (139-meter) wide canyon, and of course the incredible view of the raging Capilano River 230 feet (70 meters) below. The massive red cedars and Douglas firs towering around it only serve to make the bridge seem narrower and more fragile than it really is! There is also a gift shop where native sculptors often work in season, plus a snack bar.

The attraction for garden lovers are the beautiful flower beds full of colorful annuals and perennials, highlighted by totem poles, located between the gift shop/admissions office and the bridge. There is also a walking trail leading to a 200-foot (94-meter) drop and a spectacular panorama of the gorge.

Paid admission is only required for the bridge. The gardens are free year round.

The suspension bridge allows views of the tree-lined valley 455 feet (139 meters) below.

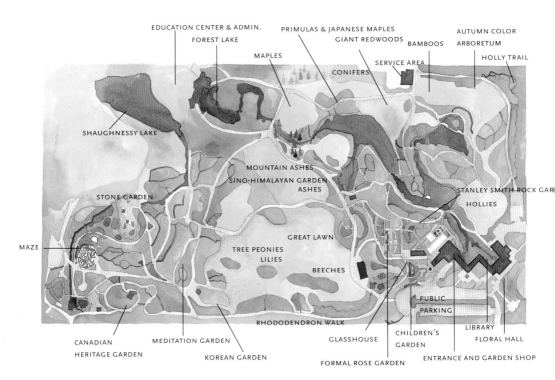

EDUCATION CENTER & ADMIN.

FOREST LAKE

MAPLES

PRIMULAS & JAPANESE MAPLES

GIANT REDWOODS

CONIFERS

SERVICE AREA

BAMBOOS

AUTUMN COLOR
ARBORETUM

HOLLY TRAIL

SHAUGHNESSY LAKE

MOUNTAIN ASHES

SINO-HIMALAYAN GARDEN
ASHES

STONE GARDEN

STANLEY SMITH ROCK GAR

HOLLIES

MAZE

GREAT LAWN

TREE PEONIES
LILIES

BEECHES

PUBLIC
PARKING

RHODODENDRON WALK

CANADIAN
HERITAGE GARDEN

MEDITATION GARDEN

KOREAN GARDEN

GLASSHOUSE

CHILDREN'S
GARDEN

LIBRARY

FLORAL HALL

FORMAL ROSE GARDEN

ENTRANCE AND GARDEN SHOP

21 Vancouver: VanDusen Botanical Gardens

LOCATION: FIFTEEN MINUTES FROM DOWNTOWN VANCOUVER, AT OAK STREET AND WEST 37TH STREET

VanDusen is a rare gem among Canadian gardens, as it is both a botanical garden—with a collection of over 7,500 labeled plants—and a display garden, beautifully landscaped and impeccably maintained. It will be of interest not only to the serious gardener taking notes on new plants, but also to the casual visitor who would like to discover a beautiful paradise of flowers and greenery. The citizens of Vancouver know it well, as it has become the central focus of most of the city's garden training programs, shows, and lectures.

The site occupies fifty-five acres (twenty-two hectares) of rolling, verdant land, occupied by the Shaughnessy Golf Club from 1911 until 1960. The site was to have been sold for development as a subdivision, but local citizens objected and, in 1966, thanks notably to a donation by W.J. VanDusen, after whom the garden is named, and the involvement of various levels of government, the VanDusen Botanical Gardens Association was formed to assist the Vancouver Park Board in saving the site. Development didn't start until 1971, though, with the garden opening officially in 1975.

The vast, landscaped garden is too large to absorb in one visit, but a visitor's guide is available that points out three different walking routes, from a twenty-minute "Taste of VanDusen" stroll to the one-hour "VanDusen High Points: walk to the two-hour "World of Plants" tour. Or join a guided tour lead by a trained volunteer (phone for information). Handicapped visitors can enjoy a cart tour with a volunteer driver, usually at 1pm daily during the summer months (reservations required).

Visitors enter the garden through the main building, which houses not only the garden's administration and library, but also Floral Hall, used for conferences, shows, workshops, and other activities (phone for details), a restaurant, and the Garden Shop—which sells, among other things, packets of seed collected in the garden. Stop for a few seconds at the Plants to See display, which shows what is in bloom, as this can help orient your visit.

Many of the most interesting display gardens are located near this building, including a reflecting pool, the *White Garden* set off by a beautiful weeping blue cedar, the *Fragrance Garden*, the *Vegetable* and *Herb Gardens*, and the *Glasshouse*, featuring a bonsai display. An amusing and informative *Children's Garden*, centered around a bed of annuals planted to resemble

GARDEN OPEN: 10am to 4pm daily October 1–March 31; 10am to 6pm daily, April and Labor Day–September 30; 10am to 8pm daily, May and mid-August–Labor Day; 10am to 9pm daily, June 1–mid-August. **ADMISSION:** $5.50 adults (main season); $2.75 adults (off season).

FURTHER INFORMATION FROM:
VanDusen Botanical Garden
5251 Oak Street
Vancouver, British Columbia
V6M 4H1
(604) 878-9274
www.vandusengarden.org

NEARBY SIGHTS OF INTEREST:
Queen Elizabeth Park and Quarry Gardens, Bloedel Conservatory

OPPOSITE: *Young and old alike will enjoy the box maze.*

Hanging baskets find a home in the Lath House.

cuddly animals (the pattern changes annually) and full of amusing topiary, is just to the left of the building. Also nearby are the *Trough Garden*, the *Stanley Smith Rock Garden*, which is a small rockery specialized in dwarf conifers, and the *Formal Rose Garden*, very geometric in its Renaissance style, with a sundial at its center.

Other features not far from the entrance building include beautiful informal perennial borders with hardy perennials and dramatic ornamental grasses, *Laburnum Walk*, dripping in yellow flowers in the spring, the *Lath House* and its collection of hanging baskets, and the *Groundcover Collection*.

As you roam farther afield, you may want to take in the *Heather Garden*, the *Maze* made up of 1,018 pyramidal cedars, the *Meditation Garden*, *Rhododendron Walk*, the *Stone Garden* (featuring rocks rather than plants!), any one of the numerous lakes (particularly interesting for bird lovers, as many of the sixty varieties of birds known to frequent VanDusen congregate there), *Fern Dell*, the *Alma VanDusen Garden*, which is an open meadow of flowing, naturalized perennials and grasses, the *Meconopsis Dell* (home of the garden's blue poppies, in bloom in May), the *Meadow Ponds*, or any one of the numerous collections. These include both related plants grouped together, such as the holly collection of 147 cultivars, plus beeches, lilies, tree peonies, maples, giant redwoods, bamboos, and much more, as well as recreated habitats featuring varied plants native to a given area, such as the *Canadian Heritage Garden*, the *Sino-Himalayan Garden*, the *Southern Hemisphere Garden*, the

A monkey puzzle tree (Araucaria araucana) is featured with agaves, yuccas, columnar cacti and other exotic plants rarely grown outdoors in Canada.

Mediterranean Garden, the *Eastern North America Forest* as well as its western counterpart, and others.

Tired of flowers? The garden also includes numerous statues and fountains, plus some peaceful green lawns with benches where you can simply relax and soak up the laid-back atmosphere. Needless to say, the garden is beautiful in all seasons, with some bloom even in December and January. Spring really arrives in earnest in March, though, with the earliest spring bulbs, and from then until October, with its fall colors, the garden is a nonstop wave of changing hues.

The formal Vegetable Garden uses edible plants decoratively.

Langley: Sendall Gardens

LOCATION: IN THE CITY OF LANGLEY AT THE CORNER OF 201 A STREET AND
50TH AVENUE. FROM VANCOUVER, TAKE HIGHWAY 1A (FRASER HIGHWAY)
ABOUT TWENTY-FIVE MILES (FORTY KILOMETERS) EAST TO LANGLEY. TURN
SOUTH ONTO 200TH STREET AND THEN EAST ON 50TH AVENUE

GARDEN OPEN: dawn to dusk
daily, year-round.
ADMISSION: free.

FURTHER INFORMATION FROM:
City of Langley Parks
Department
20399 Douglas Crescent
Langley, British Columbia V3A
4B3
(604) 514-2912
len@city.langley.bc.ca

NEARBY SIGHTS OF INTEREST:
Canadian Museum of Flight
and Transportation

*Trees reflect in one of the
ponds.* City of Langley Parks
Department

This four-acre (1.5-hectare) public park was originally a private
home with extensive gardens, featuring vast plantings of rhododendrons and Japanese maples—but they had been sadly
neglected and were become overrun with brush when the City
of Langley Parks Department bought the land in the 1970s. The
gardens were slowly restored to their present state over a ten-
year period starting in 1975, and they underwent further reno-
vations in 2000.

Today the site is a series of well-tended garden rooms just
waiting to be discovered. There are extensive beds of shrubs
and perennials, plus many mature trees, including colorful
flowering cherries. There is a small greenhouse with tropical
plants next to the caretaker's cottage, as well as stands of rhododendrons and trellises covered in climbing hydrangeas and
clematis. There are also some spectacular rose arbors plus pens
for peacocks and waterfowl and a deco-
rative fountain.

There is a *natural woodland* in the
ravine to the back of the caretaker's
cottage which has been enhanced with
two ponds and plantings of flowering
shrubs and small trees such as
Chinese dogwoods. And the surprise
element of the garden is the *'Wisteria
Jungle,'* in fact a tangled mass of wisteria that has managed to work its way
well up into the tree canopy.

There is a small concession stand
open during the summer months
where visitors can pick up brochures
about the park and also restrooms and
a picnic area.

23 Port Moody: Riverview Lands

LOCATION: TWELVE MILES (TWENTY KILOMETERS) EAST OF VANCOUVER VIA HIGHWAY 7 (LOUGHEED HIGHWAY). LEFT AT COLONY FARM ROAD, AFTER INTERSECTION OF HIGHWAY 7B (MARY HILL BYPASS). RIGHT ONTO HOSPITAL GROUNDS AND FOLLOW DIRECTIONAL SIGN TO THE RIGHT

GARDEN OPEN: dawn to dusk daily, year-round.
ADMISSION: free.

FURTHER INFORMATION FROM:
Riverview Horticultural
Centre Society
P.O. Box 31005
No. 8–2929 St. John's Street
Port Moody, British Columbia
V3H 4T4
(604) 290-9910
marycb@telus.net or
rhcs@hotmail.com
www.tricitiesonline.com/river
view/Index.htm

NEARBY SIGHTS OF INTEREST:
Colony Farm Park and
Community Gardens, Mundy
Park, Riverview Forest,
Minnekhada Regional Park

This large arboretum is probably among the least known parks in British Columbia and certainly warrants much more attention from garden-loving visitors than it currently receives. That's probably because of the stigma long attached to mental hospitals such as Riverview Lands, as the provincial psychiatric hospital on which the arboretum is planted came to be known. Today, the huge institution still stands, although the hospital's population has been dramatically cut due to downsizing. The vast grounds have been partly sold off to development companies, but 244 acres (99 hectares) of forest and arboretum still remain and are now open to the public.

Riverview Lands was the site of Western Canada's first botanical garden. The land was cleared in 1904, and part of it was turned into a vegetable and fruit garden to help feed the patients. At the same period, Dr. John Davidson was appointed Provincial Botanist and established a tree nursery and botanical gardens (called Essondale Botanical Gardens) on the site, bringing in unusual trees and shrubs from all over the temperate world. By 1916, there were over 25,000 plants in the botanical garden. Although many of the trees were later transferred to other sites and the botanical garden itself was dismantled and moved to the new University of British Columbia Botanical Garden (page TK) after it was founded in Vancouver, the arboretum still contains many spectacular mature trees dating back to the beginning of the arboretum. Some examples include massive mature specimens of European beech (*Fagus sylvatica*, many different cultivars), silver linden (*Tilia tomentosa*), giant sequoia (*Sequoiadendron giganteum*), tulip tree (*Liriodendron tulipifera*), and double-flowering horsechestnut (*Aesculus hippocastanum* 'Flore Pleno').

Most of the old gardens, including the residents' vegetable garden, are gone, but one, *Finnie's Garden*, built for and by residents for therapeutic and recreation purposes, still remains as a wildlife sanctuary. Native plants mingle there with the fruit trees of yore, still a splendid sight in early spring.

Visits to the garden are free, but donations to the Riverview Horticultural Centre Society are appreciated and will be used to maintain the garden and to continue the fight to save it from development.

Many of the trees, like this Camperdown elm, are centenarians. Riverview Horticultural Centre Society

24 Chillimack: Minter Gardens

LOCATION: ABOUT 75 MILES (120 KILOMETERS) FROM VANCOUVER. HIGHWAY 1 TO HARRISON HOT SPRINGS EXIT (EXIT 135) AND FOLLOW SIGNS TO 52892 BUNKER ROAD, ROSEDALE

GARDEN OPEN: 9am to 5pm daily, April–May and September–October; 9am to 6pm daily, June; 9am to 7pm daily, July–August.

ADMISSION: $12 adults, $10.50 seniors, $6.50 youths, free children 5 years and younger, $32 family.

FURTHER INFORMATION FROM:

Minter Gardens
P.O. Box 40
Chillimack, British Columbia
V2P 6H7
(604) 749-7191 or 1 (888) 646-8377
mail@minter.org
www.mintergardens.com

NEARBY SIGHTS OF INTEREST:

Harrison Hot Springs

A foot bridge crosses a babbling brook amid ferns and Japanese maples. Minter Gardens

Minter Gardens, founded by garden personality Brian Minter in 1980, are one of Canada's foremost show gardens, at least as impressive as Butchart Gardens in Victoria, although not nearly as well known. The site itself is particularly charming; the gardens are surrounded by mountains and nestled at the very base of 7,000-foot (2,000-meter) Mount Cheam. The vegetation is particularly luxuriant due to regular rainfall—yes, umbrellas are provided!—and clement temperatures that allow growth rates far beyond what would be possible elsewhere.

There are presently eleven theme gardens scattered throughout rolling hillside of the twenty-seven-acre (eleven-hectare) park. They include the spectacular *Rose Garden*, the beautifully arranged eighteenth-century *Formal Garden* with a distinct Italian influence, the *Alpine Garden*, the *Hillside Garden*, the *Fern Garden*, the *Lake Garden*, the *Fragrance Garden*, and much more. Children and adults will also enjoy losing themselves for a few minutes in the *Evergreen Maze*. There is an impressive *penjing* (Chinese-style bonsai) collection in the *Chinese Garden* and oriental influences (and plants) abound throughout the gardens. Also on the site are a small petting zoo, aviaries, a water wheel, waterfalls, ponds, a play area, a gift shop and restaurants, plus, nearby, plant sales areas.

The most impressive element of the garden, however, is its numerous examples of *carpet bedding*. This art form of the Victorian era, where closely packed annuals are used to paint floral pictures, has almost been lost in Canada and, indeed, in North America, with only a few scattered examples still remaining. At Minter Gardens, though, the art has been fully revived; there are geometric forms, abstract paintings, logos recalling community events, a huge Canadian flag, and much more, all taking advantage of the site's naturally sloping terrain, since such beds have to be seen at an angle to be appreciated. Since the carpet beds are traditionally redone annually, the exact displays change from year to year, meaning the garden is constantly being redesigned. This art has sometimes been denigrated by the horticultural elite as too simple and unsophisticated—and, true enough, it *is* easily understood by even non-gardeners. And that, perhaps, is exactly the point; making garden art

that anyone can understand requires more finesse in planning, planting, and maintenance than does the average mixed border. And that everyone can appreciate carpet bedding only helps stimulate interest in gardening in general.

Beyond two-dimensional carpet bedding, the gardens also feature some examples of even rarer three-dimensional carpet bedding, also called *floral topiary* or armature draping. Unlike true topiary (also well represented at the gardens), the forms of the Victorian ladies, the peacock, and "Olive, The Other Reindeer" are not pruned shrubs, but wire forms packed with colorful annuals. The result is amusing and colorful and adds a note of whimsy to the gardens.

The carpet bedding and floral topiaries are at their best in summer, but the gardens are colorful throughout much of the year, thanks to mass plantings of bulbs and colorful spring-flowering trees and shrubs, ensuring early color, plus chrysanthemums and flowering kale that maintain the displays through the fall. And under a winter snow, the conifers that dot the garden can be truly magical.

A "Victorian lady" topiary holds her parasol aloft.

25 Summerland: Summerland Ornamental Gardens

LOCATION: TEN MILES (SIXTEEN KILOMETERS) NORTH OF PENTICTON VIA HIGHWAY 97; TURN LEFT AT SUNOKA BEACH AND FOLLOW THE ROAD ONE MILE (1.75 KILOMETERS) TO GARDEN ENTRANCE

Formerly an active part of the Dominion Experimental Farm, established in 1914 to help solve agriculture problems in fruit-growing Okanagan Valley, the Summerland Ornamental Gardens have become over time a fascinating example of English gardening tradition transposed to semi-arid conditions. Today, the gardens remain part of what is now called the Agriculture and Agri-Food Canada Pacific Agri-Food Research Centre, whose main test gardens are located just down the road, but are operated as a public garden in partnership with the Summerland Research Station Garden Society, a non-profit, volunteer organization.

The soul of the modern garden is the *Xeriscape Garden*, near the Entry Kiosk, which demonstrates ideas for ornamental gardening under arid conditions, including a collection of plants adapted to drought. There is also a meadow garden, an English garden, a rock garden, a selection of ornamental grasses, a ground cover demonstration area, lawns, an arboretum, and a beautiful and colorful rose garden. *Friendship Plaza*, with beautiful rock walls, a wooden arbor, rustic urns, and graceful steps, is used as a natural amphitheater for music and

GARDEN OPEN: 8am to dusk daily, May–October; 9am to 5pm daily, November–March.
ADMISSION: $2 or more suggested donation.

FURTHER INFORMATION FROM:
Summerland Ornamental
Gardens
4200 Highway 97 South
Box 1363
Summerland, British
Columbia V0H 1Z0
(250) 494-6385
ejstaff@home.com
www.ohwy.com/bc/s/
suornaga.htm

NEARBY SIGHTS OF INTEREST:
Art Gallery of the South
Okanagan, Dominion Radio
Astrophysical Observatory,
Okanagan Museum

Xeriscaping—the use of drought-resistant plants in landscaping—is the major theme at Summerland.
Malcolm Lane

performing arts performances (phone for dates and details). The grandiose former superintendent's house, a 1920 English cottage, is now a museum explaining the history of the Research Centre and is also used as administration offices for the gardens.

Beyond the gardens is the *Canyon Walk* nature walk leading to a superb view of Trout Creek Canyon and historic Kettle Valley Railway Bridge.

Admission is through a donation to the society, which can be deposited in any number of boxes placed in the gardens for that purpose. There is a picnic area, but bring beverages, as there is no water fountain on the site.

26 Kelowna: Guisachan Heritage Park

LOCATION: **1060** CAMERON AVENUE, KELOWNA

Kelowna is a major center for fruit, vegetable, and grape production in the celebrated Okanagan Valley. It also has several very nice parks, including the main one, City Park; another is the one described here, Guisachen Heritage Park.

The history of this house dates back to the late 1800s, when Lord Aberdeen, a member of the British House of Lords, visited Canada and became enchanted with the Okanagan Valley, just starting at that time to give signs of its future as a fruit-producing region. He and his wife settled at Coldstream Ranch, in Vernon, British Columbia in 1891, and then built Guisachan House (from the Gaelic word for "place of firs") as a summer residence. The house later become the property of the Cameron family, both avid gardeners, and locals still call the garden "Cameron Gardens."

The Indian bungalow-style house with large verandahs has been completely restored and turned into an upscale restaurant while one of the outbuildings, the Cameron Milkshed, is now a gift shop. The 2.4-acre (one-hectare) gardens have also been restored, thanks largely to the copious notes taken by Mrs. Cameron in her journals on just what the gardens looked like from the 1920s through the 1940s. There is a large rock garden and a beautiful rose garden, vast perennial borders, and even an herb garden serving the restaurant's cuisine.

GARDEN OPEN: dawn to dusk daily, year-round.
ADMISSION: free.

FURTHER INFORMATION FROM:
Guisachan Heritage Park
1060 Cameron Avenue
Kelowna, British Columbia
V1Y 8V3
(250) 862-9368

NEARBY SIGHTS OF INTEREST:
B.C. Orchard Industry Museum, Butterfly World and Botanical Gardens

Guisachan Heritage Park.
Guisachan Heritage Park

Index